T0214271

Lecture Notes in Computer Science 12135

More information about this series at http://www.springer.com/series/7411

Anne Remke · Valerio Schiavoni (Eds.)

Distributed Applications and Interoperable Systems

20th IFIP WG 6.1 International Conference, DAIS 2020
Held as Part of the 15th International Federated Conference
on Distributed Computing Techniques, DisCoTec 2020
Valletta, Malta, June 15–19, 2020
Proceedings

 Springer

Editors
Anne Remke
University of Münster
Münster, Germany

Valerio Schiavoni (iD)
University of Neuchâtel
Neuchâtel, Switzerland

ISSN 0302-9743   ISSN 1611-3349   (electronic)
Lecture Notes in Computer Science
ISBN 978-3-030-50322-2   ISBN 978-3-030-50323-9   (eBook)
https://doi.org/10.1007/978-3-030-50323-9

LNCS Sublibrary: SL5 – Computer Communication Networks and Telecommunications

This Springer imprint is published by the registered company Springer Nature Switzerland AG
The registered company address is: Gewerbestrasse 11, 6330 Cham, Switzerland

Foreword

The 15th International Federated Conference on Distributed Computing Techniques (DisCoTec 2020) took place during June 15–19, 2020. It was organized by the Department of Computer Science at the University of Malta, but was held online due to the abnormal circumstances worldwide affecting physical travel.

The DisCoTec series is one of the major events sponsored by the International Federation for Information Processing (IFIP). It comprises three conferences:

- The IFIP WG6.1 22nd International Conference on Coordination Models and Languages (COORDINATION 2020)
- The IFIP WG6.1 19th International Conference on Distributed Applications and Interoperable Systems (DAIS 2020)
- The IFIP WG6.1 40th International Conference on Formal Techniques for Distributed Objects, Components and Systems (FORTE 2020)

Together, these conferences cover a broad spectrum of distributed computing subjects, ranging from theoretical foundations and formal description techniques to systems research issues. As is customary, the event also included several plenary sessions in addition to the individual sessions of each conference, that gathered attendants from the three conferences. These included joint invited speaker sessions and a joint session for the best papers from the respective three conferences.

Associated with the federated event, two satellite events took place:

- The 13th International Workshop on Interaction and Concurrency Experience (ICE 2020)
- The First International Workshop on Foundations of Consensus and Distributed Ledgers (FOCODILE 2020)

I would like to thank the Program Committee chairs of the different events for their help and cooperation during the preparation of the conference, and the Steering Committee and Advisory Boards of DisCoTec and their conferences for their guidance and support. The organization of DisCoTec 2020 was only possible thanks to the dedicated work of the Organizing Committee, including Davide Basile and Francisco "Kiko" Fernández Reyes (publicity chairs), Antonis Achilleos, Duncan Paul Attard, and Ornela Dardha (workshop chairs), Lucienne Bugeja (logistics and finances), as well as all the students and colleagues who volunteered their time to help. Finally, I would like to thank IFIP WG6.1 for sponsoring this event, Springer's *Lecture Notes in Computer Science* team for their support and sponsorship, EasyChair for providing the reviewing framework, and the University of Malta for providing the support and infrastructure to host the event.

June 2020   Adrian Francalanza

Preface

This volume contains the papers presented at the 20th IFIP International Conference on Distributed Applications and Interoperable Systems (DAIS 2020), sponsored by the IFIP (International Federation for Information Processing) and organized by the IFIP WG6.1. The DAIS conference series addresses all practical and conceptual aspects of distributed applications, including their design, modeling, implementation, and operation, the supporting middleware, appropriate software engineering methodologies and tools, as well as experimental studies and applications.

DAIS 2020 was meant to be held during June 15–19, 2020, in Valletta, Malta, as part of DisCoTec, the 15th International Federated Conference on Distributed Computing Techniques. However, due to the COVID-19 pandemic, the organizers decided to turn the conference into a virtual event to be held completely online.

There were 30 initial abstract registrations for DAIS, which were then followed by 17 full papers. Each submission was reviewed by up to three Program Committee (PC) members. The review process included an in-depth discussion phase, during which the merits of all papers were discussed by the PC. The committee decided to accept ten full papers, one short paper, and one invited paper.

Accepted papers address challenges in multiple application areas, including system support for machine learning, security and privacy issues, experimental reproducibility and fault-tolerance, as well novel networking approaches for future network generations. Researchers continue the trend of focusing on trusted execution environments, for instance in the case of database systems. Instead, we notice fewer research efforts devoted to blockchain topics.

The virtual conference, especially during these last months full of unpredictable events, was made possible by the work and cooperation of many people working in several committees and organizations, all of which are listed in these proceedings. In particular, we are grateful to the Program Committee members for their commitment and thorough reviews and for their active participation in the discussion phase, and all the external reviewers for their help in evaluating submissions. Finally, we also thankful to the DisCoTec general chair, Adriano Francalanza, and the DAIS Steering Committee chair, Rui Oliveira, for their constant availability, support, and guidance.

June 2020

Anne Remke
Valerio Schiavoni

Organization

General Chair

Adrian Francalanza — University of Malta, Malta

Program Committee Chairs

Anne Remke — University of Münster, Germany
Valerio Schiavoni — University of Neuchâtel, Switzerland

Steering Committee

Rocco De Nicola — IMT Lucca, Italy
Pascal Felber — University of Neuchâtel, Switzerland
Kurt Geihs — University of Kasel, Germany
Alberto Lluch Lafuente — DTU, Denmark
Kostas Magoutis — ICS-FORTH, Greece
Elie Najm (Chair) — Télécom ParisTech, France
Manuel Núñez — Universidad Complutense de Madrid, Spain
Rui Oliveira — University of Minho, Portugal
Jean-Bernard Stefani — Inria Grenoble, France
Gianluigi Zavattaro — University of Bologna, Italy

Program Committee

Pierre-Louis Aublin — Keio University, Japan
Sonia Ben Mokhtar — LIRIS-CNRS, France
Sara Bouchenak — INSA, France
Antoine Boutet — INSA, France
Silvia Bonomi — Università degli Studi di Roma La Sapienza, Italy
Damiano Di Francesco Maesa — University of Cambridge, UK
Davide Frey — Inria, France
Paula Herber — University of Münster, Germany
Mark Jelasity — University of Szeged, Hungary
Evangelia Kalyvianaki — University of Cambridge, UK
Vana Kalogeraki — Athens University of Economics and Business, Greece
Rüdiger Kapitza — Technical University of Braunschweig, Germany
João Leitão — Universidade Nova de Lisboa, Portugal
Daniel Lucani — Aarhus University, Denmark
Miguel Matos — INESC-ID, University of Lisboa, Portugal
Kostas Magoutis — University of Ioannina, Greece

Claudio Antares Mezzina	University of Urbino, Italy
Alberto Montresor	University of Trento, Italy
Daniel OKeeffe	Royal Holloway University of London, UK
Emanuel Onica	Alexandru Ioan Cuza University of Iasi, Romania
Marta Patino	Universidad Politecnica de Madrid, Spain
José Orlando Pereira	Universidade do Minho, INESC-TEC, Portugal
Hans P. Reiser	University of Passau, Germany
Etienne Riviére	École Polytechnique de Louvain, Belgium
Romain Rouvoy	University of Lille 1, France
Pierre Sutra	Télécom SudParis, France
Spyros Voulgaris	Athens University of Economics and Business, Greece

Additional Reviewers

Isabelly Rocha	University of Neuchâtel, Switzerland
Philipp Eichhammer	University of Passau, Germany
Christian Berger	University of Passau, Germany
Vania Marangozova-Martin	IMAG, France

DisCoTec Organizing Committee

Adrian Francalanza (General Chair)	University of Malta, Malta
Davide Basile (Publicity Chair)	ISTI-CNR, Italy
Kiko Fernández-Reyes (Publicity Chair)	Uppsala University, Sweden
Antonis Achilleos (Workshops Chair)	Reykjavik University, Iceland
Duncan Attard (Workshops Chair)	University of Malta, Malta
Ornela Dardha (Workshops Chair)	University of Glasgow, UK
Lucienne Bugeja (Logistics)	University of Malta, Malta

Contents

Privacy and Security

On the Trade-Offs of Combining Multiple Secure Processing Primitives for Data Analytics

Hugo Carvalho[✉], Daniel Cruz, Rogério Pontes, João Paulo, and Rui Oliveira

INESC TEC and Universidade do Minho, Braga, Portugal
{hugo.a.carvalho,daniel.c.cruz,rogerio.a.pontes,
joao.t.paulo,rui.oliveira}@inesctec.pt

Abstract. Cloud Computing services for data analytics are increasingly being sought by companies to extract value from large quantities of information. However, processing data from individuals and companies in third-party infrastructures raises several privacy concerns. To this end, different secure analytics techniques and systems have recently emerged. These initial proposals leverage specific cryptographic primitives lacking generality and thus having their application restricted to particular application scenarios. In this work, we contribute to this thriving body of knowledge by combining two complementary approaches to process sensitive data.

We present SafeSpark, a secure data analytics framework that enables the combination of different cryptographic processing techniques with hardware-based protected environments for privacy-preserving data storage and processing. SafeSpark is modular and extensible therefore adapting to data analytics applications with different performance, security and functionality requirements.

We have implemented a SafeSpark's prototype based on Spark SQL and Intel SGX hardware. It has been evaluated with the TPC-DS Benchmark under three scenarios using different cryptographic primitives and secure hardware configurations. These scenarios provide a particular set of security guarantees and yield distinct performance impact, with overheads ranging from as low as 10% to an acceptable 300% when compared to an insecure vanilla deployment of Apache Spark.

Keywords: Data analytics · Privacy · Trusted hardware

1 Introduction

Data analytics plays a key role in generating high-quality information that enables companies to optimize the quality of their business while presenting several advantages such as making faster business decisions, predicting users

© IFIP International Federation for Information Processing 2020
Published by Springer Nature Switzerland AG 2020
A. Remke and V. Schiavoni (Eds.): DAIS 2020, LNCS 12135, pp. 3–20, 2020.
https://doi.org/10.1007/978-3-030-50323-9_1

behaviours, elaborating better marketing plans, and improving relationships with customers. As the amount of data to be analysed grows, companies tend to resort to cloud services due to their high levels of reliability, flexibility, and efficiency, as well as competitive costs. However, using cloud services to store and process data increases the risk of unauthorized access to it, thus presenting serious issues to the users, given that some data may contain private or sensitive information, such as personal e-mails, and medical or financial records. The problem can arise internally, for instance when a system administrator manages confidential data inappropriately [1], or externally through, for instance, the exploitation of bugs in the cloud infrastructure [4,6,7]. Also, the existence of regulations such as the European General Data Protection Regulation (GDPR) [3] stresses the need for a new set of security measures for sensitive data being stored and processed at third-party services.

Current secure data analytics solutions aiming at overcoming the previous challenges can be broadly divided into two groups. Applications in the first one operate over encrypted data or protected data to be more generic. These are based on cryptographic techniques such as deterministic [8,30] or homomorphic [24] encryption that allow doing different types of computations (e.g., equality, order, and arithmetic operations) over encrypted data. The second group of solutions uses hardware-based protected environments or trusted hardware as it is commonly known, such as Intel SGX [15] or Arm TrustZone [9], to process data analysis with privacy and integrity guarantees. As expected, each approach has its advantages and limitations as we will elaborate on below in Sect. 2.

With SafeSpark we combine, in a modular and extensible manner, both approaches in a secure data analytics framework. To the best of our knowledge, it is the first tool to do so. The contribution of this paper is threefold. We present a modular and extensible framework capable of combining a growing set of cryptographic data processing techniques with trusted hardware processing devices. We have implemented a prototype that extends the Apache Spark framework with secure operations using standard encryption, deterministic encryption, order-preserving encryption techniques, and the Intel SGX technology while remaining full Spark SQL compliant. And we thoroughly evaluate the prototype with the TPC-DS Benchmark under three scenarios using different cryptographic primitives and secure hardware configurations.

The remainder of the paper is organized as follows. Section 2 presents relevant background and Sect. 3 reviews the state of the art for secure data analytics. Section 4 describes SafeSpark's architecture and Sect. 5 details its prototype implementation. Section 6 presents the experimental evaluation. Section 7 concludes the paper.

2 Background

This section describes the cryptographic techniques we use and their security guarantees as well as the Intel SGX technology.

2.1   Cryptographic Schemes

Current privacy-preserving solutions use different encryption techniques to ensure data privacy [22,29].

STD is a symmetric encryption scheme that provides *Indistinguishability under Chosen-Plaintext Attack* (IND-CPA) security which ensures that no information is disclosed from ciphertexts [20]. This scheme has a strong security definition but does not support any kind of computation over encrypted data. As such, SafeSpark's prototype uses STD to protect data that does not need to be processed at the untrusted premises.

The DET scheme ensures that multiple encryption operations over the same plaintext, and with the same encryption key, will result in the same ciphertext. Therefore, this scheme leaks encrypted values that correspond to the same value in plaintext, thus providing *Indistinguishability under Distinct Chosen-Plaintext Attacks* (IND-DCPA) [30] security. Also, the DET scheme allows performing equality comparisons over ciphertexts, for instance, it can be used to support SQL queries such as GROUP BY, COUNT, or DISTINCT.

The OPE scheme allows comparing the order of two ciphertexts, which is preserved from the original plaintexts [12]. With this scheme, range queries like MAX, MIN, COUNT, ORDER BY and GROUP BY can be applied directly over encrypted data. Since the OPE scheme preserves more properties from the original plaintext data it also has weaker security guarantees - *Indistinguishability under Ordered Chosen-Plaintext Attack* (IND-OCPA).

Other schemes, such as Paillier Encryption [24] or Secure Multi-Party Computation [18] can also be used for building secure data processing systems. However, their performance impact is high thus affecting the practicality of the resulting solution [34]. Nevertheless, SafeSpark has a modular and extensible design capable of supporting additional schemes such as these in the future.

2.2   Intel SGX

Intel SGX [15] is a trusted hardware solution contemplating protected execution environments - called Enclaves - whose security relies on the processors' instructions and a set of keys only accessible to the hardware. Enclaves have isolated memory addresses with the assurance that no malicious external environment, such as the operating system or hypervisor can compromise their security.

SGX splits an application into a trusted and an untrusted environment. When a user wants to compute data using SGX, she starts by creating an Enclave, which is placed in a trusted memory region. Then, when the user's application calls a trusted function (*i.e.*, a function that runs within SGX Enclaves), the execution of the application and the input data needed for that function, are transferred to the enclave. Therefore, by exchanging encrypted data with the enclave, and securely transmitting the corresponding encryption keys, applications can safely execute operations over the plaintext of sensitive data without leaking information to the server where the operation is deployed [15].

Enclaves also provide sealing capabilities that allow encrypting and authenticating the data inside an enclave so that it can be written to persistent memory without any other process having access to its contents. Also, SGX relies on software attestation, which ensures that critical code is running within a trusted enclave. One of the main advantages of SGX against its predecessors is its lower Trusted Computing Base (TCB). This factor defines the set of components, such as hardware, firmware, or software components that are considered critical to system security. With SGX, TCB only includes the code that users decide to run inside their enclave. Thus, SGX provides security guarantees for attacks from malicious software running on the same computer.

2.3 Threat Model

SafeSpark considers a trusted and untrusted site. The Spark client resides on the trusted site (e.g.: private infrastructure) and the Spark cluster is deployed on the untrusted one (e.g.: public cloud). We assume a semi-honest, adaptive adversary (internal attacker) with control over the untrusted site, with the exception of the trusted hardware. The adversary observers every query, its access patterns and can also replay queries. However, our model assumes that the adversary is honest-but-curious and thus does not have the capability of modifying queries nor their execution. The parameters and results of queries are encrypted with a secret key only available to the client and enclaves.

3 Related Work

Current secure data analytics platforms fall into two broad approaches. One, like the Monomi [33] system, resort to cryptographic schemes such as DET and OPE to query sensitive data on untrusted domains. The other, relies on hardware-based protected environments.

Monomi, in particular, splits the execution of complex queries between the database server and the client. The untrusted server executes part of the query, and when the remaining parts cannot be computed on the server or can be more efficiently computed on the client-side, the encrypted data is sent to the client, which decrypts it and performs the remaining parts of the query. Seabed [25] has a similar approach with an architecture based on splitting the query execution between the client and the server. This platform proposes two new cryptographic schemes, ASHE and SPLASHE which allow executing arithmetic and aggregation operations directly over the cryptograms.

Contrarily, VC3 [31] and Opaque [35] follow a trusted hardware approach. Namely, they use Intel SGX [16] to create secure enclaves where sensitive data can be queried in plaintext without revealing private information. VC3 uses SGX to perform secure MapReduce operations in the cloud, protecting code and sensitive data from malicious attackers. Opaque is based on Apache Spark and adds new operators that, in addition to ensuring the confidentiality and integrity of the data, ensure that analytical processing is protected against inference attacks.

These additional security guarantees lead however to a high impact on performance, with Opaque being up to 62 times slower than the original Spark.

Segarra et al. in [32] propose a secure processing system build on top of Spark Streaming that uses Intel SGX to compute stream analytics over public untrusted clouds. This solution offers security guarantees similar to those proposed in Opaque without requiring changes to applications code.

Unlike previous work, this paper aims at exploring the combination of both cryptographic and trusted hardware primitives for the Spark SQL engine. To the best of our knowledge, this approach is still unexplored in the literature and, as shown in the paper, provides novel trade-offs in terms of performance, security, and functionality that better suit a wider range of data analytics applications.

4   Architecture

SafeSpark's architecture is based on the Apache Spark platform [10], which currently does not support big data analytics with confidentiality guarantees. In this section, we describe a novel modular and extensible architecture that supports the simultaneous integration of cryptographic and trusted hardware primitives.

4.1   Apache Spark

Apache Spark is an open-source data analytics engine for large-scale distributed and parallel data processing. Spark uses in-memory processing, which makes it way faster than its predecessors, such as Apache Hadoop [19]. Our work is based on Spark SQL, which is an upper-level library for structured data processing. Spark SQL provides a programming abstraction, called DataFrames, which presents a data table with rows and named columns, similar to a database table, and on which one can perform traditional SQL queries [10].

Spark's architecture, depicted by the white boxes in Fig. 1, consists of three main components. The *Driver Program* is responsible for managing and scheduling the queries submitted to the Spark cluster, while the *Cluster Manager* allocates resources (*e.g.*, CPU, RAM) to each query, dividing it into smaller tasks to be processed by the *Spark Workers*. Spark proposes a distributed architecture that scales horizontally. Namely, by launching *Spark Workers* on new servers, the queries being processed by the Spark cluster can leverage the additional computational resources of such servers.

Spark considers a *Data Storage* phase where information is uploaded to a given data source (*e.g.*, Apache HDFS). Stored data is then loaded into tabular representation (in-memory DataFrames) that can be efficiently queried.

During the *Data Processing* phase, clients start by creating a *SparkContext* object, that connects the program being executed (*Driver Program*) to the Spark environment. Then, each client submits queries to the system through the Spark SQL component, which generates an execution plan that is sent to the *Cluster Manager*. The latter divides the execution plan into multiple tasks and assigns each task to a subset of *Spark Workers* with available resources (*e.g.*, CPU,

RAM). When all the tasks are completed, the result is sent from the *Spark Workers* to the *Driver Program*, which returns the output to the clients.

4.2 SafeSpark

SafeSpark extends Spark's architecture [10] by integrating multiple secure processing primitives that can be combined to offer different performance, security and functionality trade-offs to data analytics applications. Figure 1 shows the proposed architecture which contemplates four new components: *SafeSpark Worker, Handler, CryptoBox* and *SafeMapper*.

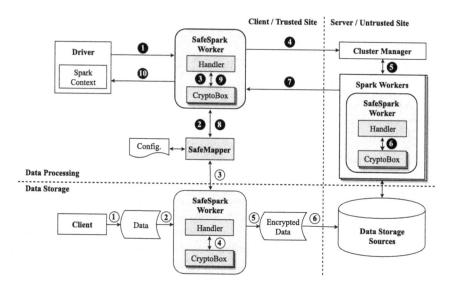

Fig. 1. SafeSpark's architecture

During the *Data Storage* phase, sensitive data is encrypted on the trusted site before being uploaded to the untrusted Spark data source. For this, the user must first specify in a configuration file how the data will be represented in a tabular form. Then, for each data column, the user will specify the type of cryptographic scheme (*e.g.* STD, DET, OPE) or trusted hardware technology (*e.g.* Intel SGX) to be employed.

The *SafeMapper* module is responsible for parsing the information contained in the configuration file and forwarding it to the *SafeSpark Worker*. The latter will intercept the plaintext data being uploaded to the untrusted data source and will encrypt each data column with the specified secure technique. The conversion of plaintext to encrypted data is actually done by the *Handler* component, which provides *encode()* and *decode()* methods for encrypting and decrypting information, respectively. Moreover, the *Handler* uses modular entities, called *CryptoBoxes*, each one corresponding to a different cryptographic technique or trusted hardware technology. Each *CryptoBox* contains an API with methods that allow generating a key, as well as methods to encrypt and decrypt data using the respective *CryptoBox* key.

The *SafeSpark Worker* is present on both sites and has the goal of abstracting the integration of cryptographic techniques and trusted hardware into the system. In addition to the *encode()* and *decode()* methods, it also implements a *process()* method that is used on the untrusted side to execute secure operations, during the *Data Processing* phase. This method is essential to enable the execution of secure operations, such as sums or averages, at the trusted hardware enclaves deployed on the untrusted premises.

The proposed architecture allows exploring different trade-offs between performance, privacy, and functionalities through the combination of different secure processing and storage primitives. Also, SafeSpark's modular design aims at easing the integration of new cryptographic algorithms and trusted hardware technologies, such as ORE [13], into the platform.

4.3   Flow of Operations

To exemplify the flow of operations in our platform let us consider the use-case of a company that wishes to store and query their employees' information in a third-party cloud service. The company's database will have an *Employees* table holding the *Salary*, *Age*, and *Category* of each employee (database columns). These columns contain sensitive information so the company's database administrators define a secure schema using SGX for the *Salary*, OPE for the *Age* and DET for the *Category*.

Firstly, the database's information must be uploaded to the corresponding cloud service (①). Given the sensitive nature of this data, the upload request is intercepted by the *SafeSpark Worker* (②) that initializes the SGX, OPE, and DET *CryptoBoxes* specified in the configuration schema (③), while using them to encrypt the corresponding data columns (④). The resulting encrypted data columns (⑤) are then uploaded into the untrusted data storage source (⑥).

Note that for encrypting data with the SGX technology, we consider a symmetric cipher similar to the STD scheme. During SafeSpark's bootstrap phase, the client application, running on the trusted premises must generate this key and exchange it with the enclave, through a secure channel, so that encrypted data can be decrypted inside the secure enclave and the desired operations can be done privately over plaintext data. This paper tackles the architectural challenges of integrating Intel SGX and other cryptographic primitives in Spark. Thus, we do not focus on the protocols of secure channel establishment or key exchange between clients and remote enclaves. Such challenges have been addressed in [11,27], which SafeSpark can rely upon in a real-world instantiation and that would not require any code changes at Spark's core codebase.

After completing the database's loading phase, clients can then query the corresponding information. Let us consider a SQL query that averages employees' salaries who are between 25 and 30 years and then groups the results by category.

```
SELECT Category, avg(Salary)
FROM Employees
WHERE Age BETWEEN 25 AND 30
GROUP BY Category
```

By sending the query through the *Spark Context* (❶), the request is intercepted by the *SafeSpark Worker*, which verifies the user-defined configuration file (❷), checking whether it is necessary to change the query, in order to invoke secure operators from *CryptoBoxes* (❸). Since stored values for the column *Age* are encrypted with OPE, the *SafeSpark Worker* encrypts the values "25" and "30" by resorting to the same OPE *CryptoBox* and key. Moreover, as the *Salary* column is encrypted using SGX, the operation *avg* needs to be performed within secure SGX enclaves. Therefore, SafeSpark provides a new operator that allows computing the average within SGX enclaves, while the *SafeSpark Worker* replaces the common operator *avg* by this new operator (*AVG_SGX*).

Then, after protecting sensitive query arguments at the trusted premises, the request is sent to the untrusted premises, namely to the *Cluster Manager*, which dispatches the tasks to *Spark Workers* (❺). Since the GROUP BY and BETWEEN operators internally perform equality and order comparison operations, and considering that *Category* and *Age* columns are encrypted with DET and OPE schemes, Spark is able to execute the operation directly over ciphertexts. However, the operation *avg* needs to be executed by the *SafeSpark Workers* using the *process()* method of the *CryptoBox* SGX (❻). At the SGX enclave, this method receives the input data to calculate *avg* and decrypts it with the previously agreed key. Then it does the *avg* calculation in plaintext and encrypts the result before sending it back to the untrusted Spark engine.

The query's encrypted result is sent to the Spark Client (❼) and intercepted by *SparkWorker* that, based on the *SafeMapper* component (❽), decrypts it using the appropriate *CryptoBox* (❾). Lastly, the plaintext result is sent back to the client (❿).

5   Implementation

SafeSpark's prototype leverages the *SafeMapper* and *CryptoBox* components used by SafeNoSQL [22]. Thereby, the STD and DET schemes were implemented with an AES 128-bit key in CBC mode with and without a random initialization vector, respectively, and by using the OpenSSL cryptographic library [5]. For the OPE scheme, we follow the implementation proposed by *Boldyreva et al.*, using the OpenSSL and MPFR (Multiple-Precision Floating-Point) libraries [5,17]. On the other hand, since the SafeNoSQL platform does not consider the use of SGX technology, we extended the library of *CryptoBox* components, in order to support arithmetic and relational operations using SGX. Next, we describe the implementation of the other SafeSpark components.

5.1   Data Storage

The conversion of plaintext data to encrypted one, during the data storage phase (Fig. 1), is done by using Parquet files [26] as these provide the standard format for Spark environments [14]. Parquet is a column-oriented data storage format that provides optimizations that make it very efficient, particularly for analytical processing scenarios. Our converter was implemented using the JAVA programming language, and it provides encode and decode (*i.e.*, encrypt and decrypt) methods that allow protecting sensitive data based on a secure database configuration schema. Thus, each column at the Parquet file is encrypted with the chosen encryption methods before being uploaded to the untrusted premises.

5.2   Data Processing

For the data processing phase the *SafeSpark Worker*, deployed at the untrusted site, is able to natively perform equality and order operations over columns protected with DET and OPE. However, when the SGX technology is being used, operations must be redesigned to execute within secure enclaves. For this reason, we resorted to Spark *Used-Defined Functions* (UDF) and *User-Defined Aggregate Functions* (UDAF's) since these allow us to change Spark's behaviour without directly changing its source code. The Scala programming language was used to implement these UDF/UDAFs. However, since SGX technology does not support the Scala programming language, we used the *Java Native Interface* (JNI) to call functions, developed in the C language, that are able to perform arithmetic and comparison operations using the SGX technology.

Considering this new set of functionalities, the SQL query presented at Sect. 4.3 is translated by the *SafeSpark Worker*, by invoking the corresponding SafeSpark operators, in the following way:

```
SELECT Category, AVG_SGX(Salary)
FROM Employees
WHERE Age BETWEEN OFC6AC2E AND OFC6D497
GROUP BY Category
```

Note that the *avg* operator is replaced by *AVG_SGX*, which is a new operator provided by SafeSpark that computes the salary average within secure SGX Enclaves. Moreover, the values "25" and "30" are replaced by "0FC6AC2E" and "0FC6D497", respectively, which is the hexadecimal representation for the output produced by the OPE encryption operation.

As a drawback of the current implementation, the Spark's framework does not yet provide a stable API for enabling a developer to define their own *User-Defined Types* (UDT). Therefore, if a specific data column was protected with SGX and that column is included in a GROUP BY or ORDER BY clause, its execution is not attainable since it is not possible to specify a UDF or UDAF for these two clauses. To solve this problem, we adopt a column duplication strategy. Thereby, when a data column is encrypted using SGX and one needs to perform GROUP BY or ORDER BY operations over it, that column is duplicated and protected with a DET or OPE primitive, respectively. However, this approach is not suitable for nested arithmetic and order operations, for instance, a SUM operation followed by an ORDER BY operation applied to the same column. Furthermore, as proposed by SafeNoSQL [22], this column duplication strategy is also used to improve the performance impact of decrypting data protected with the OPE scheme. Since this is a time-consuming operation, a duplicate column with the STD scheme is introduced so that, whenever a value encrypted with OPE needs to be retrieved in plaintext to the client (*e.g.*, the age of an employee) a faster decryption method is applied. The performance and storage space overhead trade-offs of these optimizations are further analysed in Sect. 6.

Finally, Spark SQL's DataFrames API was extended by creating a new operator, called *collectDecrypt*, that is responsible for decrypting the result of a query before presenting it to the user.

6   Experimental Evaluation

SafeSpark's prototype was evaluated to understand the impact of combining different privacy-preserving techniques. Namely, we compared Spark Vanilla against three different secure settings, on which we alternate the cryptographic and trusted hardware primitives being used and the data these are applied to.

6.1   Experimental Setup and Methodology

The experiments consider a distributed cluster composed of five nodes, configured with Cloudera Manager v.6.1.1. We used version 2.4 of Apache Spark and version 3.0.0 of HDFS for data storage. For the Client node, which is responsible for executing the queries and managing the cluster, we used a node equipped with an Intel Core i3-4170 CPU 3.70 GHz, 15.9 GiB (DDR3) of RAM, a SATA3 119 GiB SSD and with a Gigabit network interface. The nodes with data processing function (Workers) are equipped with an Intel Core i3-7100 CPU 3.9 GHz (with Intel SGX support), 7.8 GiB (DDR3) of RAM, a SATA3 119 GiB SSD and with a Gigabit network interface. During the data storage phase, we used a separate server to encrypt the data. This is equipped with an Intel (R) Xeon (R) CPU E5-2698 v4 @ 2.20 GHz, 31.3 GiB (DDR3), and a Gigabit network interface.

We used the TPC-DS [23] benchmark, which models the decision support functions of a retail product supplier, considering essential components of any decision support system: data loading, multiple types of queries, and data maintenance. To explore different user behaviors for a decision support system, the TPC-DS benchmark provides four classes of SQL queries, each one representing a different database user activity in this type of system: Iterative, Data Mining, Reporting, and Ad-Hoc queries. For the experiments, we selected two queries from each group based on previous work [21,28]. Namely, we chose queries 24 and 31 from the Iterative OLAP class, queries 27 and 73 from the Reporting class, queries 37 and 82 from the Ad-Hoc class, and queries 40 and 46 from the

Data Mining class. TPC-DS was configured with a $10\times$ scale factor, corresponding to a total of 12 GB of data to be loaded into Spark's storage source.

We performed ten runs of each TPC-DS query for Spark Vanilla, which computes over plaintext data, and for the different SafeSpark setups, which run on top of encrypted data. For each query, we analyzed the mean and standard deviation of the execution time. Also, the *dstat* framework [2] was used at each cluster node to measure the CPU and memory consumption, as well as the impact on disk read/write operations and on the network traffic. Moreover, we analyzed the data storage times and the impact of encrypted data on storage space.

6.2 SafeSpark Setups

The evaluation considers three SafeSpark setups with specific combinations of secure primitives for protecting TPC-DS's database schema, namely:

SafeSpark-SGX. This setup aims at maximizing the usage of SGX for doing queries over sensitive information at the TPC-DS database schema. Thus, the data columns which are used within arithmetic operations or filters of equality and order were encrypted using SGX. The OPE scheme was used for all the columns contemplating ORDER BY operations since this type of operation is not supported by the SGX operator, as explained in Sect. 5.2. For the remaining columns contemplating equality operations as GROUP BY or ROLL OUT, we used the DET scheme.

SafeSpark-OPE. This scenario aims at maximizing the use of cryptographic schemes, starting by using OPE and followed by the DET scheme. Therefore, in this case, SGX was only used for operations that are not supported by DET and OPE, namely arithmetic operations, sums or averages. Thus, OPE was used for all the operations containing order and equality comparisons, as ORDER BY, GROUP BY or BETWEEN clauses. For the remaining columns, that only require equality operations, the DET scheme was used.

SafeSpark-DET. As in the previous scenario, this one also maximizes the use of cryptographic schemes. However, it prioritizes the DET primitive instead of the OPE one, thus reducing the number of OPE columns that were being used in GROUP BY and ROLL UP operations in the previous scenario. Thus, SGX was only used for operations not supported by OPE or DET primitives. For columns that need to preserve equality, we used DET. For columns requiring order comparisons, we used the OPE scheme. In some cases, it was necessary to duplicate some columns already protected with the DET scheme. For example, when a column is targeted simultaneously by a GROUP BY (equality) and ORDER BY (order) operation.

Finally, we used the STD scheme to protect all columns on which no server-side data processing is performed. The secure setups used are further detailed at https://hugocarvalho9.github.io/safespark/testing-setups.html where it is shown the different secure primitives used for the TPC-DS schema.

6.3   Results

This section presents the results obtained from the experimental evaluation.

6.3.1   Loading and Storage

Table 1 shows that Spark Vanilla took 4.7 min for the storage phase. For the SafeSpark configurations, we considered not only the loading time but also the time used to encrypt the data. The SafeSpark-SGX setup took 697.1 min to encrypt and load the data, and the stored data size increased by 4.73×. The SafeSpark-OPE loading time was 735.1 min, and the data size increased by 6.23×. Lastly, the loading time for SafeSpark-DET was 776.3 min, and the data size increased by 6.39×.

Table 1. Loading time and data size.

Setup	Vanilla	SafeSpark-SGX	SafeSpark-OPE	SafeSpark-DET
Loading time	4.7 min	637.1 min	735.1 min	776.4 min
Data size	4.1 GB	19.4 GB	25.54 GB	26.2 GB

The impact shown throughout the storage phase can be explained by the use of the OPE scheme to encrypt data since it has a longer encoding time comparing with the other schemes, especially when the plaintext size is larger [22]. Also, the cryptograms produced by this scheme are significantly larger than the original plaintext, which can sustain the observed increase for the stored data size. In some situations, the cryptogram's size increases up to 4× when compared to the size of the original plaintext. It is important to note that all setups resort to the OPE primitive. However, SafeSpark-SGX is the setup that uses least this primitive and so has the fastest loading time. On the other hand, SafeSpark-DET has a higher loading time because it duplicates some columns to incorporate both DET and OPE primitives, as explained in Sect. 6.2.

6.3.2   Latency

Figure 2 presents the query latency results for the three SafeSpark configurations and Vanilla Spark. The values reflect each query execution time, as well as the time used to encrypt the query's parameters and to decrypt the query results when these are sent back to the client.

As expected, SafeSpark has worse performance than Spark Vanilla due to the secure primitives performance overhead. The SafeSpark-SGX scenario exhibits the highest overhead, while its best result occurs for query 24 with a 1.54× penalty and the worst for query 82 with a 4.1× penalty. These values can be justified by two factors. First, this scenario maximizes the use of SGX to protect data, leading to a wide number of data transfer and processing operations being executed within the SGX enclaves. We noted that, for example, query 31 has

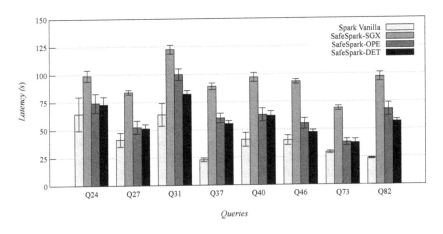

Fig. 2. Query execution times.

done approximately 4.5 million operations to SGX enclaves with an average time of 2.2 μs for each operation. Second, we use Spark SQL UDFs to perform operations on data protected with SGX. However, a limitation of Spark is that it currently does not support query plan optimizations for UDFs. Thus, the same query running on Spark Vanilla and SafeSpark may generate different execution plans, which can compromise the performance values obtained.

The SafeSpark-OPE maximizes the use of cryptographic schemes, thereby reducing the number of operations that are performed within SGX Enclaves. As we can observe in the Fig. 2, this testing scenario is more efficient than the previous one. This improvement is justified not only by the lower number of operations within Enclaves but also by reducing the use of UDFs, which leads Spark to generate optimized query execution plans. The best (1.15× penalty) and worst (2.86× penalty) execution times are still visible at queries 24 and 82, respectively. Although SafeSpark-OPE improves the results presented by SafeSpark-SGX, there are some queries where the execution time is significantly penalized by the time to encrypt the query parameters and decrypt the query results. For example, we noticed that query 31 took on average 14,226 s for decrypting the results, while 13,112 s were spent on OPE's decryption operation. In fact, the use of OPE to decrypt results shows a notable impact on the execution time, considering that the process of decrypting data using OPE is significantly slower than the analogous operations for the DET or STD ciphers, especially when the size of the cryptogram is larger.

SafeSpark-DET has its best execution time also for query 24, with a penalty of 1.13×. The worst result is for query 37, which is 2.4× slower than the same query executed on Spark Vanilla. It is also worth highlighting that there are six queries (24, 27, 31, 40, 46 and 73) where the execution time penalty is between 1.13× and 1.52×. Ad-Hoc queries (37 and 82) require a higher execution time due to the usage of UDFs for arithmetic operations done within SGX enclaves.

The results also show that SafeSpark-DET alleviates the penalty of decrypting data, by reducing the usage of the OPE scheme and maximizing the usage of the DET scheme. Consequently, as the number of values decrypted with the OPE scheme decreases, so it does the query execution time.

6.3.3   Resource Usage

Overall, resource usage results were similar for all SafeSpark setups. Due to space constraints, Table 2 highlights the worst-case results obtained for each resource (*i.e.*, CPU, memory, disk and network I/O). The full results can be consulted at https://hugocarvalho9.github.io/safespark/resource-usage.html.

Table 2. Resource consumption results

Resource	Query	Setup	Master	Worker #1	Worker #2	Worker #3	Worker #4
CPU (%)	40	Spark Vanilla	16	15.2	11	15.4	15.9
		SafeSpark-DET	10.5	19.1	24.9	17.7	24.2
Memory (GB)	37	Spark Vanilla	14.8	6.6	5.6	5.8	5.9
		SafeSpark-SGX	15.8	6.5	6.7	6.4	7
Disk read (KB/s)	46	Spark Vanilla	0.7	1.4	193.9	686.2	594.9
		SafeSpark-SGX	0.9	516.3	909.5	656.2	975.9
Disk write (KB/s)	82	Spark Vanilla	84.1	2726.6	2783.4	2791	2149.2
		SafeSpark-DET	83.7	11354.4	165.3	160.6	8961.2
Network recv (MB/s)	46	Spark Vanilla	304	1570.5	1939.4	3013	3083.1
		SafeSpark-DET	301.5	4309	4501.5	4467.6	4853.2
Network send (MB/s)	46	Spark Vanilla	7.4	0.3	0.5	0.6	1
		SafeSpark-DET	15.8	0.5	0.6	0.9	0.6

The CPU and memory consumption does not show notable changes, even considering the process of decrypting the query results and the computational power used by Intel SGX. The worst CPU consumption result occurred on query 40 with SafeSpark-DET, presenting an overhead 31%, when compared to Vanilla Spark. Regarding memory consumption, the worst overhead was 10% for SafeSpark-SGX, also on query 37.

SafeSpark has an impact on disk and network I/O. Query 46 with SafeSpark-SGX shows an overhead of 107% on disk reads, and query 82 with SafeSpark-DET has a 97% overhead on disk writes, when compared with Spark Vanilla. Finally, network traffic has the highest impact on query 46 with SafeSpark-DET (approximately 87%). These overheads are justified by the fact that cryptograms generated by SafeSpark, which will be sent through network channels and stored persistently, are larger than plaintext data. This is even more relevant when using the OPE scheme as it generates larger cryptograms.

6.4   Discussion

Based on the experimental results presented, we distilled a set of considerations that are described next.

Applications that collect vast amounts of real-time data and focus on decreasing the loading time and transferred/stored data size should avoid the usage of OPE. As we have seen, this scheme generates larger cryptograms and its encryption/decryption time introduces a significant impact on the loading time. Thereby, reducing the usage of OPE leads to better results in the storage phase, as well as on network and disk I/O traffic.

Concerning the queries execution time, we observed that performance can be influenced by two main factors: i) The number of columns that need to be decrypted with the OPE scheme when the result is sent back to the client; ii) The number of operations performed within SGX enclaves.

The first could be improved by leveraging SafeSpark's modular design to integrate more efficient secure order-preserving primitives such as ORE [13].

Regarding the second challenge, a significant source of overhead comes from our current implementation relying on Spark SQL's UDF/UDAF mechanisms for supporting SGX operations. These are not integrated with Spark's query planner component and thus, do not provide optimized query execution plans. A potential approach to face this problem could be to develop our own Spark operators and optimized execution plans, as done in Opaque [35]. Also, as future work, we could devise batching strategies to enable multiple operations to be executed in a single enclave call, which would reduce the number of calls to the enclave and their inherent performance overhead.

Finally, the SafeSpark-DET setup, which only uses OPE for ORDER BY operations and SGX for operations not supported by deterministic schemes, is able to achieve the best performance results. In fact, this setup supports six queries with overheads between 13% and 52%, when compared to Spark Vanilla. Nevertheless, it is important to have in mind that, with this performance increase, one is reducing the provided security guarantees. For instance, SafeSpark-DET presents lower security guarantees than SafeSpark-SGX.

Comparing our platform with the existing state-of-the-art systems, SafeSpark differs from the hardware-based approaches [31,32,35] since it enables the use of deterministic schemes to compute equality and order operations. This functionality makes it possible to achieve better performance results while relaxing the security guarantees. On the other hand, SafeSpark distinguishes itself from Monomi and Seabed platforms by using the SGX technology to perform arithmetic operations instead of using Homomorphic Encryption schemes.

7   Conclusion

This paper presents SafeSpark, a modular and extensible secure data analytics platform that combines multiple secure processing primitives to better handle the performance, security, and functionality requirements of distinct data analytics applications. Distinctively, SafeSpark supports both cryptographic schemes and the Intel SGX technology according to users' demand.

SafeSpark's experimental evaluation shows that it is possible to develop a practical solution for protecting sensitive information being stored and processed at third-party untrusted infrastructures with an acceptable impact on application performance. Moreover, while supporting the entire Spark SQL API. When comparing SafeSpark's performance with Spark Vanilla, the prototype's overhead ranges from roughly 10% to 300%. Particularly, with the SafeSpark - DET configuration, we show that for a majority of queries it is possible to maintain the performance overhead below 50%.

Currently, we are working to extend SafeSpark with other secure processing primitives with different security and performance trade-offs (e.g., ORE [13]). Evaluation with even larger data sets and new types of queries is underway too.

Acknowledgements. We thank the anonymous reviewers and our shepherd Pierre-Louis Aublin for their helpful suggestions. The research leading to these results has received funding from the European Union's Horizon 2020 - The EU Framework Programme for Research and Innovation 2014–2020, under grant agreement No. 857237 and FCT - Fundação para a Ciência e a Tecnologia grant SFRH/BD/142704/2018.

References

1. The cambridge analytical files. https://www.theguardian.com/news/series/cambridge-analytica-files. Accessed 2019
2. Dstat: versatile resource statistics tool. http://dag.wiee.rs/home-made/dstat/. Accessed 2020
3. Eu general data protection regulation. https://eugdpr.org/. Accessed 2020
4. Isaac, M., Frenkel, S.: Facebook security breach exposes accounts of 50 million users. https://www.nytimes.com/2018/09/28/technology/facebook-hack-data-breach.html. Accessed 2020
5. Openssl - cryptography and SSL/TLS toolkit. https://www.openssl.org/. Accessed 2020
6. Perlroth, N.: All 3 billion yahoo accounts were affected by 2013 attack. https://www.nytimes.com/2017/10/03/technology/yahoo-hack-3-billion-users.html. Accessed 2020
7. Roman, J.: Ebay breach: 145 million users notified. https://www.bankinfosecurity.com/ebay-a-6858. Accessed 2020
8. Agrawal, R., Kiernan, J., Srikant, R., Xu, Y.: Order preserving encryption for numeric data. In: Proceedings of the 2004 ACM SIGMOD International Conference on Management of Data, pp. 563–574. ACM (2004)
9. ARM, A.: Security technology building a secure system using trustzone technology (white paper). ARM Limited (2009)
10. Armbrust, M., et al.: Spark SQL: relational data processing in spark. In: Proceedings of the 2015 ACM SIGMOD International Conference on Management of Data, pp. 1383–1394. ACM (2015)
11. Bahmani, R., et al.: Secure multiparty computation from SGX. In: Kiayias, A. (ed.) FC 2017. LNCS, vol. 10322, pp. 477–497. Springer, Cham (2017). https://doi.org/10.1007/978-3-319-70972-7_27

12. Boldyreva, A., Chenette, N., Lee, Y., O'Neill, A.: Order-preserving symmetric encryption. In: Joux, A. (ed.) EUROCRYPT 2009. LNCS, vol. 5479, pp. 224–241. Springer, Heidelberg (2009). https://doi.org/10.1007/978-3-642-01001-9_13

13. Boneh, D., Lewi, K., Raykova, M., Sahai, A., Zhandry, M., Zimmerman, J.: Semantically secure order-revealing encryption: multi-input functional encryption without obfuscation. In: Oswald, E., Fischlin, M. (eds.) EUROCRYPT 2015. LNCS, vol. 9057, pp. 563–594. Springer, Heidelberg (2015). https://doi.org/10.1007/978-3-662-46803-6_19

14. Chambers, B., Zaharia, M.: Spark: The Definitive Guide: Big Data Processing Made Simple. O'Reilly Media Inc, Sebastopol (2018)

15. Costan, V., Devadas, S.: Intel SGX explained. IACR Cryptology ePrint Archive 2016(086), 1–118 (2016)

16. Durak, F.B., DuBuisson, T.M., Cash, D.: What else is revealed by order-revealing encryption? In: Proceedings of the 2016 ACM SIGSAC Conference on Computer and Communications Security, pp. 1155–1166. ACM (2016)

17. Fousse, L., Hanrot, G., Lefèvre, V., Pélissier, P., Zimmermann, P.: MPFR: a multiple-precision binary floating-point library with correct rounding. ACM Trans. Math. Softw. (TOMS) 33(2), 13 (2007)

18. Goldreich, O.: Secure multi-party computation. Manuscript. Preliminary version 78 (1998)

19. Hadoop, A.: Apache hadoop. http://hadoop.apache.org. Accessed 2020

20. Katz, J., Lindell, Y.: Introduction to Modern Cryptography. CRC Press, Boca Raton (2014)

21. Kocberber, O., Grot, B., Picorel, J., Falsafi, B., Lim, K., Ranganathan, P.: Meet the walkers: accelerating index traversals for in-memory databases. In: Proceedings of the 46th Annual IEEE/ACM International Symposium on Microarchitecture, pp. 468–479. ACM (2013)

22. Macedo, R., et al.: A practical framework for privacy-preserving NoSQL databases. In: 2017 IEEE 36th Symposium on Reliable Distributed Systems (SRDS), pp. 11–20. IEEE (2017)

23. Nambiar, R.O., Poess, M.: The making of TPC-DS. In: Proceedings of the 32nd International Conference on Very Large Data Bases, pp. 1049–1058. VLDB Endowment (2006)

24. Paillier, P.: Public-key cryptosystems based on composite degree residuosity classes. In: Stern, J. (ed.) EUROCRYPT 1999. LNCS, vol. 1592, pp. 223–238. Springer, Heidelberg (1999). https://doi.org/10.1007/3-540-48910-X_16

25. Papadimitriou, A., et al.: Big data analytics over encrypted datasets with seabed. In: 12th {USENIX} Symposium on Operating Systems Design and Implementation ({OSDI} 16), pp. 587–602 (2016)

26. Parquet, A.: Apache parquet. Accessed 2020

27. Pass, R., Shi, E., Tramèr, F.: Formal abstractions for attested execution secure processors. In: Coron, J.-S., Nielsen, J.B. (eds.) EUROCRYPT 2017. LNCS, vol. 10210, pp. 260–289. Springer, Cham (2017). https://doi.org/10.1007/978-3-319-56620-7_10

28. Poess, M., Nambiar, R.O., Walrath, D.: Why you should run TPC-DS: a workload analysis. In: Proceedings of the 33rd International Conference on Very Large Data Bases, pp. 1138–1149. VLDB Endowment (2007)

29. Popa, R.A., Redfield, C., Zeldovich, N., Balakrishnan, H.: CryptDB: protecting confidentiality with encrypted query processing. In: Proceedings of the Twenty-Third ACM Symposium on Operating Systems Principles, pp. 85–100. ACM (2011)

30. Rogaway, P., Shrimpton, T.: Deterministic authenticated-encryption. Citeseer (2007)
31. Schuster, F., et al.: VC3: Trustworthy data analytics in the cloud using SGX. In: 2015 IEEE Symposium on Security and Privacy (SP), pp. 38–54. IEEE (2015)
32. Segarra, C., Delgado-Gonzalo, R., Lemay, M., Aublin, P.-L., Pietzuch, P., Schiavoni, V.: Using trusted execution environments for secure stream processing of medical data. In: Pereira, J., Ricci, L. (eds.) DAIS 2019. LNCS, vol. 11534, pp. 91–107. Springer, Cham (2019). https://doi.org/10.1007/978-3-030-22496-7_6
33. Tu, S., Kaashoek, M.F., Madden, S., Zeldovich, N.: Processing analytical queries over encrypted data. In: Proceedings of the VLDB Endowment, vol. 6, pp. 289–300. VLDB Endowment (2013)
34. Van Dijk, M., Juels, A.: On the impossibility of cryptography alone for privacy-preserving cloud computing. HotSec 10, 1–8 (2010)
35. Zheng, W., Dave, A., Beekman, J.G., Popa, R.A., Gonzalez, J.E., Stoica, I.: Opaque: an oblivious and encrypted distributed analytics platform. In: NSDI, pp. 283–298 (2017)

Capturing Privacy-Preserving User Contexts with INDOORHASH

Lakhdar Meftah[1]([⊠])(iD), Romain Rouvoy[2]([⊠])(iD), and Isabelle Chrisment[3]([⊠])

[1] Inria/University Lille, Lille, France
`lakhdar.meftah@inria.fr`
[2] University Lille/Inria/IUF, Lille, France
`romain.rouvoy@univ-lille.fr`
[3] LORIA-TELECOM Nancy/University Lorraine, Lorraine, France
`isabelle.chrisment@loria.fr`

Abstract. IoT devices are ubiquitous and widely adopted by end-users to gather personal and environmental data that often need to be put into context in order to gain insights. In particular, location is often a critical context information that is required by third parties in order to analyse such data at scale. However, sharing this information is *i)* sensitive for the user privacy and *ii)* hard to capture when considering indoor environments.

This paper therefore addresses the challenge of producing a new location hash, named INDOORHASH, that captures the indoor location of a user, without disclosing the physical coordinates, thus preserving their privacy. This location hash leverages surrounding infrastructure, such as WiFi access points, to compute a key that uniquely identifies an indoor location.

Location hashes are only known from users physically visiting these locations, thus enabling a new generation of privacy-preserving crowdsourcing mobile applications that protect from third parties re-identification attacks. We validate our results with a crowdsourcing campaign of 31 mobile devices during one month of data collection.

Keywords: Location hash · Mobile computing · User privacy

1 Introduction

In order to meet the user expectation, mobile apps are supposed to understand the user environment and act accordingly. To better capture the surrounding context, these mobile apps rely on data gathered from embedded sensors and user location data sits at the top of the list of key context information. However, the processing of raw location data may leak some privacy-sensitive knowledge

© IFIP International Federation for Information Processing 2020
Published by Springer Nature Switzerland AG 2020
A. Remke and V. Schiavoni (Eds.): DAIS 2020, LNCS 12135, pp. 21–38, 2020.
https://doi.org/10.1007/978-3-030-50323-9_2

that the end user might not accept. Furthermore, embedded location sensors (*e.g.*, GPS) fail at locating the end user once indoor, which seriously prevents the deployment of location-based services at a small scale (*e.g.*, offering location-based services in a mall).

To address these two challenges, we propose a new data structure to accurately capture the indoor location of end users without disclosing their physical location. By inferring such a logical location or place, we intend to leverage the development of location-based services that can work in indoor environments without exposing the user privacy. More specifically, our contribution consists in the definition of a new similarity hash function (also known as *simhash*), named INDOORHASH, which encodes the indoor location of an end user in a privacy-preserving way. Interestingly, this INDOORHASH is robust to re-identification attacks, as the physical location cannot be inferred by an adversary, but allows location-based services to compare the similarity of locations through pairwise comparisons. In this paper, we report on the robustness and accuracy of INDOORHASH built from WiFi scan data, which is a lightweight contextual information to collect. As a matter of evaluation, we embedded INDOORHASH in a mobile app that has been deployed during one month to capture the daily routine of 31 users. Our results show that INDOORHASH succeeds to accurately capture the location of end users by inferring stable logical places, while preserving their privacy.

The remainder of this paper is organized as follows. Section 2 discusses the related work. Section 3 introduces our implementation of a privacy-preserving indoor location hash, named INDOORHASH. Section 4 evaluates INDOORHASH along an empirical deployment we conducted. Section 5 illustrates the benefits of INDOORHASH for building privacy-sensitive location-based services. Finally, Sect. 6 concludes on this work.

2   Related Work

Mobile devices are equipped with a wide panel of embedded sensors that mobile apps can use to acquire key insights about the surrounding environment and the user activities. Among the context information of critical importance, GPS location and WiFi networks are common data that are heavily exploited to locate the user. More specifically, when it comes to indoor location, most of *indoor positioning systems* and *WiFi fingerprinting systems* use the surrounding scanned WiFi access points to locate users indoor or to track users' places.

2.1   WiFi Indoor Positioning Systems

Due to the absence of the *Global Positioning System* (GPS) signal inside buildings, many systems have been proposed as an indoor positioning system [12]. Among these systems, WiFi-based systems, which take advantage of the legacy WiFi *Access Points* (APs) to estimate the location of a mobile device down to 1.5 meters precision using the WiFi signal strength [14]. While some research works require a prior training phase (online mode) to map the location of the antennas [26,36], other proposals have been proposing an automatic way to build a radio map without any prior knowledge about the antennas [16,18,32]. In particular, Liu *et al.* [17] propose a peer-assisted localization method to improve localization accuracy. Li *et al.* [15] introduce a privacy-preserving WiFi indoor localization system. However, they argue that the localization query can inevitably leak the client location and lead to potential privacy violations. Jin *et al.* [13] propose a real-time WiFi positioning algorithm with the assistance of inertial measurement unit to overcome the *Received Signal Strength* (RSS) variation problem. Pulkkinen *et al.* [26] present an automatic fingerprinting solution using theoretical properties of radio signals, they rely on the locations of WiFi APs and collecting training measurements. Salamah *et al.* [29] use the *Principle Component Analysis* (PCA) to reduce the computation cost of the WiFi indoor localization systems based on machine learning approach. Yiu *et al.* [37] apply training measurements and a combined likelihood function from multiple APs to measure the indoor and the outdoor user position. Capurso *et al.* [4] present an indoor and outdoor detection mechanism, which can be used to optimize GPS energy usage. Yiu *et al.* [36] review the various methods to create the radiomap. Then, they examined the different aspects of localization performance like the density of WiFi APs and the impact of an outdated radiomap. Ahmed *et al.* [1] provide a new optimized algorithm for fast indoor localization using WiFi channel state information. Caso *et al.* [5] introduce an indoor positioning system that relies on the RSS to generate a discrete RSS radiomap. Li *et al.* [16] present SoiCP, a seamless outdoor-indoor crowdsourcing positioning system without requiring site surveying. Crowdsourced WiFi signals are used to build a radiomap without any prior knowledge.

Synthesis. Indoor location systems leveraging WiFi scans are proven to be very useful and accurate. However, existing indoor location systems remain limited to a restricted number of buildings, which have to be either equipped specifically to locate users from WiFi APs, or have to consider a large number of users to reduce the location errors. Most approaches propose to learn the position of these WiFi antennas for every building. In our work, we do not require any prior knowledge about the building and the location of the WiFi antennas. Moreover, we do not intend to physically locate the user, but to capture her context by observing if she is located in a different place or not, which can be answered without an *a priori* knowledge of a map. Then, we consider the related work that uses WiFi fingerprinting to capture the user context.

2.2   WiFi Fingerprinting Systems

Given the attractive cost of considering WiFi signals instead of GPS [38], the state of the art has been extensively considering WiFi signals to capture both indoor and outdoor user contexts. Surrounding WiFi APs can be exposed to mobile apps and act as a place fingerprint—different WiFi AP signals received thus result in different places. As such, using WiFi scans, one can track end users for several hours and obtain valuable information about activities [24], personality traits [23] and routines [27]. However, these WiFi scans can also be used to establish a unique user fingerprint [8,39], extract social networks [33] or track users offline [31,35]. Furthermore, by knowing the location of WiFi APs, the location of users can be inferred from their fingerprint. In particular, some research works are focusing on optimizing the similarity distance between two WiFi fingerprints [2,9,20,37]. Zhang *et al.* [40] introduce POLARIS, a location system using cluster-based solution for WiFi fingerprints. They explain how to collect and compress city-scale fingerprints, and then, how to find the location of a user using similar WiFi fingerprints. Sakib *et al.* [28] present a method to contextualize the mobile user using the WiFi APs fingerprints, with a clustering algorithm that creates a place for each group of WiFi APs. They validate their results with cellular cell ids datasets. Sapiezynski *et al.* [30] use WiFi to enhance GPS traces composed of one GPS location per day, they can locate 80% of mobility across the population. Wind *et al.* [34] use WiFi scans to infer stop locations for users, their algorithm can tell if a user is moving or in a stationary state using just WiFi fingerprints. Finally, Choi *et al.* [7] propose a method for an energy efficient WiFi scanning for user contextualization, they try to minimize the number of scans depending on the scanned WiFi APs.

Synthesis. While a lot of work have been done to localize the user using WiFi indoor location techniques, most of them require either a training phase or user input to locate the user using the WiFi antennas. Several research works have been focusing on the WiFi fingerprinting based on the clustering algorithms and similarity distances, but they do not report on the utility of the collected data, its cost or its privacy-preserving methods. Furthermore, they do not provide any library or framework in order for their methods to be adopted, evaluated and further improved.

3 Introducing INDOORHASH

This section introduces our current design of INDOORHASH and the properties we build on to control the number of relevant hashes.

3.1 Computing an INDOORHASH

To design our INDOORHASH, we implement a modified version of the SimHash algorithm [6]. SimHash is a technique for quickly estimating how similar two sets are. This algorithm was reported to be used by the Google Crawler to find near duplicate pages.

In the context of INDOORHASH, we tokenize the words from the SimHash algorithm as pairs of digits in the hexadecimal MAC address format—*e.g.*, we convert the MAC address 00:FF:AB:0F:C2:C7 into the set of words $\{\langle 00 : 1\rangle, \langle FF : 1\rangle, \langle AB : 1\rangle, \langle 0F : 1\rangle, \langle C2 : 1\rangle, \langle C7 : 1\rangle\}$. Then, the input text we use is the list of all WiFi APs MAC addresses that is returned when triggering a

WiFi scan. This list is therefore converted into a set of unique words weighted by the apparition frequencies resulting. For example, a list of 3 MAC addresses can result in the following input set $\{\langle 00 : 3 \rangle, \langle FF : 2 \rangle, \langle AB : 2 \rangle, \langle OF : 3 \rangle, \langle C2 : 2 \rangle, \langle C7 : 1 \rangle, \langle C7 : 1 \rangle, \langle D0 : 1 \rangle, \langle 02 : 1 \rangle, \langle DD : 1 \rangle, \langle BE : 1 \rangle\}$. From this input set, we compute a SimHash whose $size$ can be defined according to the targeted precision (cf. Algorithm 1).

Algorithm 1. INDOORHASH Algorithm.

---

function TOKENIZESCAN($scan$)
   $tokens \leftarrow \emptyset$
   for all $\langle bssid \rangle \in scan$ **do**
      $words \leftarrow$ SPLIT($bssid$, ' : ')
      for all $word \in words$ **do**
         if $word \in tokens$ **then**
            $frequency \leftarrow$ GETFREQUENCY($tokens, word$)
            $tokens \leftarrow tokens \cup \langle word : frequency + 1 \rangle$
         else
            $tokens \leftarrow tokens \cup \langle word : 1 \rangle$
         end if
      end for
   end for
   return $tokens$
end function

function COMPUTEINDOORHASH($scan, size$)
   $tokens \leftarrow$ TOKENIZESCAN($scan$)
   return SIMHASH($tokens, size$)
end function

3.2   Comparing an INDOORHASH

Unlike standard hashing algorithms, hashes computed by the SimHash algorithm can be compared to estimate the similarity of their respective input sets. To compute this similarity, INDOORHASH computes the Hamming distance between the two input hashes to report on the ratio of similar bits (cf. Algorithm 2).

However, applying standard SimHash similarity on INDOORHASH tends to report a ratio above 0.50, due to the high probability of sharing words between dissimilar MAC addresses. We therefore chose to expand our similarity range, and only consider the values between 0.50 and 1.0 as relevant similarity values. This approach improves the sensibility of the INDOORHASH when comparing their values.

Algorithm 2. INDOORHASH Similarity.

function COMPAREINDOORHASH(*hash1, hash2*)
    distance ← HAMMINGDISTANCE(*hash1, hash2*)
    sim ← 1 − (*distance*/SIZE(*hash1*))
    if *sim* < 0.5 **then**
        return 0
    end if
    return (*sim* − 0.5) × 2   ▷ Expand the similarity score
end function

3.3 Indexing an INDOORHASH

We store an INDOORHASH in a *K-Nearest Neighbors* (KNN) graph that organizes all the computed INDOORHASH according to their pairwise similarity (cf. Algorithm 3). The INDOORHASH storage procedure searches and binds to the closest neighbors in the KNN graph. If the most similar INDOORHASH is already connected to k other hashes, the farest hash is propagated among the remaining neighbors.

Algorithm 3. INDOORHASH Storage.

procedure STOREINDOORHASH(*from,hash*)
    similarity ← COMPAREINDOORHASH(*hash, from*)
    neighbors ← GETKNNNEIGHBORS(*from*)
    maxsim, simnode ← MAX(*hash, neighbors,* COMPAREINDOORHASH)
    if *similarity* < *maxsim* **then** ▷ Propagates *hash* to the most similar neighbor
        STOREINDOORHASH(*hash, simnode*)
    else   ▷ *from* is the most similar hash
        k ← SIZE(*neighbors*)
        if *k* < K_MAX **then**
            ADDKNNNEIGHBOUR(*from, hash*)
        else   ▷ Replaces the least similar neighbor by *hash*
            minsim, node ← MIN(*hash, neighbors,* COMPAREINDOORHASH)
            REMOVEKNNNEIGHBOUR(*from, node*)
            ADDKNNNEIGHBOUR(*from, hash*)
            STOREINDOORHASH(*from, node*)
        end if
    end if
end procedure

This indexing structure allows to quickly search for a similar INDOORHASH in the KNN graph by starting from any random node in this graph and converging through the closest neighbors—*i.e.*, most similar INDOORHASH in our case. The similarity search (SIMSEARCH) returns a node if the similarity of the closest neighbor with the input INDOORHASH is above an expected similarity *threshold* (cf. Algorithm 4).

Algorithm 4. INDOORHASH Search.

function SIMSEARCH(*storage, hash, threshold*)
    seed ← RANDOMNODE(*storage*)
    simnode ← SEARCHINDOORHASH(*seed, hash, ratio*)
    similarity ← COMPAREINDOORHASH(*hash, simnode*)
    if *similarity* >= *threshold* **then**
        return *simnode*
    end if
    return NONE
end function

function SEARCHINDOORHASH(*from, hash*)
    similarity ← COMPAREINDOORHASH(*from, hash*)
    neighbors ← GETKNNNEIGHBORS(*from*)
    maxsim, simnode ← MAX(*hash, neighbors*, COMPAREINDOORHASH)
    if *similarity* > *maxsim* **then**   ▷ *from* is the most similar neighbor
        return *from*
    end if
    return SEARCHINDOORHASH(*simnode, hash*)
end function

3.4 Classifying an INDOORHASH

INDOORHASH leverages the SimHash algorithm [6] to generate a robust hash from a list of visible WiFi APs. Depending on situations, we can consider that:

1. INDOORHASH refers to a *new hash*—*i.e.*, whenever a hash is stable for more than 5*mn*, a new INDOORHASH is stored locally,
2. INDOORHASH refers to a *known hash* when it is stored locally,
3. INDOORHASH refers to a *commuting hash* when no hash can be computed or the hash keeps changing after every scan.

Algorithm 5 describes how we classify an INDOORHASH along the above situations. This context classification algorithm allows not only the device to adjust its behavior accordingly, but also avoid an explosion of the number of collected INDOORHASH. Indeed, by setting an appropriate DELAY and SIMILARITY threshold, one can filter out any candidate INDOORHASH that is considered as irrelevant (*e.g.*, spending less than 5*mn* in a place does not require to be remembered). By adjusting the reference *storage*, the algorithm can leverage a graph of shared location hashes to quickly classify it as a known location, without waiting for the classification delay to be elapsed.

3.5 Sharing an INDOORHASH

INDOORHASH does not make any strong assumption on the mobile device that is used to capture the current indoor location. As such, it can therefore be shared among users to ease the detection of known locations, and even used as a location

Algorithm 5. INDOORHASH Classification.

```
function CLASSIFYINDOORHASH(storage, timestamp, hash)
    if hash <> lastHash then
        lastHash ← hash
        lastTimestamp ← timestamp
        return COMMUTING_HASH
    else
        found ← SIMSEARCH(storage, hash, SIMILARITY)        ▷ Similarity search
        if found then
            return KNOWN_HASH
        else
            if timestamp − lastTimestamp > DELAY then
                STOREINDOORHASH(storage, hash)
                return KNOWN_HASH
            end if
            return NEW_HASH
        end if
    end if
end function
```

key to store some context information. For example, whenever an INDOORHASH is computed, a device can query a cloud service to obtain some information associated to this location. The remote service can adjust the similarity score to constrain how similar two indoor locations should be in order to share the associated information, thus avoiding adversaries accessing any information shared online. Conversely, the remote storage service only manipulates INDOORHASH and cannot learn about the physical location of the end user, thus avoiding any leak of sensitive geolocated information (cf. Sect. 4.1). Furthermore, at scale, the remote storage of known INDOORHASH can leverage the indexing structure introduced in Sect. 3.3 to quickly find the most similar INDOORHASH among the graph of known hashes shared online.

4   Empirical Evaluation

This section reports on the empirical evaluation we conducted to assess INDOORHASH as a robust indoor location hash that can be used to capture the current indoor location of a user, while preserving her privacy. We therefore start by conducting a privacy analysis of our contribution, before introducing the DAYKEEPER app we deployed to assess the accuracy of INDOORHASH to capture indoor locations.

4.1   Privacy Analysis

Recover the GPS Location of INDOORHASH. Existing WiFi fingerprinting methods exploit raw MAC addresses to recover a GPS location from crowdsourced datasets that share key-value pairs of MAC addresses and the associated GPS location [30]. In our case, INDOORHASH shares the hash of a set of MAC addresses. Hashing a single MAC address is not enough to preserve the user privacy, as a rainbow table could be created for all the hashes. In our solution, we therefore hash all detected MAC addresses of WiFi APs, which adds a huge entropy to the generated hash and therefore reduces the risk to infer the physical location captured by a given INDOORHASH. Concretely, to recover all the possible hashes, a rainbow table would have to be created for 240 bits—when assuming hashes built from 5 MAC addresses (48 bits)—which is far beyond the state of the art. Additionally, as INDOORHASH does not make any assumption on the number of input MAC addresses, such an attack becomes impracticable.

Identify Users from Clusters of INDOORHASH. As no GPS location can be recovered from an INDOORHASH, the state-of-the-art geo-spatial attacks, like the ST-DBSCAN [3], fail to cluster the user locations. Therefore, running a similar attack on a set of INDOORHASH can only produce clusters of hashes grouped by similarity, which fails to disclose any sensitive information about the user. Indeed, even though an INDOORHASH can be considered as *Point of Interest* (POI), no metadata (label, location, category, etc.) can be exploited by an adversary to infer some privacy sensitive knowledge.

Conclusion. INDOORHASH provides a robust location hash that captures the physical context of a user, without disclosing any privacy sensitive information regarding the locations she visited. Yet, the adoption of INDOORHASH does not prevent developers from carefully anonymizing any payload that could be attached to such a hash (*e.g.*, IP address, device model, user identifier) to avoid indirect privacy breach.

4.2 DayKeeper Android App

To demonstrate and assess INDOORHASH in the wild, we developed an Android app that embeds our INDOORHASH as a software library. This Android app, named DAYKEEPER, aims at keeping track of the daily activities of end users in order to report on the time they spent in different locations (home, office, shopping, leisure). When users opt in, INDOORHASH and some metrics (cf. Sect. 4.3) are also periodically synchronized on a remote server, using the APISENSE platform [10], for *postmortem* analysis purpose. This data collection campaign conforms to the *Institutional Review Board* (IRB) approval associated to the exploitation of the APISENSE platform.[1]

Figure 1 depicts some screenshots of the DAYKEEPER Android app.[2] In particular, users of DAYKEEPER are free to navigate through daily (cf. Fig. 1a), weekly (cf. Fig. 1b) and monthly views (cf. Fig. 1c) and to eventually label the

---

[1] https://apisense.io.
[2] Available from https://play.google.com/store/apps/details?id=io.apisense.netqulity.

reported INDOORHASH to keep track of their personal timeline. With DAY-
KEEPER, we aim at demonstrating that INDOORHASH can offer a fine grain
analysis of user activities by splitting different activities observed in a single
building (*e.g.*, office, meeting, cafetaria, gym). Furthermore, as DAYKEEPER
leverages the WiFi APs, it provides a lightweight activity logger that does not
drain the device battery by continuously requesting the GPS sensor.

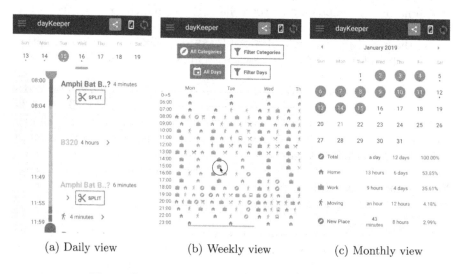

(a) Daily view   (b) Weekly view   (c) Monthly view

Fig. 1. Screenshots of the DAYKEEPER Android App.

The INDOORHASH is continuously updated by DAYKEEPER using a background service that periodically scans the surrounding WiFi APs, computes the
associated INDOORHASH (cf. Sect. 3.1) and classifies it with regards to *known
hashes* (cf. Sect. 3.4). In DAYKEEPER, *known hashes* are reflected as a continuous timeline of a given color, while *commuting hashes* are displayed as a
transition 'Moving' between two *known hashes*.

4.3   Deployment Statistics

Overall, we can report that the DAYKEEPER has been installed by 31 users along
one month. During this period, users have detected 58, 500 unique WiFi APs,
resulting in 12, 201 INDOORHASH. The remainder of this section covers the statistics we collected along our experimentation period (cf. Fig. 2). One should note
that we filtered out 9 users of DAYKEEPER who used our mobile app, but did
not opt in the sharing of their metrics. As users come and go and can activate
or deactivate the context acquisition, the data contributed by each user varies
greatly. Figure 2a therefore depicts the number of WiFi scans triggered per user
as a more representative indicator of the activity of registered users.

Then, Fig. 2b reports on the number of unique WiFi AP per user, this number reflects the diversity of locations that have been visited by a user: the more the user moves, the more WiFi APs. Figure 2c shares some indications on the number of WiFi APs that can be captured along a scan. This number depends on the density of WiFi APs exposed to a user, but it clearly shows that users are often exposed to more than 5 MAC addresses, thus strengthening the resilience of INDOORHASH against rainbow table attacks (cf. Sect. 4.1). Finally, Fig. 2d reports the average number of WiFi APs per hour for each user, thus giving a clear signal about the continuous WiFi coverage of users.

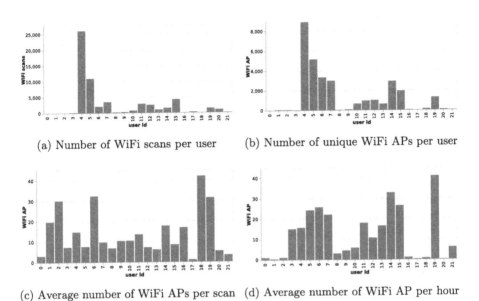

(a) Number of WiFi scans per user   (b) Number of unique WiFi APs per user

(c) Average number of WiFi APs per scan (d) Average number of WiFi AP per hour
per user

Fig. 2. DAYKEEPER App Deployment Statistics.

Overall, Figs. 2 delivers some insightful feedback about the diversity of profiles of DAYKEEPER users—e.g., whether they are moving or stationary. For example, we can observe that the user with the identifier 20 was mostly stationary, as her device contributed a lot of hours (cf. Fig. 2a), but with only 57 unique WiFi APs (cf. Fig. 2b) and an average of 0.10 WiFi APs per hour (cf. Fig. 2d). On the other side, the user with identifier 19 has been using the DAYKEEPER app for a shorter period of time, but exhibiting a more active profile. The rest of our evaluation considers all the users who have been sharing their INDOORHASH with our remote storage server, no matter their profile.

4.4   INDOORHASH Evaluation

This section focuses on a quantitative evaluation of the INDOORHASH. To assess our contribution, we compare it to alternative hashing and similarity algorithms adopted by the state of the art, as described below.

Evaluation Metrics. In the context of this evaluation, we focus on assessing the robustness of the location hash to accurately capture the context of a user. We therefore consider the following metrics:

- **Total period** represents the total number of hours of activities recognized by the algorithms for all of the users (the higher the better). This metrics reflects the capability of the algorithm to classify the context of the user;
- **Max period** reflects the maximum number of hours assigned to a single location hash (the higher the better). This metrics highlights the capability of each algorithm to detect known locations;
- **Max occurrences** represents the maximum number of occurrences that can be observed for one location hash (the higher the better). This metrics demonstrate the capability of the algorithms to infer similar location hashes for recurrent locations;
- **Hashes with 1+ hour** represents the number of location hashes that last for more than one hour (the higher the better). This metrics highlights the capability of the location hash to capture stationary conditions;
- **Max detected hashes** represents the maximum number of distinct location hashes for a given location (the lower the better). This metrics reflects the quality of the generated location hashes.

Hashing and Similarity Algorithms. We start by comparing INDOORHASH with the most-related similarity algorithms:

- The JACCARD index is the baseline algorithm that we apply to compare raw scans including plain MAC addresses of detected WiFi APs,
- The SIMHASH correspond to the standard SimHash algorithm [6] applied to plain MAC addresses,
- The INDOORHASH refers to the approach described in this paper.

For all the algorithms, we consider a similarity threshold of $0.60f$ as a conservative policy to classify the inferred location hashes.

Table 1. Comparison of alternative hashing and similarity metrics

Variant	Overall period	Max period	Max occurrences	Hashes of 1+ hour	Max detected hashes
JACCARD	2,077	524	3,684	58	22
SIMHASH	1,112	350	3,127	50	63
INDOORHASH	**2,022**	**524**	**3,684**	**59**	**23**

Overall, we can observe in Table 1 that INDOORHASH competes with the JACCARD index while providing stronger privacy guarantees. The missing 55 h that are not recognized by INDOORHASH refers to short periods of time ($<5\,$min) where the recognition algorithm of INDOORHASH considers the location as a new hash (cf. Algorithm 5).

Impact of MAC addresses. To further evaluate INDOORHASH, we consider 3 variants of INDOORHASH to evaluate the impact of the number of MAC addresses on the stability of the computed hashes. Table 2 shows the metrics for the following variants:

- **No limit** refers to the baseline INDOORHASH that does not limit the number of MAC addresses to be included in the computation of the hash;
- **10 MAC** is a variant that limits the computation of the INDOORHASH to the first 10 MAC addresses return by the scan;
- **5 MAC** is a variant that limits the INDOORHASH computation to the first 5 MAC addresses.
- **1 MAC** is the extreme variant that only consider the first MAC address to compute an INDOORHASH.

Table 2. Impact of the MAC addresses on the stability of INDOORHASH.

Variant	Overall period	Max period	Max occurrences	Hashes of 1+ hour	Max detected hashes
No limit	2,022	524	3,684	59	23
10 MAC	2,001	524	3,772	59	30
5 MAC	1,958	524	2,192	62	41
1 MAC	1,847	524	1,776	61	233

Overall, one can observe that limiting the number of MAC addresses has a harmful impact on the privacy (cf. Sect. 4.1), but also on the accuracy of INDOORHASH. Indeed, the variant considering a single MAC address offers the worst performances: the maximum number of occurrences drops to $1,776$ compared to the default variant that captures up to $3,684$ occurrences. This can result in some physical places not being recognized by the algorithm. At the same time, one can see that most important places (*Hashes with 1+hour*) keep being recognized with the same accuracy as the baseline, thus indicating that limiting MAC addresses tends to reduce the capability to capture places visited for shorter periods.

5 Towards Privacy-Preserving Location-Based Services

In this paper, we believe that *Location-Based Services* (LBS) require to guarantee the user privacy by design, in order to avoid any potential risk of data leaks that might contribute to learn sensitive knowledge from visited locations (*e.g.*, home, office, leisure). Such privacy-preserving LBS cannot collect and process the raw user locations, but should rather build on location hashes that reveal the necessary bits of information that are required to implement the service. This section therefore lists candidate LBS features that could benefit from INDOORHASH in the future.

Points of Interest (POIs) refer to known physical locations that may reveal sensitive information about the habits and tastes of end users (*e.g.*, shopping mall, restaurants) and can be used by third parties to feed recommendation algorithms. INDOORHASH can be considered as fine-grained POI that does not reveal any semantics about the location visited by a user, but can still be used to recommend alternative nearby locations by comparing similar hash histories among users.

Social networking is another example of LBS that can benefit from INDOORHASH by comparing the hash histories in order to identify potential connections within a crowd of users without revealing the exact locations where these users use to meet. INDOORHASH can therefore support the definition of proximity datasets that are commonly used for various purposes, such as mobile testing [22], by reporting on the colocation of end users and potential connections in a crowd that can support the evaluation of dissemination protocols [19,21].

Context prediction can also leverage the history of INDOORHASH to understand the mobility of end users and possibly predict the next location (*e.g.*, using markov chains or *n*-grams) of a given user in order to anticipate some actions, like fetching some content or buffering a video before loosing an Internet connection [25]. This context prediction can also be used to support the development of context-aware applications whose behaviors can adjust accordingly. For example, maintaining a different profile of a web browser to avoid that a private or professional web history being exploited by third-party cookies in a different context, which might be unknown and thus sensitive.

Routine analysis refers to the detection of user activities to better understand her daily habits. While DAYKEEPER (cf. Sect. 4.2) provides an example of personal activity tracker built on top of INDOORHASH, we believe that one can provide advanced features to detect if a user is in or out of a routine and react accordingly. Such a mechanism can help the user to focus on her tasks (*e.g.*, by enabling a *do not disturb* mode) or trigger specific assistance when she is not in a routine.

Mobile crowdsourcing consists in gathering field measurements from a crowd of participants. In mobile crowdsourcing systems, the user location is often used to group data along spatial dimensions to build some specific maps (*e.g.*, the open signal initiative)[3]. In such cases, beyond raw GPS locations, Geohash and Pluscode[4] provide a compact encoding of any physical location on earth. While both of them can fuzz the user location by adjusting their encoding scheme, they keep disclosing a critical information for the end user. Yet, user location may only be required to group or aggregate field measurements by location without sharing the physical location with anyone. In these situation, we believe that INDOORHASH can provide a privacy-preserving spatial keys that can be

---

[3] https://www.opensignal.com/.

[4] https://plus.codes/.

used to process geolocated measurements. Interestingly, the indexing structure allows end users who can compute the INDOORHASH to access these aggregated measurements. For example, one can imagine a user getting the history of indoor air pollution using her current hash to query a remote measurement service built on top of INDOORHASH [11].

6   Conclusion

Location-Based Services (LBS) are increasingly getting adopted by end users who expect to be delivered personalized user experiences depending on their current context. However, the characterization of this context often relies on the physical location of the user which is *i)* hard to capture in indoor environments and *ii)* highly sensitive from a privacy perspective.

In this paper, we tackle both of these challenges by introducing a new indoor location hash, named INDOORHASH. More specifically, INDOORHASH captures a logical user location without disclosing the physical place visited by this user. Our contribution consists in applying the SimHash algorithm to the processing of MAC addresses exposed by WiFi APs. We show that the INDOORHASH computed from such input data offers a robust location hash that accurately capture any user location. We also implement a distributed system that allows to store and index INDOORHASH in order to ease the detection of known locations and share geolocated data with privacy guarantees.

As a matter of perspectives, we are interested in extending the INDOORHASH to a more general location hash scheme that can leverage additional signals surrounding a user, like the GSM antennas or BLE beacons in order to increase the coverage of inferred locations. We are also interested in exploring new operations on location hashes to support privacy-preserving data clustering algorithms.

References

1. Ahmed, A.U., Bergmann, N.W., Arablouei, R., Kusy, B., De Hoog, F., Jurdak, R.: Poster abstract: fast indoor localization using WiFi channel state information. In: 17th International Conference on Information Processing in Sensor Networks (IPSN 2019), pp. 120–121. IEEE, April 2018
2. Beder, C., Klepal, M.: Fingerprinting based localisation revisited: a rigorous approach for comparing RSSI measurements coping with missed access points and differing antenna attenuations. In: International Conference on Indoor Positioning and Indoor Navigation (IPIN), pp. 1–7. IEEE (2012)
3. Birant, D., Kut, A.: ST-DBSCAN: an algorithm for clustering spatial-temporaldata. Data Knowledge Eng. **60**(1), 208–221 (2007)
4. Capurso, N., Song, T., Cheng, W., Yu, J., Cheng, X.: An android-based mechanism for energy efficient localization depending on indoor/outdoor context. IEEE Internet Things J. **4**(2), 299–307 (2017)

5. Caso, G., De Nardis, L., Lemic, F., Handziski, V., Wolisz, A., Di Benedetto, M.G.: Vifi: virtual fingerprinting wifi-based indoor positioning viamulti-wall multi-floor propagation model. IEEE Transactions on Mobile Computing (2019)

6. Charikar, M.S.: Similarity estimation techniques from rounding algorithms. In: 34th ACM Symposium on Theory of Computing, pp. 380–388. ACM (2002)

7. Choi, T., Chon, Y., Cha, H.: Energy-efficient WiFi scanning for localization. Pervasive Mob. Comput. **37**, 124–138 (2017)

8. De Montjoye, Y.A., Hidalgo, C.A., Verleysen, M., Blondel, V.D.: Unique in the crowd: the privacy bounds of human mobility. Sci. Rep. **3**, 1376 (2013)

9. Del Corte-Valiente, A., Gómez-Pulido, J.M., Gutiérrez-Blanco, O.: Efficient techniques and algorithms for improving indoor localization precision on WLAN networks applications. Int. J. Commun. Netw. Syst. Sci. **2**(07), 645 (2009)

10. Haderer, N., Rouvoy, R., Seinturier, L.: Dynamic deployment of sensing experiments in the wild using smartphones. In: Dowling, J., Taïani, F. (eds.) DAIS 2013. LNCS, vol. 7891, pp. 43–56. Springer, Heidelberg (2013). https://doi.org/10.1007/978-3-642-38541-4_4

11. Hanoune, B., et al.: Conception and deployment of the Apolline sensor network for IAQ monitoring. In: 10th International Conference on Indoor Air Quality, Ventilation and Energy Conservation in Buildings (IAQVEC 2019), September 2019

12. He, S., Chan, S.H.G.: Wi-fi fingerprint-based indoor positioning: recent advances and comparisons. IEEE Commun. Surv. Tutorials **18**(1), 466–490 (2015)

13. Jin, M., Koo, B., Lee, S., Park, C., Lee, M.J., Kim, S.: IMU-assisted nearest neighbor selection for real-time WiFi fingerprinting positioning. In: International Conference on Indoor Positioning and Indoor Navigation (IPIN 2014), pp. 745–748. IEEE, October 2014

14. Krumm, J., Horvitz, E.: Locadio: inferring motion and location from wi-fi signal strengths. In: Mobiquitous, pp. 4–13 (2004)

15. Li, H., Sun, L., Zhu, H., Lu, X., Cheng, X.: Achieving privacy preservation in WiFi fingerprint-based localization. In: IEEE INFOCOM, pp. 2337–2345. IEEE, April 2014

16. Li, Z., Zhao, X., Hu, F., Zhao, Z., Carrera, J.L., Braun, T.: Soicp: a seamless outdoor-indoor crowdsensing positioning system. IEEE internet of Things J. **6**, 8626–8644 (2019)

17. Liu, H., et al.: Push the limit of WiFi based localization for smartphones. In: 18th International Conference on Mobile Computing and Networking (Mobicom 2012), p. 305. ACM, New York (2012)

18. Luo, C., Hong, H., Chan, M.C.: Piloc: a self-calibrating participatory indoor localization system. In: 13th International Symposium on Information Processing in Sensor Networks (IPSN 2014), pp. 143–153. IEEE (2014)

19. Luxey, A., Bromberg, Y.D., Costa, F.M., Lima, V., da Rocha, R.C., Taïani, F.: Sprinkler: a probabilistic dissemination protocol to provide fluid user interaction in multi-device ecosystems. In: International Conference on Pervasive Computing and Communications (PerCom), pp. 1–10. IEEE (2018)

20. Lymberopoulos, D., Liu, J.: The microsoft indoor localization competition: experiences and lessons learned. IEEE Signal Process. Magazine **34**(5), 125–140 (2017)

21. Meftah, L., Rouvoy, R., Chrisment, I.: FOUGERE: user-centric location privacy in mobile crowdsourcing apps. In: Pereira, J., Ricci, L. (eds.) DAIS 2019. LNCS, vol. 11534, pp. 116–132. Springer, Cham (2019). https://doi.org/10.1007/978-3-030-22496-7_8

22. Meftah, L., Rouvoy, R., Chrisment, I.: Testing nearby peer-to-peer mobile apps at large. In: 6th International Conference on Mobile Software Engineering and Systems (MOBILESoft 2019), pp. 1–11. IEEE (2019)

23. de Montjoye, Y.-A., Quoidbach, J., Robic, F., Pentland, A.S.: Predicting personality using novel mobile phone-based metrics. In: Greenberg, A.M., Kennedy, W.G., Bos, N.D. (eds.) SBP 2013. LNCS, vol. 7812, pp. 48–55. Springer, Heidelberg (2013). https://doi.org/10.1007/978-3-642-37210-0_6

24. Nguyen, T.B., Nguyen, T., Luo, W., Venkatesh, S., Phung, D.: Unsupervised inference of significant locations from wifi data for understanding human dynamics. In: 13th International Conference on Mobile and Ubiquitous Multimedia, pp. 232–235. MUM 2014, ACM, New York (2014)

25. Paspallis, N., Alshaal, S.E.: Improving QOE via context prediction: a case study of using wifi radiomaps to predict network disconnection. In: ICPE Companion, pp. 31–34. ACM (2017)

26. Pulkkinen, T., Verwijnen, J., Nurmi, P.: WiFi positioning with propagation-based calibration. In: 14th International Conference on Information Processing in Sensor Networks (IPSN 2015), pp. 366–367. ACM (2015)

27. Rekimoto, J., Miyaki, T., Ishizawa, T.: LifeTag: wifi-based continuous location logging for life pattern analysis. In: Hightower, J., Schiele, B., Strang, T. (eds.) LoCA 2007. LNCS, vol. 4718, pp. 35–49. Springer, Heidelberg (2007). https://doi.org/10.1007/978-3-540-75160-1_3

28. Sakib, M.N., Halim, J.B., Huang, C.T.: Determining location and movement pattern using anonymized WiFi access point BSSID. In: 7th International Conference on Security Technology (SecTech 2014), pp. 11–14. IEEE, December 2015

29. Salamah, A.H., Tamazin, M., Sharkas, M.A., Khedr, M.: An enhanced WiFi indoor localization system based on machine learning. In: 2016 International Conference on Indoor Positioning and Indoor Navigation (IPIN 2016), pp. 1–8. IEEE, October 2016

30. Sapiezynski, P., Stopczynski, A., Gatej, R., Lehmann, S.: Tracking humanmobility using WiFi signals. PLoS One 10(7), e0130824 (2015)

31. Sapiezynski, P., Stopczynski, A., Wind, D.K., Leskovec, J., Lehmann, S.: Offline behaviors of online friends. arXiv preprint arXiv:1811.03153 (2018)

32. Shen, G., Chen, Z., Zhang, P., Moscibroda, T., Zhang, Y.: Walkie-markie: indoor pathway mapping made easy. In: 10th USENIX Symposium on Networked Systems Design and Implementation (NSDI 2013), pp. 85–98 (2013)

33. Stopczynski, A., et al.: Measuring large-scale social networks with high resolution. PLoS One 9(4), e95978 (2014)

34. Wind, D.K., Sapiezynski, P., Furman, M.A., Lehmann, S.: Inferringstop-locations from WiFi. PLoS One 11(2), e0149105 (2016)

35. Xie, X., Xu, H., Yang, G., Mao, Z.H., Jia, W., Sun, M.: Reuse of WiFi information for indoor monitoring of the elderly. In: 17th International Conference on Information Reuse and Integration (IRI 2016), pp. 261–264. IEEE, July 2016

36. Yiu, S., Dashti, M., Claussen, H., Perez-Cruz, F.: Wireless RSSI fingerprinting localization (2017)

37. Yiu, S., Yang, K.: Gaussian process assisted fingerprinting localization. IEEE Internet of Things Journal 3(5), 683–690, October 2016

38. Zandbergen, P.A.: Accuracy of iphone locations: a comparison of assisted GPS, wifi and cellular positioning. Trans. GIS **13**, 5–25 (2009)

39. Zhang, H., Yan, Z., Yang, J., Tapia, E.M., Crandall, D.J.: mFingerprint: privacy-preserving user modeling with multimodal mobile device footprints. In: Kennedy, W.G., Agarwal, N., Yang, S.J. (eds.) SBP 2014. LNCS, vol. 8393, pp. 195–203. Springer, Cham (2014). https://doi.org/10.1007/978-3-319-05579-4_24

40. Zhang, N., Feng, J.: POLARIS: a fingerprint-based localization system over wireless networks. In: Gao, H., Lim, L., Wang, W., Li, C., Chen, L. (eds.) WAIM 2012. LNCS, vol. 7418, pp. 58–70. Springer, Heidelberg (2012). https://doi.org/10.1007/978-3-642-32281-5_7

Cloud and Systems

Towards Hypervisor Support
for Enhancing the Performance
of Virtual Machine Introspection

Benjamin Taubmann[✉] and Hans P. Reiser

University of Passau, Passau, Germany
{bt,hr}@sec.uni-passau.de

Abstract. Virtual machine introspection (VMI) is the process of external monitoring of virtual machines. Previous work has demonstrated that VMI can contribute to the security of cloud environments and distributed systems, as it enables, for example, stealthy intrusion detection. One of the biggest challenges for applying VMI in production environments is the performance overhead that certain tracing operations impose on the monitored virtual machine. In this paper, we show how this performance overhead can be significantly minimized by incorporating minor extensions for VMI operations into the hypervisor. In a proof-of-concept implementation, we demonstrate that the pre-processing of VMI events in the Xen hypervisor reduces the monitoring overhead for the use case of VMI-based process-bound monitoring by a factor of 18.

1 Introduction

Virtual machine introspection (VMI) is the process of analyzing the state of a virtual machine from outside, i.e., the perspective of the hypervisor [5]. Based on the external view, VMI-based monitoring has certain properties that make it appealing for many application scenarios, including solutions that aim to enhance the security in cloud environments and distributed systems [6,8]. Hence, it is not surprising that the first application for VMI was an intrusion detection system [5]. Those properties are: isolation between the monitoring and the monitored system, an untampered view on the system state, and the stealthiness of monitoring.

In the following we use the term *production virtual machine* for the virtual machine that is monitored via VMI and is performing the normal operations. The term *monitoring virtual machine* is used for the virtual machine that analyzes the production virtual machine using VMI [18]. The focus of this paper is on the Xen architecture. Hence, the term monitoring virtual machine refers to either the Dom0 of Xen or any other virtual machine with the permissions to perform VMI-based operations. The VMI application that performs the analysis does not run directly in the hypervisor.

Published by Springer Nature Switzerland AG 2020
A. Remke and V. Schiavoni (Eds.): DAIS 2020, LNCS 12135, pp. 41–54, 2020.
https://doi.org/10.1007/978-3-030-50323-9_3

There are two forms of virtual machine introspection: *asynchronous and synchronous*. The main difference between these operation modes is how the analysis is started [8]. We speak of asynchronous virtual machine introspection if the analysis is started by external events, such as timers that periodically retrieve the system state. This is useful to regularly observe the system state and retrieve information that is in memory for a longer time frame, such as the list of running processes. Synchronous virtual machine introspection is triggered by sensitive operations in the control flow of the monitored system, e.g., software breakpoints. This can be required to retrieve ephemeral information that resides in main memory only for a short period, such as the parameters of function calls.

In this paper we use the term *performance impact* to quantify the overhead induced on the execution in the production virtual machine due to VMI-based operations. The overhead is mainly caused by the fact that the production virtual machine is paused for the analysis, which has three different reasons. The first one concerns the case when the production virtual machine and monitoring virtual machine share the same physical CPU core. In this case, the production virtual machine gets paused when the monitoring system is running. This overhead factor can be reduced by using an additional CPU core or by minimizing the amount of time required for the analysis.

The second reason is that the production virtual machine must be paused to prevent that the analyzed data structure (e.g., the process list) is modified during the analysis. If the analysis were performed on a running system, memory contents changing concurrently to the analysis could result in incorrect information. In order to obtain reliable information, it is, therefore, necessary to perform the analysis in a non-modifying state in order to retrieve a consistent view of the system state. A common approach to address this problem is to take a snapshot of the contents in main memory and then run the analysis on it. However, taking a snapshot of the main memory may also require to pause the production virtual machine. Klemperer et al. [9] addressed this problem by implementing a snapshot mechanism that uses a copy-on-write strategy.

The third reason is that the production virtual machine is paused due to synchronous VMI-based mechanisms, e.g., when a breakpoint is invoked and the control flow of the production virtual machine traps to the monitoring virtual machine. The impact on the performance of the production virtual machine, in this case, depends on how often the monitored virtual machine is interrupted and the time how long the monitored system is paused for the analysis.

While the first two causes of performance overhead have adequate solutions, the third reason is an open problem that severely limits the applicability of synchronous VMI-based monitoring in practical use cases. In this paper, we focus on how to minimize the performance overhead in this third case and discuss mechanisms to enable efficient VMI-based monitoring. In detail, we discuss an approach that reduces the overhead of process-bound system call monitoring. Minimizing the overhead of synchronous VMI-based monitoring is important to implement VMI-based security solutions in production environments that tolerate only a minimal performance impact.

The contributions of this paper are:

- a presentation of different approaches that aim to minimize the performance impact of synchronous virtual machine introspection;
- a proof-of-concept implementation that minimizes the performance impact of process-bound monitoring;
- the evaluation of the proof-of-concept implementation.

The outline of the paper is as follows: Sect. 2 introduces the most important technologies used by virtual machine introspection and the most common mechanisms of synchronous virtual machine introspection. Section 3 discusses approaches on how to minimize the overhead of synchronous VMI-based monitoring. In Sect. 4, we discuss a prototype implementation that aims at minimizing the monitoring overhead of process-bound system call tracing. In Sect. 5, we measure the performance gain of the prototype. Section 6 discusses related approaches and Sect. 7 concludes the paper.

2   Virtual Machine Introspection

This section describes the technologies that are used for virtual machine introspection and synchronous monitoring.

2.1   Hardware Requirements

Synchronous virtual machine introspection requires that the CPU is able to trap to the hypervisor in order to monitor the execution of a virtual machine. For example, the hardware virtualization instruction set of Intel processors (Intel VT-x) allows trapping to the hypervisor (VM-Exit) when certain sensitive instructions are invoked in a virtual machine [7, 20]. The virtual-machine control structure (VMCS) defines for each virtual machine in which case it should trap to the hypervisor (VMX root mode). While the hypervisor handles the event, the virtual machine that invoked the sensitive operation is paused.

2.2   Hypervisor Support

The hypervisor has an important role for virtual machine introspection. For asynchronous introspection, the hypervisor must give the monitoring virtual machine the permissions to access the main memory of the production virtual machine. This can be done for example by mapping the memory pages from the production virtual machine into the address space of the monitoring virtual machine. For synchronous monitoring, the hypervisor needs to forward the information about traps to the monitoring virtual machine so that it can run analysis operations. The concepts presented in this paper are mostly hypervisor independent. However, the focus of this paper is on the design of the Xen architecture.

Xen [1] is a bare-metal hypervisor that supports the hardware virtualization instruction set of Intel. The relevant components for VMI-based operations using

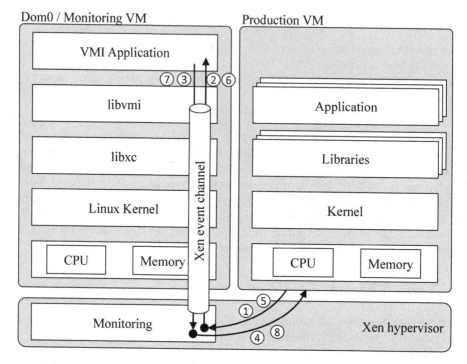

Fig. 1. VMI architecture using Xen and Libvmi. The arrows show the control flow of VM Exit/Entry-based context switches when a sensitive instruction in the production VM triggers a VMI event. The numbered items illustrate that synchronous tracing with breakpoints requires two iterations, the first to intercept the breakpoint and single-step the original instruction, the second to re-insert the breakpoint and resume the production VM.

Xen are depicted in Fig. 1. The Dom0 is the virtual machine with the most permissions and can access the main memory of all virtual machines running on this hypervisor. Thus, most VMI-based approaches implement the VMI application in Dom0. However, with the Xen security modules (XSM) it is possible to grant other virtual machines than the Dom0 the permissions required to perform VMI-based operations [17,18]. This has certain advantages and can be useful in cloud computing when it is necessary to restrict the VMI permissions of a monitoring virtual machine to the production virtual machine of a specific user.

Asynchronous VMI-based operations can be implemented with Xen by mapping the relevant memory pages of a virtual machine to the monitoring virtual machine, e.g., the Dom0. The functions that map memory pages are implemented in the libxencontrol (libxc) library and use Xen hypercalls to instruct the hypervisor. For synchronous VMI-based operations, sensitive operations in the production virtual machine cause a trap to the hypervisor. Then, the monitoring module of the hypervisor becomes active and sends the corresponding VMI event via the event channel to the VMI application in the Dom0/monitoring virtual machine. While the event is processed in the monitoring virtual machine, the production virtual machine is paused.

2.3 VMI Applications

LibVMI [13,14] is the defacto standard library that helps to build VMI-based monitoring applications. LibVMI provides the API to perform VMI-based operations on Xen and KVM. This includes, for example, functions for reading and writing content from the main memory and functions for translating virtual and physical addresses. In addition, LibVMI supports synchronous monitoring with Xen. For this purpose, it provides primitives for listening on VMI-events generated by the Xen hypervisor.

2.4 Basic Synchronous VMI Methods

The main advantages of synchronous virtual machine introspection are that it can be used to monitor the control flow of virtual machines and to extract ephemeral information such as parameters of function calls. The mechanisms of synchronous monitoring utilize the concepts of hardware virtualization that allow trapping to the hypervisor under certain conditions, e.g., when sensitive instructions are invoked. In the following, we explain the most common VMI-based monitoring techniques: breakpoints, the monitoring of the write access to CPU control registers, and system call tracing.

Breakpoints. A common approach to monitoring the control flow using virtual machine introspection is to insert software breakpoints, by using the INT3 instructions that trap to the hypervisor when they are invoked. One approach to implement a software breakpoint mechanism for virtual machine introspection requires the following eight steps. First, the software breakpoint is inserted at the function that should be monitored, either by changing the content in memory or by manipulating the page tables[1]. Second, the production virtual machine invokes the function and the CPU traps to the hypervisor. Third, the hypervisor handles the trap caused by the INT3 instruction, creates a VMI monitoring event and sends it via the Xen event channel to the virtual machine handling the event. Fourth, the monitoring virtual machine gets active and the VMI application receives the new event. Fifth, the VMI application analysis the state of the production virtual machine and re-inserts the original instruction. The VMI application finishes the investigation and tells the hypervisor that the production virtual machine should perform a single-step and execute the original instruction. Sixth, the CPU is configured to run the original instruction in the context of the production virtual machine in single-step mode. Afterward, the CPU traps

---

[1] The approach of manipulating the page tables uses the altp2m feature of Xen [10]. This approach does not modify the original memory page. Instead, it creates a new memory page that includes the software breakpoint. By switching the content in the memory tables it can activate/deactivate the breakpoint.

again to the hypervisor. Seventh, steps four and five are repeated with the difference that the VMI application inserts the original breakpoint. Eight, the VMI application tells the hypervisor to resume the production virtual machine.

In total, this procedure requires switching twice between the monitoring virtual machine and the production virtual machine. First, to handle the breakpoint, and second, to reinsert it after the original instruction is executed in single-step mode. Since a software breakpoint actually traps first to the Xen hypervisor and is then handled by a monitoring virtual machine, eight VM Exit/Entry-based context switches are required to handle a single breakpoint (see Fig. 1).

Also, since the VMI application is usually implemented as a userspace application in monitoring virtual machine, additional context switches between the kernel of monitoring virtual machine and the VMI applications are required. The actual number of required context switches depends on many factors, such as the scheduler's decision and how many processes are active in the monitoring virtual machine.

Access to Control Registers. Modifications to the control registers of a CPU can change the general behavior of the system. Hence, observing the changes is a valuable mechanism of virtual machine introspection. The most common example is the monitoring of modifications of the CR3 register. In the Intel architecture, the CR3 register holds a pointer to the directory table base (DTB) of a process. Whenever a process is dispatched by the scheduler of the operating system, it updates the contents of the CR3 register to point to the DTB of the next process. Thus, monitoring changes of the CR3 register can be used to be informed whenever a new process becomes active.

2.5 System Call Tracing

Software breakpoints can be used to monitor the invocation of system calls. To do so, the breakpoint is set on the first instruction of the system call handler function. Since the operating system kernel is used by all processes, this means that all invocations of system calls of all processes are monitored when a breakpoint is set on a system call handler. Thus, if only the system calls of one process should be monitored, this approach can have unnecessary high overhead.

There are two strategies to obtain the system call invocations of a specific process. The first one is to use post-processing. This means that the monitoring application itself filters the events in order to obtain only those system calls that belong to a process with a specific process identifier (PID). This, of course, does not have any positive impact on the performance at run-time. The second strategy is to additionally monitor modifications of the CR3 register, which indicate that a different process in the production virtual machine is being dispatched. Every time a new process is dispatched, the breakpoints can be inserted/removed from main memory so that the tracing is only active when specific processes are running. Sentanoe et al. [16] call this approach *process-bound monitoring*.

3   Improving the Performance

The methods of synchronous virtual machine introspection have a severe performance impact on the production virtual machine. One big part of that problem is the long chain of subsequent operations that are required to handle a VMI event in the hypervisor and the monitoring virtual machine while the production virtual machine is paused. Those steps are processed for each VMI event, even if the VMI application just disregards the event because it does not match a certain filter.

The processing of a breakpoint in the VMI application can be organized into three processing layers. On the lowest layer, the breakpoint is handled with the steps explained in Sect. 2.4. Then on the layer above, the VMI-events of a breakpoint are filtered and processed in the VMI application, e.g., when only breakpoints of a specific process should be monitored VMI events can be filtered based on the value stored in the CR3 register. On the highest layer, additional data from the production virtual machine, e.g., the parameters passed to a function are extracted.

In the following, we discuss possible approaches that aim at minimizing the VMI performance overhead. All of these approaches achieve this goal by reducing the time needed by the data extraction routine and the time during which the monitored virtual machine is paused.

Pre-filtering of Events: In some cases, only a few of the VMI events are necessary for a specific use case. For example, in the case of process-bound monitoring, many events are generated by changes in the CR3 register. However, only events for changes that either write the value of the DTB of the process to be monitored to CR3 or replace that value with a different value are required to enable/disable the breakpoints. All other CR3-based events (e.g., when a context switch from a not monitored to another not monitored process occurs) don't need to be observed. Nevertheless, in the usual approach to monitor CR3 events, a context switch to the monitoring virtual machine is required in all cases, even if the VMI application simply ignores irrelevant events.

One approach to solve this problem is to filter events at the hypervisor level. For example, CR3 events that are captured because of the production virtual machine changing the register from *oldDTB* to *newDTB* could be forwarded to the userspace VMI application only if either *oldDTB* or *newDTB* match the DTB of the process to be monitored.

Breakpoint Mechanism: A fast and efficient breakpoint mechanism helps to minimize the tracing overhead. Since breakpoints can occur frequently, small optimizations can make a big difference. Hence, the implementation of breakpoints should be as optimized as possible so that it requires as little time as possible.

Moreover, the breakpoint mechanism should be implemented into the hypervisor. This eliminates the need to switch to the monitoring virtual machine after a single-step operation was executed as the restoration of the original instruction is independent of the VMI application logic. So instead of switching to the

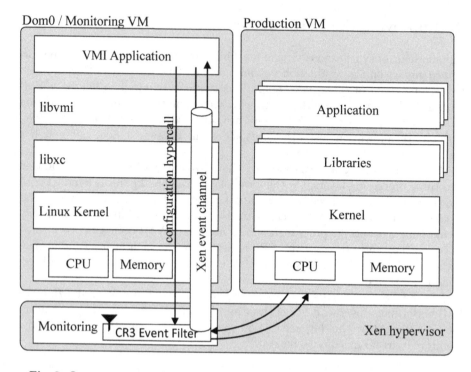

Fig. 2. Our prototype architecture that pre-filters CR3 events in the hypervisor

virtual machine with the VMI application twice, only one context switch to the VMI application is required.

Pre-processing of Events: Another approach to reducing the number of context switches of VMI-based monitoring is to integrate parts of the analysis into the hypervisor so that it is not necessary to always switch to the monitoring virtual machine. However, hypervisors should be designed to be very minimal and contain only the functions to manage virtual machines. Integrating additional VMI code would violate this principle. Thus, we propose to run only very basic information extraction routines that are necessary to access ephemeral data in the context of the hypervisor. Complex analysis of this data should still occur in the context of the monitoring virtual machine. With that approach, it should be possible to minimize the time when production virtual machine must be paused, i.e., the time to extract ephemeral data. The extracted data must then be sent to the VMI-application in the monitoring virtual machine so that it can process the data asynchronous to the execution of the production virtual machine.

4   Prototype

In the following, we describe how the performance impact of process-bound VMI-based monitoring can be minimized by implementing basic pre-filtering primitives into the hypervisor. The implemented architecture is depicted in Fig. 2. This goal of process-bound monitoring is to decrease the monitoring overhead, especially, when the production virtual machine runs many applications that are not relevant to trace for the analysis. As described in Sect. 2.4, one way to implement process-bound monitoring is to intercept write access to the CR3 register and en-/disable the breakpoints based on the fact which process becomes active. The problem of this approach is that the operating system updates the CR3 registers frequently. Hence, depending on how often the operating system changes the active process, many VMI-events must be processed by the VMI application. However, most of those events are irrelevant, because the VMI-application does not need to be informed about context switches between two processes that are not monitored.

To tackle that problem, our prototype implements a basic pre-filtering mechanism in the Xen hypervisor. The VMI application can configure the filter so that only CR3 events are forwarded to the VMI application when the current or the new value of the CR3 register matches the DTB of the monitored process. The filter can be configured at run-time using hypercalls from the monitoring virtual machine. To achieve that, we extend the hypercall API of Xen to activate or disable the monitoring and set values of CR3 events that should be forwarded. With this approach, we eliminate the need for many context switches to the monitoring virtual machine.

The changes to the Xen hypervisor are essentially the extension of the hypercall and the filtering mechanism. Both modifications require only a few lines of code in the Xen hypervisor. Additionally, the libxc used by the VMI application must be extended to support the introduced parameter of the hypercall. Finally, the VMI application must be extended to use the new CR3 filtering.

5   Evaluation

In this section, we evaluate the performance improvement of our prototype implementation for process-bound monitoring. In our evaluation, we examine whether our prototype that pre-filters VMI events in the hypervisor can help to reduce the performance overhead. For that purpose, we use a similar use case as Sentanoe et al. for the Sarracenia Honeypot [16], which aims to reconstruct the inputs and outputs of an attacker in a bash terminal session. Hence, for this use case, it is sufficient to monitor only the read, write and exec system calls invoked by the main bash process of an SSH session.

We obtain the performance impact of tracing by measuring the time that is consumed by extracting the zip file of the jansson library[2] and compiling the source code. Both the extracting of the zip file and the compilation process require the invocation of many system calls. Most of them are not important for monitoring the attacker's behavior as they belong to the compilation process. Thus, process-bound monitoring of the main bash process that only starts the extraction and compilation should help to reduce the monitoring cost.

---

[2] https://github.com/akheron/jansson.

Table 1. Measurements of the time, the number of intercepted system calls (read, write, open, close and exec) and CR3 events using four different monitoring mechanisms

Monitoring method	1	2	3	4
Mean time per run [s]	5.25 ± 0.022	148.92 ± 8.66	117.69 ± 8.66	8.31 ± 0.0078
Monitored syscalls	–	1,245,130	4	6
Monitored CR3 events	–	–	20,553,669	276
Overhead	–	2736%	2141%	58%

In our evaluation, we run this use case while monitoring with four different mechanisms:

1. No monitoring.
2. Monitoring the 6system calls of all running processes.
3. Monitoring the system calls of the bash process only. The tracing is based on the fact which process is currently running. The CR3 events are not pre-filtered in the hypervisor. This is similar to the approach of Sentanoe et al.
4. Monitoring the system calls of the bash only by en-/disabling the tracing based on the fact which process is currently running. The CR3 events are pre-filtered in the hypervisor.

The measurements are executed on an HP Elitebook 820 G4 with an Intel(R) Core(TM) i5-7200U CPU @ 2.50 GHz processor. The production virtual machine has one CPU core and 256 MB of main memory. The VMI application is running in the Dom0 and is implemented to monitor the read, write, open, close and exec system call of the bash process of an SSH session that runs the extraction and compilation. The monitoring of the system calls is implemented by placing a breakpoint on the corresponding system call handler function.

The results of our measurements are depicted in Table 1. The second row shows the average execution time of the compilation process that was executed ten times. The execution time is measured in the production virtual machine using the Linux time command. We use the elapsed real-time to quantify the run-time of the unpacking and compilation process over all ten iterations. The third and fourth rows provide the number of monitored system calls and CR3 events over all ten iterations.

At first glance, the approach of process-bound monitoring of system calls appears to be beneficial in order to reduce the impact of monitoring. However, the measurements of monitoring method three show that the required monitoring of write access to the CR3 register in the VMI application almost annihilates this positive effect. This is because the CR3 events are more frequent than system call events. Nevertheless, we measure a slight improvement in performance. The results of the method four show that implementing basic analysis mechanisms into the hypervisor can significantly reduce the impact of VMI-based monitoring. Based on method four we can estimate the overhead for a single CR3 event by dividing the overhead through the number of CR3 events. From this calculation, we get an overhead of about 11 ms per CR3 event. This long time period can be explained with the different layers in which the event is processed (see Fig. 1).

To sum up, the process of pre-filtering CR3 events decreases the run-time of the execution with process bound tracing from 148.92 s to 8.31 s, which is about 18 times faster. Additionally, these measurements show that integrating basic VMI primitives into the hypervisor can reduce the performance overhead and help to make VMI applicable in production environments. Hence, there is ample room for performance improvement in the current Xen mechanisms for VMI that needs to be addressed by future research. To further improve the performance of synchronous VMI-based monitoring, we, therefore, suggest that more VMI monitoring primitives should be implemented in the Xen hypervisor. Nevertheless, by adding VMI-based functionality to the hypervisor, an additional access control mechanism should be added to the hypervisor. Additionally, if code is loaded to the hypervisor, it must be verified that it does not affect the reliability and security of the overall system.

6   Related Work

The field of dynamic control flow instrumentation has a long history and in the last decades has been many different approaches that tackle the performance overhead. In the following, we want to discuss the most important related approaches. DTrace [3] is a tracing framework for the Solaris operating system. One of the main objectives of DTrace is to have no impact on the performance when the tracing is not implemented. This is implemented by inserting no-operation (nop) instruction at possible probing points. When the monitoring is activated, the nop instructions are replaced by jumps to the analysis routines. The monitoring actions can be implemented by users in the D programming language.

Our prototype approach follows the same approach as the eBPF filters in the Linux kernel [4,12], which have a similar concept as DTrace. The core concept of eBPF is to run application-specific tracing code in the high privileged Linux kernel in order to monitor functions in user and kernel space. This approach helps to minimize (synchronous) context switches to the user space that stalls the execution. The features of eBPF filters are very advanced and the Linux kernel is already able to run small programs, whereas our prototype for VMI-based tracing currently only allows pre-filtering tracing events in the Xen hypervisor.

Tuzel et al. [19] analyzed the performance impact of VMI-based monitoring techniques in detail. The focus of their paper is to analyze to which extent VMI-based monitoring techniques can be detected from the production virtual machine. The result of their conducted study is that VMI-based monitoring in their setup is not stealthy to applications running in the production virtual machine. The focus of our paper is to decrease the monitoring overhead to make it applicable in production environments but not to make VMI-based monitoring completely stealthy.

Klemperer [9] proposed to use copy-on-write-based snapshots in order to perform the analysis on a non-changing system state. For this purpose, they extended the KVM hypervisor and hook instructions that alter memory pages during the normal execution. If a page is modified they copy the original version of the page for the snapshot. After the analysis is finished, the snapshot gets deleted and changes to memory pages are not monitored anymore. This approach is probably most effective when larger parts of main memory must be analyzed. For the extraction of function call parameters when a breakpoint is invoked this approach is too expensive.

Drakvuf [11] is a VMI framework that uses libvmi and Xen and is mainly designed for dynamic analysis of Windows malware. It uses the altp2m approach [10] to implement software breakpoints. The advantage of this approach is that instead of replacing the original instruction with the INT3 instruction in memory, it creates a new memory page with the software breakpoint. Depending on whether a process in the production virtual machine is reading from that page or executing an instruction the memory page is swapped in the page tables. The rVMI framework designed by Pfoh and Vogl [15] is similar to Drakvuf. However, it uses a patched version of KVM and Qemu instead of Xen[3]. The communication between the VMI application and Qemu is established via the QMP interface of Qemu.

Westphal et al. [21] define a VMI monitoring language that supports the most common methods for VMI. Their prototype is implemented for the VMware KVM hypervisor. Similarly to our proposed approach, they execute VMI analysis scripts in the domain of the KVM hypervisor.

Bushouse et al. [2] implement VMI-based monitoring into Linux containers running in the Dom0 of Xen instead of running the VMI-application in a monitoring virtual machine. This should not have any positive beneficial impact on the performance.

7   Conclusions

By implementing a pre-filtering approach in the hypervisor, we significantly reduce the impact of VMI-based monitoring on the production virtual machine. Our prototype reduces the monitoring overhead for process-bound monitoring by a factor of 18. We, therefore, conclude that more complex event processing in the hypervisor, such as the implementation of a breakpoint mechanism, can help to solve the problem of minimizing the performance impact of VMI-based tracing.

Acknowledgment. This work has been supported by the German Research Foundation (DFG) in the project ARADIA (RE 3590/3-1).

---

[3] Currently, the KVM hypervisor does not support synchronous VMI-based monitoring out of the box. To use synchronous VMI-based monitoring mechanisms, the KVM hypervisor must be patched.

References

1. Barham, P., et al.: Xen and the art of virtualization. SIGOPS Oper. Syst. Rev. **37**(5), 164–177 (2003)
2. Bushouse, M., Reeves, D.: Furnace: self-service tenant VMI for the cloud. In: Bailey, M., Holz, T., Stamatogiannakis, M., Ioannidis, S. (eds.) RAID 2018. LNCS, vol. 11050, pp. 647–669. Springer, Cham (2018). https://doi.org/10.1007/978-3-030-00470-5_30
3. Cantrill, B.M., Shapiro, M.W., Leventhal, A.H.: Dynamic instrumentation of production systems. In: Proceedings of the Annual Conference on USENIX Annual Technical Conference, ATEC 2004, pp. 15–28. USENIX Association, Berkeley (2004). http://dl.acm.org/citation.cfm?id=1247415.1247417
4. Fleming, M.: A thorough introduction to eBPF (2017). https://lwn.net/Articles/740157/. Accessed 26 Sept 2019
5. Garfinkel, T., Rosenblum, M.: A virtual machine introspection based architecture for intrusion detection. In: Proceedings of the Network and Distributed Systems Security Symposium, pp. 191–206 (2003)
6. Hebbal, Y., Laniepce, S., Menaud, J.M.: Virtual machine introspection: techniques and applications. In: 2015 10th International Conference on Availability, Reliability and Security, pp. 676–685, August 2015. https://doi.org/10.1109/ARES.2015.43
7. Intel Corporation: Intel® 64 and IA-32 Architectures Software Developer's Manual (2017). https://software.intel.com/sites/default/files/managed/39/c5/325462-sdm-vol-1-2abcd-3abcd.pdf
8. Jain, B., Baig, M.B., Zhang, D., Porter, D.E., Sion, R.: SoK: introspections on trust and the semantic gap. In: IEEE Symposium on Security and Privacy, pp. 605–620 (2014)
9. Klemperer, P., Jeon, H.Y., Payne, B.D., Hoe, J.C.: High-performance memory snapshotting for real-time, consistent, hypervisor-based monitors. IEEE Trans. Depend. Secur. Comput., 1 (2018). https://doi.org/10.1109/TDSC.2018.2805904
10. Lengyel, T.K.: Stealthy monitoring with Xen altp2m (2016). https://blog.xenproject.org/2016/04/13/stealthy-monitoring-with-xen-altp2m/. Accessed 31 Jan 2019
11. Lengyel, T.K., Maresca, S., Payne, B.D., Webster, G.D., Vogl, S., Kiayias, A.: Scalability, fidelity and stealth in the DRAKVUF dynamic malware analysis system. In: Proceedings of the 30th Annual Computer Security Applications Conference, pp. 386–395 (2014)
12. McCanne, S., Jacobson, V.: The BSD packet filter: a new architecture for user-level packet capture. In: Proceedings of the USENIX Winter 1993 Conference, USENIX 1993, p. 2. USENIX Association, Berkeley (1993). http://dl.acm.org/citation.cfm?id=1267303.1267305
13. Payne, B.D.: Simplifying virtual machine introspection using LibVMI. Sandia Report, pp. 43–44 (2012). http://libvmi.com/
14. Payne, B.D., de A. Carbone, M.D.P., Lee, W.: Secure and flexible monitoring of virtual machines. In: 23rd Annual Computer Security Applications Conference (ACSAC 2007), pp. 385–397, December 2007. https://doi.org/10.1109/ACSAC.2007.10
15. Pfoh, J., Vogl, S.: rVMI - a new Paradigm for Full System Analysis (2017). https://github.com/fireeye/rvmi. Accessed 31 Jan 2019

16. Sentanoe, S., Taubmann, B., Reiser, H.P.: *Sarracenia*: enhancing the performance and stealthiness of SSH honeypots using virtual machine introspection. In: Gruschka, N. (ed.) NordSec 2018. LNCS, vol. 11252, pp. 255–271. Springer, Cham (2018). https://doi.org/10.1007/978-3-030-03638-6_16

17. Shi, J., Yang, Y., Li, C.: A disjunctive VMI model based on XSM. In: 2015 IEEE International Conference on Smart City/SocialCom/SustainCom (SmartCity), pp. 921–925, December 2015. https://doi.org/10.1109/SmartCity.2015.188

18. Taubmann, B., Rakotondravony, N., Reiser, H.P.: CloudPhylactor: harnessing mandatory access control for virtual machine introspection in cloud data centers. In: The 15th IEEE International Conference on Trust, Security and Privacy in Computing and Communications (TrustCom 2016). IEEE (2016)

19. Tuzel, T., Bridgman, M., Zepf, J., Lengyel, T.K., Temkin, K.: Who watches the watcher? Detecting hypervisor introspection from unprivileged guests. Digit. Invest. **26**, S98–S106 (2018). https://doi.org/10.1016/j.diin.2018.04.015

20. Uhlig, R., et al.: Intel virtualization technology. Computer **38**(5), 48–56 (2005). https://doi.org/10.1109/MC.2005.163

21. Westphal, F., Axelsson, S., Neuhaus, C., Polze, A.: VMI-PL: a monitoring language for virtual platforms using virtual machine introspection. Digit. Invest. **11**, S85–S94 (2014). https://doi.org/10.1016/j.diin.2014.05.016. http://www.sciencedirect.com/science/article/pii/S1742287614000590, fourteenth Annual DFRWS Conference

Fed-DIC: Diagonally Interleaved Coding in a Federated Cloud Environment

Giannis Tzouros[✉] and Vana Kalogeraki

Department of Informatics, Athens University of Economics and Business,
Athens, Greece
{tzouros,vana}@aueb.gr

Abstract. Coping with failures in modern distributed storage systems that handle massive volumes of heterogeneous and potentially rapidly changing data, has become a very important challenge. A common practice is to utilize fault tolerance methods like Replication and Erasure Coding for maximizing data availability. However, while erasure codes provide better fault tolerance compared to replication with a more affordable storage overhead, they frequently suffer from high reconstruction cost as they require to access all available nodes when a data block needs to be repaired, and also can repair up to a limited number of unavailable data blocks, depending on the number of the code's parity block capabilities. Furthermore, storing and placing the encoded data in the federated storage system also remains a challenge. In this paper we present Fed-DIC, a framework which combines Diagonally Interleaved Coding on client devices at the edge of the network with organized storage of encoded data in a federated cloud system comprised of multiple independent storage clusters. The erasure coding operations are performed on client devices at the edge while they interact with the federated cloud to store the encoded data. We describe how our solution integrates the functionality of federated clouds alongside erasure coding implemented on edge devices for maximizing data availability and we evaluate the working and benefits of our approach in terms of read access cost, data availability, storage overhead, load balancing and network bandwidth rate compared to popular Replication and Erasure Coding schemes.

1 Introduction

In recent years, the management and preservation of big data has become a vital challenge in distributed storage systems. Failures, unreliable nodes and components are inevitable and such failures can lead to permanent data loss and overall system slowdowns. To guarantee availability, distributed storage systems typically rely on two fault tolerance methods: (1) Replication, where multiple copies of the data are made, and (2) Erasure Coding, where data is stored in

© IFIP International Federation for Information Processing 2020
Published by Springer Nature Switzerland AG 2020
A. Remke and V. Schiavoni (Eds.): DAIS 2020, LNCS 12135, pp. 55–72, 2020.
https://doi.org/10.1007/978-3-030-50323-9_4

the form of smaller data blocks which are distributed across a set of different storage nodes.

Replication based algorithms as those utilized in Amazon Dynamo [1], Google File System (GFS) [2,3], Hadoop Distributed File System (HDFS) [4,5] are widely utilized. These can help tolerate a high permanent failure rate as they provide the simplest form of redundancy by creating replicas from which systems can retrieve the lost data blocks, but cannot easily cope with bursts of failures. Furthermore, replication introduces a massive storage overhead as the size of the created replicas is equal to the size of their original data e.g. 3-way replication occupies 3 times the volume of the original data block in order to provide fault tolerance.

On the other hand, Erasure Coding [6] can provide higher redundancy while also offering a significant improvement in storage overhead compared to replication. For example, a 3-way replication creates 3 replicas of a data block and causes a 3x storage overhead for providing fault tolerance, while an erasure code can provide the same services for half the storage overhead or even lower by creating smaller parity blocks that can retrieve lost data more efficiently than full-sized replicas. Thus, Erasure codes are more storage affordable than replication but their reliability is limited to the number of parity blocks for repairing erasures. For example, an erasure code that creates 3 parity chunks cannot fix a data block with 4 or more unavailable or lost chunks.

Yet the most critical challenge with erasure coding is that it suffers from high reconstruction cost as it needs to access multiple blocks stored across different sets of storage nodes or racks (groups of nodes inside a distributed system) in order to retrieve lost data [7], leading to high read access and network bandwidth latency. The majority of the distributed file systems deploy random block placement [8] and one block per rack policies [9,10] to achieve optimized reliability and load balancing for stored encoded data. However, storing data across multiple nodes and/or racks can lead to higher read and network access costs among nodes and racks during the repairing processes. For example, in the worst case, repairing a corrupted or unavailable block in a node may require traversing all nodes across different racks, causing a heavy amount of data traffic among nodes and racks. Also, in a typical cross-rack storage, the user does not have any control over the placement of the data blocks across different racks, limiting the ability of the system to tolerate a higher average failure rate.

To reduce the cost of accessing multiple nodes or racks, file systems can keep metadata records regarding the topology of the encoded data codewords (groups that contain original data blocks alongside their parity blocks) in private nodes. However, the placement of the metadata files among the system's nodes is also challenging. For example, storing a codeword in a small group of nodes while keeping metadata about the data blocks scattered throughout the public clouds instead of a specific storage node [11], will also require to traverse all nodes at worst in order to recover any failed data inside the codeword. This problem leads to high cross-node read and network access costs, despite the use of metadata.

In this paper we propose Fed-DIC (**Fed**erated cloud **D**iagonally **I**nterleaved **C**oding), a novel compression framework deployed on an edge-cloud infrastructure where client devices perform the coding operation and they interact with the federated cloud to store the encoded data. Fed-DIC's compression approach is based on diagonal interleaved erasure coding that offers improved data availability while reducing read access costs in a federated cloud environment. It employs a variation of diagonally interleaved codes on streaming data organized as a grid of input records. Specifically, the grid content is interleaved into groups that diagonally span across the grid, and then the interleaved groups of data are encoded using a simple Reed-Solomon (RS) erasure code. Next, our framework organizes the encoded data into batches based on the number of clusters in the federated cloud and places each batch to a different cluster in the cloud, while keeping a metadata index of the locations of each stored data stream. The benefit is that Fed-DIC will only access the cluster with the requested data records and retrieve the correspondent diagonals, enabling the system to efficiently extract the corresponding records.

Fed-DIC has multiple benefits: it maximizes the availability of the encoded data by ordering input data into smaller groups, based on diagonally interleaved coding, and encoding each group using the erasure coding technique. Furthermore, it supports efficient archival and balances the load by storing each version of the streaming data array in a rotational basis among the storage nodes, e.g. if we have an infrastructure with 3 file clusters, for the first version of the data array, the first batch of diagonals is stored on the first node cluster, the second batch on the second node cluster and the third batch on the third cluster. For the second version of the array, the first batch of diagonals is stored on the second cluster, the second batch on the third cluster and the third batch on the first cluster and so on. We present an approach how multiple storage usage can optimize read access costs while keeping data availability and low bandwidth cost for retrieving data by utilizing multiple storage clusters in the same cloud environment instead of storing data in a single cluster. We illustrate the effectiveness of our approach with an extended experimental evaluation in terms of read access cost, data availability, storage overhead, load balancing and network bandwidth rate compared to popular Replication and Erasure Coding schemes.

2   Background

In this section we provide some background material regarding the technologies that we utilize at Fed-DIC: the Federated Cloud environment, Erasure Coding and Diagonally Interleaved Coding.

2.1   Federated Storage Systems

Many large-scale distributed computing organizations that need to store and maintain continuous amounts of data deploy distributed storage systems, such as HDFS [4,5], GFS [2,3] (which were mentioned above), Ceph [12], Microsoft Azure

[13,14], Amazon S3 [15], Alluxio [16] etc., which comprise multiple nodes, often organized into groups called racks. Currently, most of these systems write and store large data as blocks of fixed size, which are distributed almost evenly among the system's nodes using random block placement or load balancing policies. In each system, one of the nodes operates as the master node e.g. the NameNode in HDFS, that keeps a record of the file directories and redirects client requests toward the storage API for opening, copying or deleting a file. However, these policies are limited as they depend on the size of the data stored in the systems as well as the policies followed by the specific storage nodes (*e.g.*, load balancing policies). Our framework assumes the deployment of multiple HDFS clusters within the federated cloud environment, each comprising a different master node and storage layer. The client edge device can communicate with each of the master nodes with a different interface in order to store different groups of data into separate HDFS clusters.

2.2   Erasure Codes

Distributed systems deploy erasure codes as a storage-efficient alternative to replication so as to guarantee fault tolerance and data availability for their stored data. Erasure codes are a form of Forward Error Correction (FEC) codes that can achieve fault tolerance in the communication between a sender and a receiver by adding redundant information in a message; this enables the detection and correction of errors without the need for re-transmission. For instance, a sender node encodes a file with erasure coding and generates a data codeword or a stripe containing original and redundant parity data. Next, the sender node sends sequentially the blocks of the encoded stripe to a receiver node. In its turn, the receiver node detects whether there is a sufficient number of available blocks in order to decode them into their original content. If no original blocks are received, the parity blocks can repair them up to a finite range.

The most commonly used erasure code algorithm is the Reed-Solomon (RS), a maximum distance separable code (MDS) which is expressed as a pair of parameters (b, k) ($RS(b, k)$) where b is the number of input chunks on a data block and k is the number of parity chunks created by the erasure code. The parity chunks are generated by utilizing Cauchy or Vandermonde matrices over a $GF(2^m)$ Galois Field, where 2^m is the number of elements in the field and m is the word size of encoding. The code constructs a matrix of size $k \times d$ which contains values from the $GF(2^m)$ field that correspond to the dimensions of the matrix and represent the positions of the input chunks. Next, the RS code derives an inverse $k \times k$ submatrix from the previous matrix. The original matrix is multiplied by the inverse submatrix in order to convert the top square of the former into a $k \times k$ identity matrix which will keep the content of the original data chunks unaltered during the encoding and decoding processes. The result is a stripe of length $n = b + k$, that contains the b chunks of the original data and the k parity chunks generated by the code. RS is k-fault tolerant due to the fact that the original data can be recovered for up to k lost chunks. In other words, while replication needs to copy and store the original data $n + 1$ times,

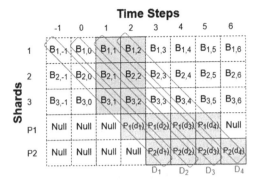

Fig. 1. A pictorial representation of diagonally interleaved coding for an input message with $(c, d, a) = (2, 5, 2)$. The data blocks are rearranged into diagonals and each diagonal is encoded into stripes ($D_1...D_4$) by the systematic code. B Symbols in time steps from -1 to 0 and from 3 to 6 are assumed to have zero, null or non-positive values, and they are not part of the input message.

erasure codes only require to store the data $\frac{n-k}{n}$ times, which costs considerably less compared to replication.

Reed-Solomon codes are also characterized by linearity [17]. In other words, they perform linear coding operations based on the Galois field arithmetic. More formally, given an (b, k) code, let $B_1, B_2, ..., B_b$ be the b original data chunks and $P_1, P_2, ..., P_k$ be the k parity chunks. Each parity chunk P_j ($0 < j < k$) can be expressed as $P_j = \sum_{i=1}^{b}(c_{ji} \cdot B_i)$, where $c_{ji} \subset GF(2^m)$ is a coding coefficient specified by the RS code for computing P_j.

This technique is limited as the redundancy provided by simple RS codes can repair up to k unavailable nodes. If there are more than k chunk erasures, the code will not be able to fully repair their original data. Our framework tries to deal with limited redundancy by deploying a more advanced erasure coding technique based on Reed-Solomon and Diagonally Interleaved Coding, the latter of which we describe in the next section.

2.3   Diagonally Interleaved Coding

Leong et al. have studied a burst erasure model in [18], where all erasure patterns with limited-length burst erasures are admissible so that they can construct an asymptotically optimal convolutional code that achieves maximum message size for all available patterns. This code involves stripes derived from one or more data messages interleaved in a diagonal order.

For a set of parameters (c, d, k), where c is the interval between input messages, d is the total number of symbols in the encoded message (original data and parity symbols) and k is the number of generated parity symbols, an input message is equally split into a vector of c columns and $d - k$ rows. Next, tables of blank or null symbols are placed around the message table that represent non-existent messages before and after the input message. The symbols of the entire table are interleaved in diagonal pattern, forming well-defined diagonals containing at least one symbol from the input message. Finally, a systematic block code is used to create k parity symbols for every diagonal, thus constructing a convolutional code with $d - 1$ diagonal stripes that can repair up to k lost symbols in each diagonal and span across d consecutive time steps. As a result, diagonally interleaved codes are able to handle an extended number of erasure bursts in one message and allow smaller erasures to be fixed without accessing massive amounts of data. In Fig. 1 we illustrate with an example how diagonally interleaved coding is applied for a single data block.

The process of splitting an input message into a vector can be applied only if the input data is organized in single data stripes. To optimize data availability, our framework uses a derived version of diagonally interleaved coding that takes as input data organized in a grid and interleaves all content into diagonals before encoding them with a Reed-Solomon code.

3 Challenges

In this section we present the challenges of existing schemes and how we propose to address them in our Fed-DIC framework.

High Read Access and Network Bandwidth Costs During Data Retrieval. One major challenge in typical cloud environments is the lack of user-oriented control in data distribution and storage. Most cloud systems store data blocks in randomly chosen nodes and nodes within racks in their clusters without balancing the load. For example, a system that uses an $RS(b, k)$ to encode its streamed data, will distribute the $d = b + k$ chunks of the generated codeword to d different nodes in a random order. However, in cases of node failures, the system needs to retrieve data from other nodes within the rack or even across racks to retrieve parity data, leading to high read access costs and network overhead, which can considerably slow down the repair process.

Fed-DIC deals with this problem by uploading and distributing the encoded data to a federated cloud with multiple autonomous Hadoop clusters in the same network, each with a unique NameNode. To retrieve a particular data record, the framework keeps a metadata file containing the locations of the stored encoded data. The metadata file is created and can be accessed by the edge device in order to locate the requested data record and retrieve it faster with a significantly reduced read access latency, limited to the cluster where the specific data record is stored, without the need to traverse all nodes or maintain scattered metadata among nodes or clusters. Fed-DIC's topology in terms of the stored data among the clusters of the federated cloud, combined with the reduced storage size of the data chunks generated from its encoding process, provide significantly smaller read access costs and transfer bandwidth overhead for nodes in the cloud.

Limited Data Availability. Distributed systems deploy erasure coding methods to achieve higher redundancy than replication with more affordable storage cost. However, the availability provided by simple erasure codes such as Reed-Solomon codes for the encoded data is restricted to the number of parity chunks generated by the code. More specifically, a Reed-Solomon code that creates k parity data chunks from b original data chunks ($RS(b, k)$) can repair up to k failures between the original or parity data. If there are more than k unavailable or failed chunks in the stripe, the RS code will not be able to restore the data back to their original state.

To deal with this challenge, several advanced erasure codes have been presented, including alpha entanglement codes [19] and diagonally interleaved codes [18]. Fed-DIC uses a variation of diagonally interleaved coding on a group of streaming data containing input records from multiple sensor groups (columns) across multiple days (rows). The array data are interleaved diagonally and encoded with multiple parity chunks for each arranged diagonal pattern, achieving higher data availability and greater repairing range than conventional erasure coding methods.

Load Balancing Unreliability. Most large-scale distributed systems deploy load balancing policies for node distribution or utilizing one-node-per-rack [8–10] to balance the storage load across the cluster. However, most load balancing policies require the use of sophisticated techniques which may lead to load imbalances among nodes, especially when the number of the data chunks in a stripe exceeds the number of nodes that comprise a cluster.

Fed-DIC groups the encoded data diagonals into batches before they are stored to multiple node clusters in a non-random order. If the user decides to upload a data array and store it over the old one, the framework rotates the directions of the clusters in which the new batches will be stored in order to achieve good load balancing.

4   Design of the Fed-DIC Framework

To deal with the above problems of conventional erasure coding on federated clouds, we designed and developed Fed-DIC (**Fed**erated cloud **D**iagonally **I**nterleaved **C**oding), a framework that utilizes diagonal interleaving and erasure coding on streaming data records in a federated edge cloud environment. The goal of our framework is to reduce the read access cost and network overhead caused by accessing multiple nodes in a federated cloud while maximizing data availability for the data stored in the federated cloud environment. Fed-DIC also supports load balancing by storing multiple versions of the data records among clusters in a rotational order, while keeping storage availability, using the techniques we have developed and its API for distributing the data and balancing them across the clusters. In cases of high load in a cluster due to data congestion or unavailable nodes, Fed-DIC can reconfigure the number of batches and the content size of each batch in order to achieve load balancing by storing data to a smaller number of clusters with more nodes and larger storage space.

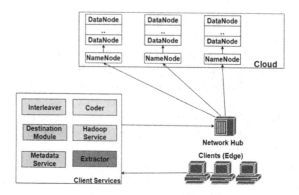

Fig. 2. The architecture of Fed-DIC, which comprises the client devices, where all operations are performed, the network hub, which connects the clients with the cloud and the federated cloud, which contains multiple independent storage clusters.

4.1   Framework Architecture

As illustrated in Fig. 2 Fed-DIC comprises three main components: the client side (edge devices), a federated cloud comprising multiple independent clusters where each cluster consists of multiple independent nodes, and a network hub that connects the two other components through the network. The client devices are operated by the user and provide six services: (1) The `Interleaver module` which re-orders the input data set into a grid and interleaves them into diagonal groups, (2) the `Coder module` which encodes all diagonal groups prior to the uploading process and decodes received diagonal stripes containing user-requested data, (3) the `Destination module` which splits the encoded stripes into batches and configures the order of destination clusters where the batches will be stored, (4) the `Hadoop Service` which communicates with the NameNodes of each cluster in order to upload the diagonal stripe batches, (5) the `Metadata service` which creates a metadata index file during the upload process and provides a query interface for the user during the retrieval process, and (6) the `Extractor module` which searches through a received diagonal stripe in order to extract the data record requested by the user and store it to a new file.

Our framework works as follows: A client takes as input a set of streaming data records and organises them into a grid of D columns and G rows. The data records in the grid are re-ordered into $C = D + G - 1$ diagonal groups, which are then encoded with Reed-Solomon, generating up to k parity chunks per diagonal using an 8-bit Galois Field. Next, Fed-DIC groups the diagonal stripes into H batches and stores each batch into a different cluster in the federated cloud. Simultaneously, the client creates a metadata file that contains information for each stored data record: The day the record was created, the group of sensors that generated the record and the diagonal stripe in which the record was interleaved. To retrieve selected data records, the client receives user-created request queries about data records and communicates with their correspondent clusters to download the stripes that include the records so as to extract their contents in output files. To upload a new version of the already stored data while archiving the older versions, the cluster destinations are rotated in a stack order by setting the first cluster destination at the position of the last cluster destination in a circular pattern. In that way, Fed-DIC achieves not only the maintenance of multiple versions, but also load balancing throughout all clusters within the federated cloud. If Fed-DIC kept uploading newer versions into the same clusters each time, there could have been inconsistencies between the clusters. Especially, the first and last clusters in the cloud would have smaller data load than the other clusters.

4.2 Read Access Latency

The read access cost for a data query q from a group of Q queries, is given by the sum of the access time a client needs to traverse l lines in the metadata file to find the requested data, the latency needed to access any h clusters that contain the data ($h \leq H$) and the search delay caused by any missing d data chunks in a cluster. The probability p_i shows if a chunk is available for transferring. If $p_i = 0$, the chunk is missing. This is computed by the following formula:

$$T_q = l \cdot r_{md} + h \cdot r_h + \sum_{i=1}^{d} ((1 - p_i) \cdot t_m)$$

where r_{md} is the time a client needs to read a line from the metadata file, r_h is the time to access a cluster in the federated cloud and t_m is the search delay caused by missing data chunks in the cloud. The read access latency L_q for downloading and extracting a requested data query q is given by the access cost T_q which was computed previously, plus the time required to download all available d chunks in the diagonal stripe that includes the data using an internet connection of B bandwidth and the computation time T_q^{dec} a client needs to decode the diagonal stripe so as to extract the result. The formula for the overall query storage latency is given below:

$$L_q = T_q + \frac{\sum_{i=1}^{d}(p_i \cdot t_p)}{B} + T_q^{dec}$$

where t_p is the elapsed time for an available data chunk to be transferred from the federated cloud to a client device. Similarly, the total read access latency L_Q is the sum of the read access latency for all Q queries:

$$L_Q = \sum_{q=1}^{Q} (L_q)$$

The read access latency for erasure coding is computed in a similar way to L_q, with the only difference that the metadata access time is not taken into account.

4.3 Data Loss Percentage

When stored chunks are missing or unavailable in the federated cloud due to failures or nodes being disabled in the cloud's clusters, erasure codes try to utilize any available parity chunks in order to reconstruct the damaged encoded file. However, if a decent amount of chunks are not available in a cluster, there may be permanent loss of the original data, due to the number of available data chunks being insufficient for use with erasure codes. The data loss percentage D_C of a fault tolerance method is measured by the fraction of the probability p_i of a data chunk c_i being available with the total number of data chunks in the entire cloud, subtracted from 1, as follows:

$$D_C = (1 - \frac{\sum_i^C (p_i \cdot c_i)}{C}) \cdot 100$$

4.4   Framework API

Fed-DIC provides an API with the following four operations:

Encode(). This operation interleaves the input data set into D diagonal data groups of varied length. Then, it merges data in each group into new data blocks so as to be encoded with a unique Reed-Solomon erasure code.

Store(). This operation groups the encoded diagonal data stripes into H batches containing an equal number of (D/H) codewords in each batch and communicates with all the NameNodes of the federated cloud in order to upload and store each batch in a different cluster, while keeping track of the data locations and information in a metadata file stored in the client devices. The metadata file can be shared and backed up in all clients in order to avoid any corruptions. If, for any reason, the cloud changes the location of its clusters, the clients need to update the metadata accordingly. However, a small non-significant access overhead may occur in the case that the client device that performs the Store() process becomes unavailable and the metadata have to be accessed from another client. Due to the integrity of our private client nodes, the probability of this situation is extremely rare, so it is not considered when measuring the read access latency.

Retrieve(). This method provides an interface to the user for entering multiple queries regarding a data record the user aims to retrieve. Once the user issues his queries, the method searches for each requested data record the diagonal stripe in which it is included and downloads it accessing immediately the corresponding storage cluster.

Decode(). Once the clients receive the diagonal stripes with the data requested by the user, this operation decodes any available chunks in a stripe into its original merged data block and extracts the requested result from the block before deleting it.

4.5   Uploading and Downloading Algorithms

We describe the two main algorithms implemented by our framework:

Storing Data to the Federated Cloud: A client takes as input the data records to be uploaded, these correspond to G sensor data groups over a time period R days, stored in .csv files. The client invokes the $Encode()$ operation to organize the content into a grid with dimensions $G \times R$, where its elements are interleaved into C dynamic diagonal arrays of varied length (as shown in Fig. 1). Records are inserted into the grid according to the day and sensor group indicated on the record. Starting with the record of the last sensor group during the first day, the client forms a diagonal line from bottom right to top left and inserts any existing grid elements in the diagonal line, into a dynamic diagonal array. The diagonal arrays span through the entire grid with the last one containing only the record of the first sensor group during the last day. Next, in each diagonal array, the data in the elements are merged into a single data object and encoded using a (b, k) Reed-Solomon code. The encoding process splits each merged data object into equally sized b chunks and generates k parity chunks, creating a stripe of length $d = b + k$. Next, the client uses the operation $Store()$ to group the diagonal stripes into H batches containing an equal number of (C/H) stripes in each batch and to upload the batches into the different clusters of the federated cloud by communicating with every NameNode within the cloud. Once the NameNode of a cluster receives the data, it distributes the chunks in random order to its nodes. During the storage process, the clients write and store metadata records about the stored data, their version, the date and sensor group as well as the number of the diagonal stripes they belong to. The metadata file helps the edge devices to access the stored data faster and more easily by reducing the access costs among the HDFS clusters. The distribution of the batches is performed in a sequential way. For example, in a federated cloud of F clusters, the first data batch is stored into the first cluster and so on until the last batch is stored in the F-th cluster. When the user wants to upload a new version of the data over the already stored versions, the clients swap the order of the cluster destinations by placing the first cluster destination right after the last cluster destination of the older version in a Last In, First Out (LIFO) order. In our example, for the second version of our data, the first batch will be uploaded into the F-th cluster, the second one to the first cluster and so on with the last cluster being uploaded to the $(F\text{-}1)$-th cluster. The way data records are stored in Fed-DIC enables us to traverse 1–2 clusters at most to recover any data segment. Whereas, conventional (b, k) Reed-Solomon would merge r_1 with every other record in the input into a single data block, split it into b original chunks and encode it using a Galois Field matrix to generate k parity chunks which are distributed to the cloud via Hadoop. Thus, even if a small part of data must be recovered, the data encoded with RS need to be restored in their entirety, which may require traversing all clusters in the cloud, incurring a heavy read access cost.

Retrieving Data from the Federated Cloud: The clients provide an interface to the user awaiting response queries. When the user issues a query, the clients gather all entered queries into a list array and use *Retrieve()* to search through the metadata file generated from the uploading process for the diagonal stripes where the query data are stored. For every entry in the query list, the client connects to the correspondent cluster to download the diagonal stripe with the requested data. If the edge device fails to download sufficient amount of chunks for restoring the stripe into its original data, it informs the user that the queried data from that diagonal stripe cannot be recovered. If it receives enough chunks from the stripe, it deploys *Decode()* to restore the diagonal stripe using $RS(b, k)$ back to its original content. Finally, the clients search through the recovered data objects for the requested record entries and extract them as a result. When there are multiple concurrent requests from users, the clients schedule the requests to the hub in multiple rows according to the source cluster of the requested data and return the result for the oldest request each time.

5   Experimental Evaluation

In this section we evaluate Fed-DIC in terms of data loss, maximum transfer network rate and storage overhead, compared to the Replication and conventional Reed-Solomon Erasure Coding techniques. The client machines we used were desktop computers with an Intel i7-7700 4-core CPU at 3.5 GHz per core, with 16 GB RAM and a Western Digital WD10EZEX-08WN4A0 hard disk drive of 1 TB. The machines run Microsoft Windows 10 and are connected to the network using a Cisco RV320 Dual Gigabit WAN VPN Router with a data throughput of 100 Mbps and support of 20,000 concurrent connections. The router operates as our network hub and due to its specifications, the probability of a failure or bottleneck is extremely small. Although there are several ways to deal with such failures, this is outside the scope of our paper. For the experiments, we deploy via Oracle VirtualBox 4 clusters each comprising 4 nodes, 16 virtual machines (VMs) in total running Apache Hadoop 3.1.1 in Linux Lubuntu 16.04 for evaluating Fed-DIC against Replication and Reed-Solomon. For memory and disk allocation reasons, the VMs are running across 2 real desktop machines: Our client device and a second machine with the same hardware specifications as the first, which is connected to the same network. 8 VMs are running on each machine, connected to the same network as the client machines using a bridged adapter. Our setup is restricted to the equipment and network availability in our local computing and communication environment, however the algorithms we have developed can adapt well to accommodate larger clusters with thousands of nodes by modifying the number of batches in which the encoded data will be grouped as well as the content size in each batch. Also, we can set the batches to be stored in clusters with higher reliability within a large cloud. Our data set for the experiments is a collection of transport values obtained from SCATS sensors that are deployed in the Dublin Smart City [20]. This data set contains a huge amount of records with information regarding the specific sensor

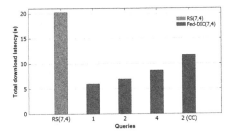
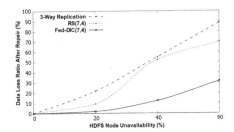

Fig. 3. Read access latency for Reed-Solomon and Fed-DIC (multiple queries)

Fig. 4. Data Loss rate among Replication, Erasure Coding and Fed-DIC

that captured the snapshot and its capture date; the data needs to be stored and maintained in the cloud to be further analyzed by the human operators (i.e., to identify congested streets and entire geographical areas over time). Fed-DIC is responsible to store and recover this data to and from the cloud.

Our first experiment involves the total read latency of recovering data with Fed-DIC (7, 4) compared to Reed-Solomon (7, 4). For RS (7, 4) we merge the input files of the data grid used by Fed-DIC to a single .csv file. When the file is encoded to a stripe of 11 chunks (7 original and 4 parity), we distribute 3 chunks to each of the first 3 clusters, with the last 2 being stored in the last cluster. Note, that Reed-Solomon could retrieve the encoded file traversing only 3 clusters instead of going through all 4 clusters. In fact, Fed-DIC could also be easily configured (by appropriately setting the number of batches where diagonal stripes are grouped) to store and retrieve the data successfully utilizing only 3 clusters. However, in order to take advantage of the entire experimental environment (4-cluster cloud system with a total of 16 nodes) we utilize all 4 clusters for both techniques, to avoid load imbalances (data distributed in 3 clusters, while the 4th cluster is unused) and minimize the impact on the data loss percentage (in cases of failures). Due to the data chunks spanning across all 4 clusters, a simple decoding process with RS takes almost 20 s to complete, as seen in Fig. 3. This happens due to the clients having to access all 4 clusters in order to download all the chunks needed for recovering the stripe's original data. Even if we request a small portion of the encoded data, Reed-Solomon has no built-in features that allow us to retrieve a specific part of data, so it will still have to retrieve and decode the entire file content in order to give us an output. Our Fed-DIC technique on the other hand, reduces the total access latency by returning only requested parts of the stored data instead of the entire data content by accessing 1 to 2 clusters at most. For 1 to 4 queries for data inside the same cluster, Fed-DIC achieves at least 60% lower read access latency compared to RS. Even in the case that we request 2 data queries that are stored in two different clusters, Fed-DIC still reads the data in a shorter time compared to RS.

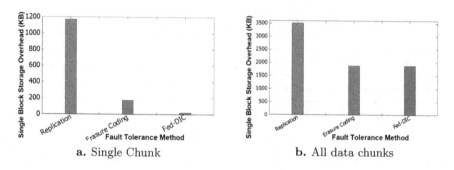

a. Single Chunk   **b.** All data chunks

Fig. 5. Storage overhead for Replication, Erasure Coding, and Fed-DIC

Our second experiment evaluates the reliability between 3-way Replication, RS (7, 4) and Fed-DIC (7, 4) in the data loss scenario. We performed 3 runs of experiments. As Fig. 4 indicates, due to its organized multi-cluster storage policies, Fed-DIC manages to achieve lower data loss rates than RS. Even when only up to 40% of the nodes are available in the federated cloud, Fed-DIC may be able to maintain a sufficient number of chunks in some diagonal stripes, which allows it to restore a portion the original data.

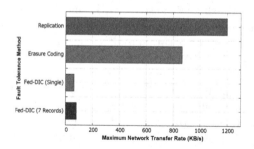

Fig. 6. Comparing Replication, Erasure Coding and Fed-DIC in terms of maximum network transfer rate (single record retrieval and 1 diagonal retrieval)

The next experiment we evaluate the storage overhead and the maximum network transfer rate between these fault tolerance methods. As Fig. 5a shows, Replication stores the entire data content inside the cluster without splitting it, causing a large storage overhead even for single blocks, compared to a chunk produced by simple Erasure Coding and Fed-DIC. In Fig. 5b we present the total storage overhead for all three methods. 3-Way replication occupies a massive portion of the storage with all 3 replicas combined, while all chunks generated by Erasure Coding and Fed-DIC produce lower overheads, with the latter occupying slightly less storage than erasure coding due to the varied sizes of the chunks. We also measured the rates during data transferring using performance monitoring programs included with Lubuntu OS. As seen in Fig. 6 due to the size of the replicas, Replication severely burdens the network with a high transfer rate of 1.2 MBps, followed by Erasure Coding with a transfer rate of 900 KBps. Fed-DIC operates with smaller data transfers and thus provides smaller and less burdening network data rates when transferring one or multiple queried data records.

Finally, Fig. 7 shows the load balancing achieved in the three fault tolerance methods between 4 4-node clusters, while uploading 4 different data streams with similar sizes. Due to the random distribution of replicas and chunks in the HDFS cloud, Replication and client-side Reed-Solomon erasure codes are very inconsistent in terms of load balancing. Specifically, a majority of data may be stored to one cluster, while other clusters store less data, even though Erasure Coding seems more consistent than Replication. It is worth to note that we do not consider HDFS server-side erasure coding since it requires a code with higher parameters, which generates a number of chunks equal to the number of nodes in a single cluster. Meanwhile, Fed-DIC, using the rotational stack policy for cluster destinations described previously, it can store new streams in the federated cloud's clusters in a different order for every stream. Since our framework stores data of different size in each cluster in every uploading process, it can maintain an almost perfect load balance between H clusters for each H uploaded streams. For example, in Fig. 7 for every 4 streams uploaded in the cloud, Fed-DIC can achieve storage consistency and good load balancing between the 4 clusters.

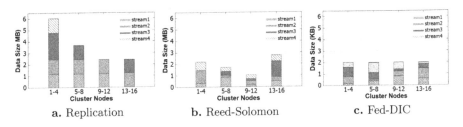

Fig. 7. Load balancing between 4 file clusters for all fault methods including Fed-DIC

6   Related Work

Several approaches over the last decade have been proposed for improving read access costs and the reliability of erasure coding in cloud storage environments. In particular, a method that drastically improves read access costs and data reconstruction in erasure coded storage systems is Deterministic Data Distribution, or D^3 for short [7]. D^3 maximizes the reliability of a storage system and reduces cross rack repair traffic by utilizing deterministic distribution of data blocks across the storage system. D^3 uses orthogonal arrays to define the data layout in which the data will be distributed across multiple racks, ignoring the one block per rack placement, while balancing the load among nodes across the system's racks. This implementation works on single HDFS clusters with multiple racks but it does not seem to support federated clouds or other systems with independent clusters, unlike our approach with Fed-DIC. Even if we modify D^3 to support multiple clusters, the clusters need to contain a certain number of nodes in order to apply server-side erasure coding, whereas in Fed-DIC, erasure coding is performed by the client devices.

Simple erasure codes provide efficient fault tolerance but their reliability is restricted to the parameters set by the user. Advanced erasure coding techniques like Alpha entanglement codes by Estrada et al. [19], increase the reliability and the integrity of a system compared to normal Reed-Solomon codes by entangling old and new data blocks and creating robust, flexible meshes of interdependent data with multiple redundancy paths. Also in the Ring framework for key-value stores (KVS) [21], Taranov et al. introduce Stretched Reed-Solomon (SRS) codes which support a single key-to-node mapping for multiple resilience levels. These lead to higher and more expanded reliability compared to conventional Reed-Solomon codes. However, this work is only restricted to key-value stores and is not available to conventional databases for use. Also, unlike our work, the reliability ranges of SRS are limited only to the parameters of specific key-to-node mappings.

Hybris [11] by Dobre et al. is a hybrid cloud storage system that scatters data across multiple unreliable or inconsistent public clouds, and it stores and replicates metadata information within trusted private nodes. The metadata are related to the data scattered across the public clouds, providing easier access and strong consistency for the data, as well as improved system performance and storage costs compared to existing multi-cloud storage systems. In our case, Fed-DIC uses metadata containing information about the topology of data stored in a federated cloud so that the client can connect immediately to the cluster that contains a requested portion of the data, thus drastically reducing the read access cost in these systems compared to simple erasure codes.

7   Conclusion

In this paper, we presented Fed-DIC, our framework that integrates Diagonal Interleaved Coding with organized storage of the encoded data in a federated cloud environment. Our framework takes as input data organized in a grid, interleaves them into diagonal stripes that are encoded using a Reed-Solomon erasure code. The encoded diagonal stripes are grouped into batches which are stored to different clusters in the cloud. The user issues queries to retrieve portions of the data without the need for the clients to access every cluster in the cloud, thus reducing the access cost compared to other methods like Replication and simple Erasure Codes. Our experimental evaluations illustrate the benefits of our framework compared to other fault tolerance methods in terms of total read access latency, data loss percentage, maximum network transfer rate, storage overhead and load balancing. For future work, one direction we are following is to deploy

Fed-DIC in a federated environment with different hardware equipment where we plan to evaluate the working and benefits as well as the corresponding costs of our approach when different types of equipment are utilized.

Acknowledgment. This research has been supported by the Computer Systems and Communications Laboratory at AUEB. The authors would like to thank Dr. Davide Frey for shepherding the paper. This research has been supported by European Union's Horizon 2020 grant agreement No 734242.

References

1. DeCandia, G., et al.: Dynamo: Amazon's highly available key-value store. In: ACM SIGOPS Operating Systems Review, vol. 41, no. 6. ACM (2007)
2. Ghemawat, S., Gobioff, H., Leung., S.-T.: The Google file system (2003)
3. Wang, M., et al.: Formalizing Google file system. In: 2014 IEEE 20th Pacific Rim International Symposium on Dependable Computing, pp. 190–191. IEEE (2014)
4. Shvachko, K., et al.: The hadoop distributed file system. In: MSST, vol. 10, pp. 1–10 (2010)
5. Karun, A.K., Chitharanjan, K.: A review on Hadoop—HDFS infrastructure extensions. In: 2013 IEEE Conference on Information & Communication Technologies, pp. 132–137. IEEE (2013)
6. "Erasure coding vs. Replication: A quantitative comparison"
7. Li, Z., et al.: D^3: deterministic data distribution for Ecient data reconstruction in erasure-coded distributed storage systems. In: 2019 IEEE International Parallel and Distributed Processing Symposium (IPDPS), pp. 545–556. IEEE (2019)
8. Ambade, S.V., Deshpande, P.: Hadoop block placement policy for different file formats. Int. J. Comput. Eng. Technol. (IJCET) **5**(12), 249–256 (2014)
9. Sathiamoorthy, M., et al.: Xoring elephants: novel erasure codes for big data. arXiv preprint arXiv:1301.3791 (2013)
10. Muralidhar, S., et al.: f4: Facebook's warm {BLOB} storage system. In: 11th {USENIX} Symposium on Operating Systems Design and Implementation (fOSDIg 2014), pp. 383–398 (2014)
11. Dobre, D., Viotti, P., Vukolić, M.: Hybris: robust hybrid cloud storage. In: Proceedings of the ACM Symposium on Cloud Computing, pp. 1–14. ACM (2014)
12. Weil, S.A., et al.: Ceph: a scalable, high-performance distributed file system. In: Proceedings of the 7th Symposium on Operating Systems Design and Implementation, pp. 307–320 (2006)
13. Chappell, D., et al.: Introducing Windows Azure. In: Microsoft, Dec (2009)
14. Calder, B., et al.: Windows Azure storage: a highly available cloud storage service with strong consistency. In: Proceedings of the Twenty-Third ACM Symposium on Operating Systems Principles, pp. 143–157 (2011)
15. Amazon, E.: Amazon web services, November 2012. http://aws.amazon.com/es/ec2/
16. Chang, X., Zha, L.: 'The performance analysis of cache architecture based on Alluxio over virtualized infrastructure. In: 2018 IEEE International Parallel and Distributed Processing Symposium Workshops (IPDPSW), pp. 515–519. IEEE (2018)
17. MacWilliams, F.J., Sloane, N.J.A.: The Theory of Error-Correcting Codes, vol. 16. Elsevier (1977)

18. Leong, D., Qureshi, A., Ho, T.: On coding for real-time streaming under packet erasures. In: 2013 IEEE International Symposium on Information Theory, pp. 1012–1016. IEEE (2013)
19. Estrada-Galinanes, V., et al.: Alpha entanglement codes: practical erasure codes to archive data in unreliable environments. In: 2018 48th Annual IEEE/IFIP DSN, pp. 183–194. IEEE (2018)
20. SCATS. https://data.smartdublin.ie/dataset/traffic-volumes/resource/4d45af2f-5ec1-4728-820a-a0fe350ad1dd
21. Taranov, K., Alonso, G., Hoee, T.: Fast and strongly-consistent peritem resilience in Key-Value Stores. In: EuroSys, pp. 39–1 (2018)

TailX: Scheduling Heterogeneous Multiget Queries to Improve Tail Latencies in Key-Value Stores

Vikas Jaiman[1,2] , Sonia Ben Mokhtar[3] , and Etienne Rivière[2(✉)]

[1] Institute of Data Science (IDS), Maastricht University,
Maastricht, The Netherlands
v.jaiman@maastrichtuniversity.nl
[2] ICTEAM, UCLouvain, Ottignies-Louvain-la-Neuve, Belgium
etienne.riviere@uclouvain.be
[3] INSA Lyon, LIRIS, CNRS, Villeurbanne, France
sonia.benmokhtar@insa-lyon.fr

Abstract. Users of interactive services such as e-commerce platforms have high expectations for the performance and responsiveness of these services. Tail latency, denoting the worst service times, contributes greatly to user dissatisfaction and should be minimized. Maintaining low tail latency for interactive services is challenging because a request is not complete until all its operations are completed. The challenge is to identify bottleneck operations and schedule them on uncoordinated backend servers with minimal overhead, when the duration of these operations are heterogeneous and unpredictable. In this paper, we focus on improving the latency of multiget operations in cloud data stores. We present TailX, a task-aware multiget scheduling algorithm that improves tail latencies under heterogeneous workloads. TailX schedules operations according to an estimation of the size of the corresponding data, and allows itself to procrastinate some operations to give way to higher priority ones. We implement TailX in Cassandra, a widely used key-value store. The result is an improved overall performance of the cloud data stores for a wide variety of heterogeneous workloads. Specifically, our experiments under heterogeneous YCSB workloads show that TailX outperforms state-of-the-art solutions and reduces tail latencies by up to 70% and median latencies by up to 75%.

Keywords: Distributed storage · Performance · Scheduling

1 Introduction

Serving users requests in interactive applications or websites generally involves handling a number of operations to backend services and databases. For instance, the display of a social network page may involve fetching and aggregating a

© IFIP International Federation for Information Processing 2020
Published by Springer Nature Switzerland AG 2020
A. Remke and V. Schiavoni (Eds.): DAIS 2020, LNCS 12135, pp. 73–92, 2020.
https://doi.org/10.1007/978-3-030-50323-9_5

number of images, posts, ads, etc. NoSQL cloud databases increasingly offer *multi-get* operations in their APIs, enabling to fetch values associated with a collection of keys with a single call [3,17,27,32]. In practice, multiget requests vary in the number of accessed keys and value size. A workload analysis at Facebook [32] shows that a request contains an average of 24 keys while 5% of the requests contain more than 95 keys. Another analysis from a SoundCloud trace presented by the authors of Rein [35] shows a heavy-tailed distribution of the number of keys: 40% of the requests involve multiple keys with an average size of 8.6 keys and the maximum number of keys reaches up to ~2,000 keys. Similarly, another analysis of key-value stores production workloads at Facebook [4] shows that value size typically ranges from a few Bytes to several MBs: Value sizes are highly skewed towards smaller sizes but very few large value sizes consume a large share of computational resources [11].

A multiget request finishes when all of its operations complete. The response time of a request depends on the response time of the slowest operation in that multiget request and, as a result, multiget operations are affected more often by high *tail latencies* [11,15,17,28]. Reducing tail latency is of uttermost importance in online services, as high service delays may have serious consequences on user quality-of-experience and satisfaction.

Several past works have considered the problem of reducing tail latency by scheduling single-key requests in key-value stores [20,24,37]. These approaches offer solutions to the *head-of-line-blocking* problem that results from the heterogeneity in the value sizes stored in the database: single-key requests for small values may get scheduled after a request for a large value (incurring, therefore, a long processing time). Requests for small values may be delayed after requests for large values, increasing average and tail latencies. In contrast, other works have considered the scheduling of multiget requests in key-value stores [14,35], but under the assumption of homogeneous service times for operations, i.e., of requests for fixed-size values. Scheduling multiget requests is more involved than scheduling single-key requests but also offers more opportunities when it is performed in a task-aware manner, i.e., when taking into account the entirety of the request for scheduling its constituents rather than considering these constituents independently. In particular, as the completion time of a multiget requests is, *in fine*, that of its longest operation, a task-aware scheduling algorithm may decide to delay the processing of non-critical operations of a multiget request in favor of more critical operations of another multiget request. The occurrence of long operations is intrinsically linked with the number but also with the size of the values fetched by these requests and, thus, by the heterogeneity in the size of queried data.

Contributions. We present TailX, a task-aware multiget scheduling algorithm that reduces tail latencies under heterogeneous workloads i.e. (i) when multiget requests are formed of operations for values of different sizes and (ii) when the number of operations for different multiget requests vary. TailX addresses two key challenges associated with the scheduling of multiget requests in a distributed, horizontally-scalable key-value store:

- First, a multiget request arrives at an entry point server in the key-value store, called the *coordinator*, which must split it into multiple sub-requests called *opset*, fetch values from different replicas, and send an aggregated response to the client. Selecting the appropriate replica for each opset must be performed in an online fashion, and service time cannot be known *a priori* and based solely on the keys. In other words, requests are processed in a non-clairvoyant fashion [31]. This is a result of two factors: (i) the load at the different replicas (amount of pending requests) is unknown by the coordinator and (ii) the size of the values corresponding to the keys is known by the replicas who hold them, but unknown to the coordinator that performs request splitting and replica selection.
- Second, once an opset reaches the selected replica, it must be scheduled for execution at that replica based on the overall execution time for the corresponding multiget request. Ideally, opset that are more critical for the overall execution time of a multiget query should be executed with higher priority than opset that are not as critical. The notion of "criticality" of a specific opset is, however, unknown to the replica, as the knowledge of the overall multiget requests is at the coordinator. As a result, a replica may take non-optimal decisions in processing opset, such as answering opset that could have been postponed without impacting the latency of the corresponding multiget requests, and conversely postponing critical opset.

TailX implements the sharing of information between coordinators and replicas and associated algorithms for end-to-end, task-aware scheduling of multiget requests:

- For coordinators, it enables awareness of the load of the different replicas and awareness of the size of values associated with given keys. The necessary information is exchanged between all nodes (coordinators and replicas-in many designs, nodes assume both roles) using an efficient and fast gossip protocol. The load of replicas, as indicated by the length of their queues of pending requests, enables avoiding overloads and reduces the impact of head-of-line-blocking. As sharing globally a map between all keys and the size of corresponding values would be impractical in terms of costs and scalability, and as request splitting and scheduling happen in the critical path of the request/response loop, TailX favors the pragmatic and efficient use of a compact data structure–a Bloom filter [6]–that probabilistically indicates keys that are associated to large values (i.e. above a threshold size).
- For replicas, TailX scheduling takes into account the possible influence of opset on tail latency and supports *procrastinating* non-critical opset in favor of the execution of more critical opset. These decisions are based on information embedded by the coordinator in an opset, indicating how much this opset is estimated to be allowed to *wait* before it can influence negatively the latency of its enclosing multiget request.

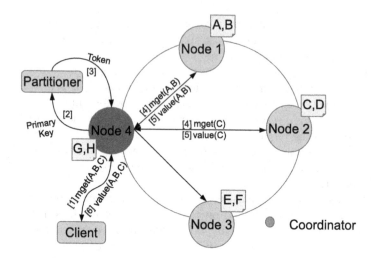

Fig. 1. Handling of a multiget request in Cassandra.

We implement TailX in the industry-grade key/value store Cassandra [25]. We compare TailX with Rein [35], a state-of-the-art algorithm for multiget requests scheduling, using a deployment on a cluster of 16 servers on the Grid'5000 testbed [5]. We use YCSB [10] to generate workloads that contain various proportions of accessed keys and value size, based on the description of production traces by Facebook [4]. Compared to Rein, TailX improves median latency by 75% as well as tail latency by up to 70%.

The remaining of this paper is structured as follows. We first present background on multiget scheduling in key-value stores (Sect. 2) and explain state-of-the-art algorithms. Next, we further detail the design of TailX (Sect. 3) and present its implementation and performance evaluation (Sect. 4). Finally, we discuss related work (Sect. 5) and conclude the paper (Sect. 6).

2   Multiget Requests in Key-Value Stores

We detail the execution of multiget queries in key-value stores with the example of Cassandra [25]. We note that the operation of other horizontally scalable, hash-partitioned key-value stores [3,17,27,32] supporting multiget queries are very similar. In the example of Fig. 1, nodes 1, 2 and 3 are replicas for the values associated with keys (A, B), (C, D) and (E, F) respectively. The example uses a single replica per key, but replication is used in practice to guarantee data availability. A client sending a multiget request mget(A, B, C) connects to any of the nodes that will act as coordinator (step 1). The coordinator uses a partitioner that returns tokens, as hash values for these keys (steps 2 and 3). These tokens together with the knowledge of the replication policy allow identifying the replicas holding copies of the values associated with the keys. The coordinator is in charge of (1) splitting the multiget request into a set of requests for one or

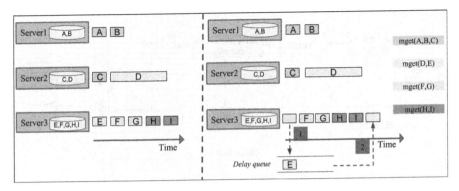

Fig. 2. An example scenario. *Left:* Requests assigned to server facing delayed response time. *Right:* Procrastinate opsets into delay queue to take benefits of delay allowance

more keys and (2) fetching the values from the corresponding replicas (steps 4 and 5). When all opsets have been answered, the coordinator may serialize the result and send it back to the client (step 6).

We illustrate the difficulty in scheduling multi-get requests efficiently to obtain low overall latencies with an example in Fig. 2 where the same request mget(A, B, C) is processed in a system where other single-key and multiget requests are ongoing. On the left of Fig. 2 servers 1, 2, 3 hold values for keys (A, B), (C, D) and (E, F, G, H, I) respectively. A small box represents a request to a small value and a large rectangle box (in this example for key D) represents a request to a large value. For the sake of simplicity, we assume that all replicas have a service time of 1 operation per unit time for serving a small value and of 5 unit time for serving a large value. For the request mget(A, B, C), (A, B) and (C) are the two opsets. With a FIFO scheduling as shown on the left of the figure, mget(A, B, C), mget(D, E), mget(F, G) and mget(H, I) will complete in 2, 6, 3 and 5 time units respectively, yielding an average response time of 4 time units.

We note that task awareness in scheduling individual opset at the replicas can allow reducing the average response time. A key observation is that each opset can be associated with a *delay allowance* that the replica can use to schedule other operations from its queue with higher priority (and, therefore, not necessarily in FIFO order). The delay allowance can be calculated as the difference in time between an approximated execution time for the largest or costliest opset. In the multiget request mget(D, E), the collection of D takes 6 time units whereas the collection of E will take 1 time unit. It is, therefore, possible to postpone (or *procrastinate*) the request for key E by at most 5 time units, leaving way for other requests. In this scenario, on the right side of the figure, mget(A, B, C), mget(D, E), mget(F, G) and mget(H, I) will complete in 2, 6, 2 and 4 time units respectively yielding an average response time of 3.5 time units.

Multiget Scheduling State-of-the-Art. The state-of-the-art in multiget requests scheduling is represented by Rein [35]. It uses two policies which include

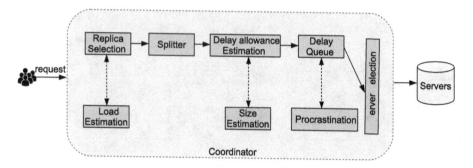

Fig. 3. Overview of TailX.

the Shortest Bottleneck First (SBF) and Slack-Driven Scheduling (SDS). In SBF, every operation of a multiget request has a priority which corresponds to the cost of the bottleneck opset while in SDS, it deprioritizes the operations based on how long they can afford to be slacked. The goal of Rein is to improve tail latency. To this end, Rein predicts which of the operations will likely be a bottleneck, i.e. create a head-of-line-blocking situation. This detection is based on the number of keys in the opset. The opset(s) with the highest number of keys is or are simply considered as the bottleneck opset. Based on this information, Rein uses a client-side priority assignment that prioritizes multiget requests with a smaller number of keys in their bottleneck opset. The determination of the bottleneck requests in Rein, however, does only take into account the number of keys in the opset but never the size of the corresponding values. The result is that the detected bottleneck opset may execute much faster than another opset from the same multiget query that is not detected as such.

3   TailX Design and Implementation

An overview of the architecture of TailX is given by Fig. 3. When a request is issued, the coordinator node selects the best replica out of total target replicas based on the past read performance of replica servers. An appropriate replica selection mechanism (dynamic snitching [39]) is applied to select the best replica.

Afterwards, the request goes to a *splitter* where it is split into opsets by a partitioner (Murmur3 [34]). The number of operations and value sizes associated with keys varies in these opsets. Among these, some opsets that contain smaller operations with shorter execution time will finish earlier whereas opsets that contain operations with larger execution time finish later. To execute a multiget request with minimum latency, all the opsets should finish at the approximately same time. Therefore, to correctly estimate the total execution time of each opset, TailX identifies the operations that take more time. For this, it passes through *size estimation* module. The objective of this module is to estimate whether a given operation will access a *small* or a *large* value. It keeps track of keys that associated with large values and store the keys of those operations.

Once the value size of an operation is identified, *delay allowance estimation* module estimates the cost of each opset i.e. approximate total execution time and calculates the approximate delay allowance that occurred by each opset. This delay allowance is inserted as metadata in each operation of an opset. After delay allowance assignment, opsets go through the *delay queue*. The objective of this step is to procrastinate each opset which has delay allowance and let other requests execute at that time. If an operation has delay allowance then it inserted in a delay queue with given procrastinating time. The operations reside in the delay queue until the given procrastinate time expires.

Finally, operations go to the required server that is holding the data. Once the operations finish, they return the data to the coordinator. We present in the following sections the details of all proposed modules. First, we present the replica selection mechanism based on the load estimated among servers (Sect. 3.1). Next, we describe the request splitting based on the data storage (Sect. 3.2). Finally, we explain the delay allowance policies including delay estimation of operations and scheduling mechanism (Sect. 3.3) (Fig. 4).

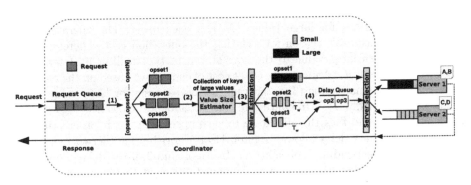

Fig. 4. Operating principle of TailX scheduling.

3.1   Load Estimation and Replica Selection

The operations of a multiget request select the target replicas according to the hash-based mechanism followed by the replica server. The number of replicas depends on the replication factor followed by the storage systems. Afterwards, a replica selection algorithm (dynamic snitching [25] which considers past read performance of the replicas) is applied for scoring the replicas and a faster replica is chosen to complete the operation. The role of this component is to select the replica that is expected to serve a given request faster than other replicas.

3.2   Request Splitting

In a key-value store, all storage nodes are divided into hash-based token ranges. After selecting the intended replica, request splits into opset according to the partitioner (e.g. Murmur3 [34]). Each opset goes to a different replica server and contains a varied number of operations with different value size. Our goal is to schedule the operations in a way that can complete each opset at the approximately same time. This gives better flexibility to other requests to execute at that time.

3.3   Delay Allowance Policies

The algorithms for delay allowance policies are described in Algorithm 1 and Algorithm 2. The role of these algorithms is to procrastinate the opsets which are finishing earlier than the other opsets.

Every opset has a different completion time due to the variations in value size and the number of operations in it. Therefore, some operations of an opset have to wait for bottleneck operations. This results in increasing the latency of the overall request.

To overcome this situation, the delay allowance module calculates the cost of each opset (*opcost*) i.e. opset execution time on the server. Calculation of the opset cost is based on the value size estimation since we need to know the number of operations for large values (N_L) in each opset. The operations of large values are the sole reason for inflating the operation cost. Therefore, we match the keys of large value to the keys stored in Bloom filter [6] (step 4 of Algorithm 1). Next, it calculates the opset cost of each opset based on the request service time for small value (T_S) and request service time for large value (T_L) (step 5 of Algorithm 1). Afterwards, it calculates delay allowance T_w (step 8 of Algorithm 1) and tags the allowance to each opset. Finally, it procrastinates operations that have delay allowance (step 11 of Algorithm 1) otherwise send the opset to the corresponding replica server. In Algorithm 2, if the delay allowance time has finished then the request is dequeued and sent to the corresponding replica server.

Delay Allowance Estimation. The role of delay estimation is to estimate the approximate execution cost of each opset and calculate the approximate delay allowance which can be occurred at each opset. The calculation of delay allowance is based on the value size estimation of each operation.

Value Size Estimation. An important question that TailX addresses is to determine whether an operation will access a large or a small value. In this context, we set a threshold (say THR_L) where values above this threshold are considered as large by TailX. We assume that this choice is application dependent and that it is up to the database administrator to set the value of THR_L according to the data distribution over her database.

TailX uses Bloom filters to keep track of keys corresponding to large values. A Bloom filter [6] is a space-time efficient probabilistic data structure that allows performing to test whether a given item belongs to a predefined set. It is a vector of m bits initially set to 0, with an associated set of k hash functions (generally $k \ll m$). Inserting an element in the Bloom filter is done by hashing the element using the k hash functions and setting the corresponding bit positions to 1. Testing the presence of an element in the Bloom filter is done similarly by hashing the element using the k hash functions and testing whether all the corresponding bit positions are set to 1. Querying a Bloom filter may lead to false-positive but will never lead to false-negative.

After identifying keys that correspond to the large value, it calculates the opset cost i.e. how much time the opset will take to execute. To estimate the opset cost (*opcost*), it calculates the service time of operations for large values (T_L) and small values (T_S). Afterwards, it multiplies them by their respective number of operations to get the overall cost of the opset.

Further, it calculates the delay allowance (T_w) for each opset. Delay allowance is calculated based on the cost difference of maximum opset cost (*opcost$_{max}$*) and cost of opset for which it is calculating the delay allowance. It means every opset has the allowance time in which it can wait and let other operations to complete.

Delay Scheduling. The role of a delay queue is to procrastinate the opset which has some delay allowance. This gives better flexibility for other queries to execute in the delay allowance time.

Delay Queue Design. Delay queue (Q_d) is an unbounded blocking queue implemented in Java for opsets which have delayed allowance. The idea of the delay queue is to procrastinate some operations. An element can be taken out once the delay has expired. The element which is at the head of the queue has the expired delay furthest in the past.

Scheduling of Requests Which has Delay Allowance. If the request is tagged by delay allowance ($T_w > 0$) during delay estimation then the request will be sent to delay queue. The scheduler adds the system current time in the delay allowance i.e. procrastinate time (T_d), which helps to correctly estimate the procrastinated opset.

Scheduling of Requests with Zero Delay Allowance. If the request is tagged by delay allowance ($T_w == 0$) during delay estimation then the request will be sent directly to the server without delay. Since these are the requests which take time to execute and don't offer any allowance for slacking that opset.

Finally, operations are sent to the intended server directly or after completion of the procrastination time.

4   Evaluation

We implement TailX as an extension of Cassandra [25], a very popular key-value store. We evaluate its effectiveness in reducing tail latency using synthetic

---

Algorithm 1: Opset delay allowance algorithm

Data: $ksName$ = keyspace name, K = set of keys, CF = tablename, op = opset,
$opcost_{max}$ = max opset cost, req = multiget request, $opsets$ = set of opsets, N_L = set
of keys correspond to large values in an opset, Q_d = delay queue, BF = bloom filter;
Input: req $(ksName, K, CF)$;
Output: Procrastinated opsets.

```
1  begin
2  |   opcost_max = 0;
3  |   for op ∈ opsets do
   |   |   /* Calculate number of keys correspond to large values
   |   |      in an opset                                          */
4  |   |   N_L := {opr ∈ op | match(BF, opr.key) = 1};
   |   |   /* Calculate opset cost                                 */
   |   |   // T_L= request service time (in nanosec) for large value
   |   |   // T_S= request service time (in nanosec) for small value
   |   |   // opsize = number of keys in an opset
5  |   |   opcost = T_L * |N_L| + T_S * (opsize - |N_L|);
   |   |   /* Calculate max opset cost                             */
6  |   |_  opcost_max = max(opcost, opcost_max);
7  |   for op ∈ opsets do
   |   |   /* Calculate delay allowance                            */
8  |   |   T_w = opcost_max - op.opcost;
   |   |   /* Tag T_w to each opset                                */
9  |   |   tag(T_w, op);
   |   |   /* Calculate procrastinating time                       */
   |   |   // T_current = current system time
10 |   |   T_d ⟵ T_current + T_w;
11 |   |   if op.T_w > 0 then
   |   |   |   /* insert opset in delay queue                      */
12 |   |   |_  Q_d.enqueue(op, T_d);
13 |   |   else
14 |   |_  |_  send op to corresponding replica;
```

T_L = request service time (in nanosec) for large value

T_S = request service time (in nanosec) for small value

opsize = number of keys in an opset

$opcost = T_L * |N_L| + T_S * (opsize - |N_L|)$;

$opcost_{max} = max(opcost, opcost_{max})$;

$T_w = opcost_{max} - op.opcost$;

$tag(T_w, op)$;

$T_{current}$ = current system time

$T_d \longleftarrow T_{current} + T_w$;

if $op.T_w > 0$ then

$Q_d.enqueue(op, T_d)$;

send op to corresponding replica;

Algorithm 2: Opset dequeue algorithm

```
1  begin
2  |   while Q_d ≠ ∅ && T_current - T_d ≥ 0 do
3  |   |   deque from Q_d;
4  |   |_  send op to corresponding replica;
```

---

dataset generated using the Yahoo! Cloud Serving Benchmark (YCSB) [10]. We compare different latency percentiles, particularly the tail, under TailX, against state-of-the-art algorithm i.e. Rein. We conduct extensive experiments on Grid'5000 [5], exploring the impact of varying ratios of multiget request sizes and their value sizes. Overall, our evaluation answers the following questions:

1. How does TailX performance effects by the multiget request sizes in the key-value stores? (Sect. 4.2)
2. How does TailX performance effects by the proportion of large values in the key-value stores? (Sect. 4.2)

We start this section by presenting our evaluation setup (Sect. 4.1) before presenting our results (Sect. 4.2).

4.1   Experimental Setup

Experimental Platform. We evaluate TailX on Grid'5000 [5]. We use a 16 node cluster in which each machine is equipped with 2 Intel Xeon X5570 CPUs (4 cores per CPU), 24 GB of RAM and a 465 GB HDD. The machines are running the Debian 8 GNU/Linux operating system.

Configuration. We evaluate TailX in Cassandra. We used the industry-standard Yahoo! Cloud Serving Benchmark (YCSB) [10] to generate datasets and run our workloads. As YCSB only generates a single value size datasets for each given client, we modified its source code to allow generation of mixed size datasets. Specifically, for mixed size workloads, we kept the proportion of large values compared to small values the same. For generating client workloads, we configured YCSB on a separate node.

Moreover, in all the generated workloads, the access pattern of stored values (whether small or large) follows a Zipfian distribution (with a Zipfian parameter $\rho = 0.99$). To have an idea of the size a given synthetic dataset, we insert 20 million of small records (1 KB size) and 100 K of large records (2 MB size). This approximately represents $\tilde{4}1$ GB of data per node. We kept the replication factor as 3 which means each piece of value is available on 3 servers. Each measurement involves 1 million or 10 million requests and is repeated 5 times. Each multiget request access various operations with different value sizes. We test the cluster of its maximum attainable throughput and kept the 75% system load for all our experiments.

4.2   TailX on Variable Configurations of the Synthetic Dataset

We evaluate in this section the effectiveness of TailX along different dimensions of heterogeneous workloads, i.e., the impact of *long* operations on multiget requests and the impact of operations correspond to large values.

Impact of Multiget Requests Containing Large Number of Operations.
To study the impact of the proportion of long multiget requests (i.e. multiget request size is large) on the system performance, we fix the size of multiget request as 100 and short multiget request to 5. We keep the ratio of long multiget

request to 20% i.e. for each 100 multiget requests, 80 multiget are of size 5 and 20 multiget are of size 100. Through this, we can see the impact of long multiget over short multiget requests. We present the improvement of TailX over Rein for 1 million operations and 10 million operations in Fig. 5 and 6 respectively. Figure 7 shows the different latency percentiles to give a closer look in system. In this experiment, we start by generating datasets in which each multiget request contains 1 KB values.

Results show that TailX reduces the tail latencies over Rein by up to 63% while reducing the median latency by up to 71%. TailX achieves a better gain for median latency compare to tail latency. In terms of absolute latency (for 1 million operations), say for 99th percentile, it is 56 ms for TailX but roughly 152 ms

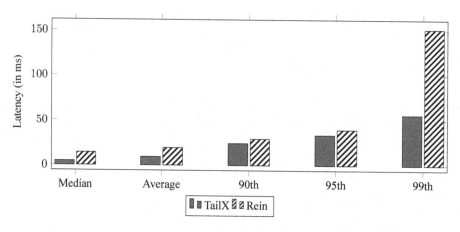

Fig. 5. Improvement of TailX over latency with different multiget request sizes (80% multiget of size 5 and 20% multiget of size 100) for 1 million operations.

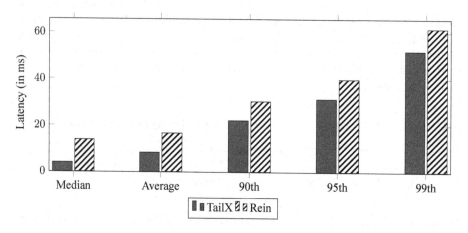

Fig. 6. Improvement of TailX over latency with different multiget request sizes (80% multiget of size 5 and 20% multiget of size 100) for 10 million operations.

for Rein respectively. For median latency, absolute value is 4.57 ms for TailX whereas it is around 14.3 ms for Rein.

Impact of Multiget Requests Having Keys of Large Value Sizes. To study the impact of the proportion of large requests (request having large value i.e. 2 MB) on the system performance, we fix the size of multiget request as 20. We keep the percentage of large multiget requests as 20% and vary the proportion of large values.

Varying Proportion of Large Value Sizes. We vary the proportion of large value from 10% to 50% in a multiget request. As specified before, these variations are only for 20% of multiget requests. We present the latency reduction of TailX over Rein for 1 million operations. In the following, we zoom into the specific percentage of large value sizes.

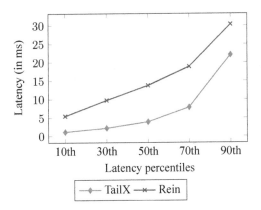

Fig. 7. Analysis of different latency percentiles for different multiget request sizes (80% multiget of size 5 and 20% multiget of size 100) for 10 million operations.

Multiget of 10% Large Values. In this experiment, 20% of each multiget contains 10% of large values. Figure 8 and 9 show the improvement of TailX over Rein i.e., 30% latency reduction in 95th and 99th percentiles. TailX achieves a better gain for median latency compare to tail latency, i.e., roughly 75% v.s. 30%. In terms of absolute latency, say for 99th percentile, it is 97 ms for TailX but roughly 135 ms for Rein respectively. For median latency, absolute value is 11 ms for TailX whereas it is around 43 ms for Rein.

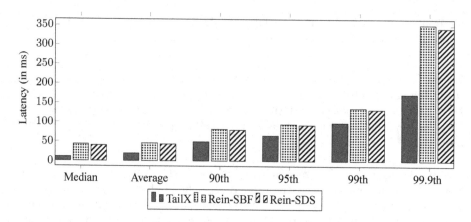

Fig. 8. Improvement of TailX over latency with different multiget request value sizes (80% of multiget requests are for small values (1 KB) and the remaining 20% multiget requests have 10% of requested large values) for 1 million operations.

Multiget of 20% Large Values. Figure 10 and 12 show the improvement of TailX over Rein i.e., 40% and 45% latency reduction in 95th and 99th percentiles respectively. TailX achieves a better gain for median latency compare to tail latency, i.e., roughly 56% v.s. 45%. In terms of absolute latency, say for 99th percentile, it is 112 ms for TailX but roughly 203 ms for Rein respectively. For median latency, absolute value is 8 ms for TailX whereas it is around 18 ms for Rein.

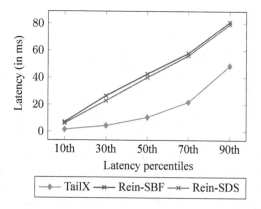

Fig. 9. Analysis of different latency percentiles for different multiget request value sizes (80% multiget requests have small values (1 KB) and rest 20% multiget requests have 10% of large values) for 1 million operations.

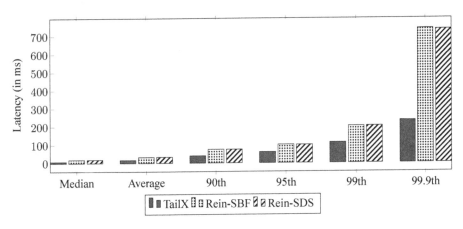

Fig. 10. Improvement of TailX over latency with different multiget request value sizes (80% multiget requests have small values (1 KB) and rest 20% multiget requests have 20% of large values) for 1 million operations.

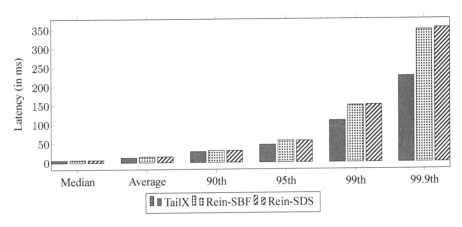

Fig. 11. Improvement of TailX over latency with different multiget request value sizes (80% multiget requests have small values (1 KB) and rest 20% multiget requests have 50% of large values) for 1 million operations.

Multiget of 50% Large Values. Figure 11 and 12 show the improvement of TailX over Rein i.e., 18% and 27% latency reduction in 95th and 99th percentiles respectively. TailX achieves a little less gain for median latency compare to tail latency, i.e., roughly 13%. In terms of absolute latency, say for 99th percentile, it is 109 ms for TailX but roughly 150 ms for Rein respectively. For median latency, absolute value is 5.9 ms for TailX whereas it is around 6.76 ms for Rein.

Summarizing, TailX outperforms Rein in most of the configurations. TailX is effective when there are some long requests in the systems. Also, the effectiveness of TailX can be seen when some multiget requests have some percentage of large values. We note that TailX is designed to handle heterogeneous workloads

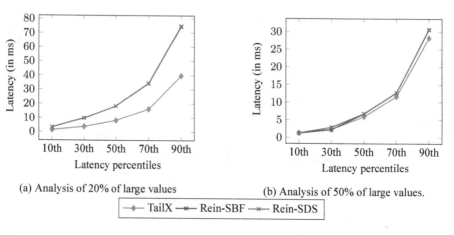

(a) Analysis of 20% of large values

(b) Analysis of 50% of large values.

TailX ——— Rein-SBF ——— Rein-SDS

Fig. 12. Analysis of different latency percentiles for different multiget request value sizes (80% multiget requests have small values (1 KB) and rest 20% multiget requests have a) 20% of large values b) 50% of large values) for 1 million operations.

that have high variance across requests sizes w.r.t number of operations and their value sizes. When the proportion of value sizes of requests increases, the impact of TailX is visible more. TailX improves the tail latency till 20% whereas while workload having 50% of large value, the improvement decreases compare to the 20%. Since TailX filter the requests with large values with bloom filter and therefore if there are bulk of requests which have large value it increases the overhead. Therefore, less impact is seen in this case. Overall in these configurations, TailX reduces the median latency up to 75% and tail latency by up to 70%.

5   Related Work

Several works addressed the problem of tail latency in distributed storage systems. Some have addressed the impact of incoming workloads that are coming on the system. We present our related work as follows:

Web Workloads. Atikoglu et al. [4] described the workload analysis of a Memcached [32] traffic at Facebook. It studies 284 billion requests over 58 days for five different Memcached use cases. It presents the CDFs of value size in different Memcached pools. ETC pool is the largest and most heterogeneous value size pool where value sizes vary from few bytes to MBs.

Network-Specific. Orchestra [8] uses weighted fair sharing where each transfer is assigned a weight and each link in the network is shared proportionally to the weight of the transfer. Baraat [15] is a decentralized task-aware scheduling system that dynamically changes the level of multiplexing in the network to avoid head-of-line-blocking. It uses task arrival time to assign a globally unique identifier and put a priority for each task. All flows of a task use this priority irrespective of the network they traverse. Varys [9] is another coflow scheduling system that decreases communication time for data-intensive jobs and provides predictable communication time. It assumes complete prior knowledge of coflow characteristics such as the number of flows, their sizes, etc. Aalo [7] is another scheduling policy that improves performance in data-parallel clusters without prior knowledge. To improve the performance in datacenters, pFabric [2] decouples flow scheduling from rate control mechanisms.

Redundancy-Specific. Redundancy is a powerful technique in which clients initiate an operation multiple times on multiple servers. The operation which completes first is considered and the rest of them is discarded. Vulimiri et al. [38] characterize the scenarios where redundancy improves latency even under exceptional conditions. It introduces a queuing model that gives an analysis of system utilization and server service time distribution. Sparrow [33], a stateless distributed scheduler that adapts the power of two choices technique [29] by selecting two random servers. It put the tasks on the server which has fewer queued tasks. Sparrow [33] uses batch sampling where instead of sampling each task it places m tasks of a job on least loaded randomly selected servers. This approach performs better for parallel jobs since they are sensitive to tail task wait time.

Task-Aware Schedulers. Hawk [13] and Eagle [12] are two systems proposing a hybrid scheduler that schedules jobs according to their sizes. In Hawk [13], long jobs are scheduled using a centralized scheduler while small jobs are scheduled in a fully distributed way. Omega [36] is a shared-state scheduler in which a separate centralized resource manager maintains a shared scheduling state.

Request Reissues and Parallelism. Kwiken [21] optimizes the end-to-end latency using a DAG of interdependent jobs. It further uses latency reduction techniques such as request reissues to improve the latency of request-response workflows. Haque et al. [19] propose solutions for decreasing tail latencies by dynamically increasing the parallelism of individual requests in interactive services. *Few-to-Many* (FM) selectively parallelizes the long running requests since that are the ones contributing the most to the tail latency. Recent efforts [22,23] show that it is challenging to schedule tasks during the arrival of variable size jobs. These works try to predict the long-running queries and parallelize them selectively. Instead of targeting the more general problem of predicting job sizes, which in some cases involves costly computations.

Jeon et al. [23] focus on the parallelizing long running queries which are few compared to the short ones. It aims to achieve consistent low response time for web search engines.

Multiget Scheduling. In key-value stores, multiget scheduling is a common pattern for scheduling requests efficiently. Systems like Cassandra [25], MongoDB [30] offer such algorithms in these systems. Rein [35] uses a multiget scheduling algorithm to schedule the multiget request in a fashion that can reduce the median as well as tail latency.

Tail Latency Specific. Minos [14] is another in-memory key-value store that uses size aware sharding to send small and large requests to different cores. It ensures that small requests never wait due to the large request which improves tail latencies. Metis [26] is an auto-tuning service to improve tail latency by using customized Bayesian optimization. SyncGC [18] tries to reduce the tail latency in Cassandra by proposing a synchronized garbage collection technique that schedules multiple GC instances to sync with each other. Sphinx [16] uses a thread-per-core approach to reduce tail latency in a key-value store by using application-level partitioning and inter-thread messaging. Some authors [1] provide bounds on tail latency for distributed storage systems by using erasure coding. It helps to provide optimization to minimize weighted tail latency probabilities.

6   Conclusion

In this paper, we addressed the problem of tail latencies in key-value stores under heterogeneous workloads for multiget requests. For multiget scheduling, an in-depth study of state-of-the-art has highlighted the fact that it doesn't perform well under heterogeneous workloads. We proposed TailX, a task-aware multiget scheduling algorithm that effectively deals with heterogeneous multiget requests. It identifies the bottleneck operations apriori and procrastinates them to avoid head-of-line-blocking. The result is an improved overall performance of the key-value store for a wide variety of heterogeneous workloads. Specifically, our experiments under heterogeneous YCSB workloads in a Cassandra based implementation shows that TailX outperforms state-of-the-art algorithm and reduces the tail latencies by up to 70% while reducing the median latency by up to 75%.

Acknowledgments. Experiments presented in this paper were carried out using the Grid'5000 testbed, supported by a scientific interest group hosted by Inria and including CNRS, RENATER and several Universities as well as other organizations. This work was partially supported by the *European Union's Horizon 2020 research and innovation programme* under grant agreement No 692178 (EBSIS project), by CHIST-ERA under project DIONASYS, and by the Swiss National Science Foundation (SNSF) under grant 155249.

References

1. Al-Abbasi, A.O., Aggarwal, V., Lan, T.: Ttloc: taming tail latency for erasure-coded cloud storage systems. IEEE Trans. Netw. Serv. Manag. **16**(4), 1609–1623 (2019)
2. Alizadeh, M., et al.: pFabric: minimal near-optimal datacenter transport. In: SIGCOMM (2013)
3. Ananthanarayanan, G., et al.: Pacman: coordinated memory caching for parallel jobs. In: NSDI (2012)

4. Atikoglu, B., Xu, Y., Frachtenberg, E., Jiang, S., Paleczny, M.: Workload analysis of a large-scale key-value store. In: SIGMETRICS (2012)
5. Balouek, D., et al.: Adding Virtualization capabilities to the Grid'5000 testbed. In: Ivanov, I.I., van Sinderen, M., Leymann, F., Shan, T. (eds.) CLOSER 2012. CCIS, vol. 367, pp. 3–20. Springer, Cham (2013). https://doi.org/10.1007/978-3-319-04519-1_1
6. Bloom, B.H.: Space/time trade-offs in hash coding with allowable errors. Commun. ACM **13**(7), 422–426 (1970)
7. Chowdhury, M., Stoica, I.: Efficient coflow scheduling without prior knowledge. In: SIGCOMM (2015)
8. Chowdhury, M., Zaharia, M., Ma, J., Jordan, M.I., Stoica, I.: Managing data transfers in computer clusters with orchestra. In: SIGCOMM (2011)
9. Chowdhury, M., Zhong, Y., Stoica, I.: Efficient coflow scheduling with varys. In: SIGCOMM (2014)
10. Cooper, B.F., Silberstein, A., Tam, E., Ramakrishnan, R., Sears, R.: Benchmarking cloud serving systems with YCSB. In: SoCC (2010)
11. Dean, J., Barroso, L.A.: The tail at scale. Commun. ACM **56**(2), 74–80 (2013)
12. Delgado, P., Didona, D., Dinu, F., Zwaenepoel, W.: Job-aware scheduling in Eagle: divide and stick to your probes. In: SoCC (2016)
13. Delgado, P., Dinu, F., Kermarrec, A.M., Zwaenepoel, W.: Hawk: hybrid datacenter scheduling. In: USENIX ATC (2015)
14. Didona, D., Zwaenepoel, W.: Size-aware sharding for improving tail latencies in in-memory key-value stores. In: NSDI (2019)
15. Dogar, F.R., Karagiannis, T., Ballani, H., Rowstron, A.: Decentralized task-aware scheduling for data center networks. In: SIGCOMM (2014)
16. Enberg, P., Rao, A., Tarkoma, S.: The impact of thread-per-core architecture on application tail latency. In: ACM/IEEE Symposium on Architectures for Networking and Communications Systems (ANCS) (2019)
17. Fan, B., Andersen, D.G., Kaminsky, M.: Memc3: compact and concurrent memcache with dumber caching and smarter hashing. In: NSDI (2013)
18. Han, S., Lee, S., Hahn, S.S., Kim, J.: SyncGC: a synchronized garbage collection technique for reducing tail latency in Cassandra. In: Proceedings of the 9th Asia-Pacific Workshop on Systems, APSys (2018)
19. Haque, M.E., Eom, Y.H., He, Y., Elnikety, S., Bianchini, R., McKinley, K.S.: Few-to-many: incremental parallelism for reducing tail latency in interactive services. In: ASPLOS (2015)
20. Jaiman, V., Mokhtar, S.B., Quéma, V., Chen, L.Y., Rivière, E.: Héron: taming tail latencies in key-value stores under heterogeneous workloads. In: SRDS (2018)
21. Jalaparti, V., Bodik, P., Kandula, S., Menache, I., Rybalkin, M., Yan, C.: Speeding up distributed request-response workflows. In: SIGCOMM (2013)
22. Jeon, M., He, Y., Kim, H., Elnikety, S., Rixner, S., Cox, A.L.: TPC: target-driven parallelism combining prediction and correction to reduce tail latency in interactive services. In: ASPLOS (2016)
23. Jeon, M., et al.: Predictive parallelization: taming tail latencies in web search. In: SIGIR (2014)
24. Jiang, W., Xie, H., Zhou, X., Fang, L., Wang, J.: Understanding and improvement of the selection of replica servers in key-value stores. Inf. Syst. **83**, 218–228 (2019)
25. Lakshman, A., Malik, P.: Cassandra: a decentralized structured storage system. SIGOPS Oper. Syst. Rev. **44**(2), 35–40 (2010)
26. Li, Z.L., et al.: Metis: robustly tuning tail latencies of cloud systems. In: USENIX ATC (2018)

27. Lim, H., Han, D., Andersen, D.G., Kaminsky, M.: Mica: a holistic approach to fast in-memory key-value storage. In: NSDI (2014)
28. Misra, P.A., Borge, M.F., Goiri, I.N., Lebeck, A.R., Zwaenepoel, W., Bianchini, R.: Managing tail latency in datacenter-scale file systems under production constraints. In: EuroSys (2019)
29. Mitzenmacher, M.: The power of two choices in randomized load balancing. IEEE Trans. Parallel Distrib. Syst. **12**(10), 1094–1104 (2001)
30. MongoDB. https://www.mongodb.com/
31. Motwani, R., Phillips, S., Torng, E.: Non-clairvoyant scheduling. In: Proceedings of the Fourth Annual ACM-SIAM Symposium on Discrete Algorithms, SODA (1993)
32. Nishtala, R., et al.: Scaling memcache at Facebook. In: NSDI (2013)
33. Ousterhout, K., Wendell, P., Zaharia, M., Stoica, I.: Sparrow: distributed, low latency scheduling. In: SOSP (2013)
34. Partitioners. https://docs.datastax.com/en/cassandra/3.0/cassandra/architecture/archPartitionerAbout.html
35. Reda, W., Canini, M., Suresh, L., Kostić, D., Braithwaite, S.: Rein: taming tail latency in key-value stores via multiget scheduling. In: EuroSys (2017)
36. Schwarzkopf, M., Konwinski, A., Abd-El-Malek, M., Wilkes, J.: Omega: flexible, scalable schedulers for large compute clusters. In: EuroSys (2013)
37. Suresh, L., Canini, M., Schmid, S., Feldmann, A.: C3: cutting tail latency in cloud data stores via adaptive replica selection. In: NSDI (2015)
38. Vulimiri, A., Godfrey, P.B., Mittal, R., Sherry, J., Ratnasamy, S., Shenker, S.: Low latency via redundancy. In: CoNEXT (2013)
39. Williams, B.: Dynamic snitching in Cassandra: past, present, and future (2012). http://www.datastax.com/dev/blog/dynamic-snitching-in-cassandra-past-present-and-future

Fault-Tolerance and Reproducibility

Building a Polyglot Data Access Layer for a Low-Code Application Development Platform
(Experience Report)

Ana Nunes Alonso[1]([✉]), João Abreu[2], David Nunes[2], André Vieira[2], Luiz Santos[3], Tércio Soares[3], and José Pereira[1]

[1] INESC TEC and U. Minho, Braga, Portugal
ana.n.alonso@inesctec.pt, jop@di.uminho.pt
[2] OutSystems, Lisboa, Portugal
{joao.abreu,david.nunes,andre.vieira}@outsystems.com
[3] OutSystems, Braga, Portugal
{luiz.santos,tercio.soares}@outsystems.com

Abstract. Low-code application development as proposed by the OutSystems Platform enables fast mobile and desktop application development and deployment. It hinges on visual development of the interface and business logic but also on easy integration with data stores and services while delivering robust applications that scale.

Data integration increasingly means accessing a variety of NoSQL stores. Unfortunately, the diversity of data and processing models, that make them useful in the first place, is difficult to reconcile with the simplification of abstractions exposed to developers in a low-code platform. Moreover, NoSQL data stores also rely on a variety of general purpose and custom scripting languages as their main interfaces.

In this paper we report on building a polyglot data access layer for the OutSystems Platform that uses SQL with optional embedded script snippets to bridge the gap between low-code and full access to NoSQL stores.

1 Introduction

The current standard for integrating NoSQL stores with available low-code platforms is for developers to manually define how the available data must be imported and consumed by the platform, requiring expertise in each particular NoSQL store, especially if performance is a concern. Enabling the seamless integration of a multitude of NoSQL stores with the OutSystems platform will

---

This work was supported by Lisboa2020, Compete2020 and FEDER through Project RADicalize (LISBOA-01-0247-FEDER-017116 — POCI-01-0247-FEDER-017116) and also by National Funds through the Portuguese funding agency, FCT - Fundação para a Ciência e a Tecnologia within project UIDB/50014/2020.

A. Remke and V. Schiavoni (Eds.): DAIS 2020, LNCS 12135, pp. 95–103, 2020.
https://doi.org/10.1007/978-3-030-50323-9_6

offer its more than 200 000 developers a considerable competitive advantage over other currently available low-code offers.

Main challenges include NoSQL systems not having a standardized data model, a standard method to query meta-data, or in many cases, by not enforcing a schema at all. Second, the value added by NoSQL data stores rests precisely on a diversity of query operations and query composition mechanisms, that exploit specific data models, storage, and indexing structures. Exposing these as visual abstractions for manipulation risks polluting the low-code platform with multiple particular and overlapping concepts, instead of general purpose abstractions. On the other hand, if we expose the minimal common factor between all NoSQL data stores, we are likely to end up with minimal filtering capabilities that prevent developers from fully exploiting NoSQL integration. In either case, some NoSQL data stores offer only very minimal query processing capabilities and thus force client applications to code all other data manipulation operations, which also conflicts with the low-code approach. Finally, ensuring that performance is compatible with interactive applications means that one cannot resort to built-in MapReduce to cope with missing query functionality, as it leads to high latency and resource usage. Also, coping with large scale data sets means avoiding full data traversals by exposing relevant indexing mechanisms and resorting to approximate and incomplete data, for instance, when displaying a developer preview.

In this paper we summarize our work on a proof-of-concept polyglot data access layer for the OutSystems Platform that addresses these challenges, thus making the following contributions:

- We propose to use a polyglot query engine, based on extended relational data and query models, with embedded NoSQL query script fragments as the approach that reconciles the expectation of low-code integration with the reality of NoSQL diversity.
- We describe a proof-of-concept implementation that leverages an off-the-shelf SQL query engine that implements the SQL/MED standard [4].

As a result, we describe various lessons learned, that are relevant to the integration of NoSQL data stores with low-code tools in general, to how NoSQL data stores can evolve to make this integration easier and more effective, and to research and development in polyglot query processing systems in general. An extended version of this work is available in [1].

The rest of the paper is structured as follows. Section 2 describes our proposal to integrate NoSQL data stores in the OutSystems platform, including our current proof-of-concept implementation. Section 3 concludes the paper by discussing the main lessons learned.

2 Architecture

Our proposal is based on two main criteria. First, how it contributes to the vision of NoSQL data integration in the low-code platform outlined in Sect. 1 and how it fits the low-code approach in general. Second, the talent and effort needed for developing such integrations and then, later, for each additional NoSQL system that needs to be supported.

We can consider two extreme views. On the one hand, we can enrich the abstractions that are exposed to the developer to encompass the data and query processing models. This includes: data types and structures, such as nested tuples, arrays, and maps; query operations, ranging from general purpose data manipulation (e.g., flattening a nested structure) to domain-specific operations (e.g., regarding search terms in a text index); and finally, where applicable, query composition (e.g., with MapReduce or a pipeline).

This approach has however several drawbacks. First, it pollutes the low-code platform with a variety of abstractions that have to be learned by the developers to fully use it. Moreover, these abstractions change with support for additional NoSQL systems and are not universally applicable. In fact, support for different NoSQL systems would be very different, making it difficult to use the same know-how to develop applications on them all. Finally, building and maintaining the platform itself would require a lot of talent and effort in the long term, as support for additional systems could not be neatly separated in plugins with simple, abstract interfaces.

On the other hand, we can map all data in different NoSQL systems to a relational schema with standard types and allow queries to be expressed in SQL. This results in a mediator/wrapper architecture that allows the same queries to be executed over all data regardless of its source, even if by the query engine at the mediator layers.

This approach also has drawbacks. First, mapping NoSQL data models to a relational schema requires developer intervention to extract the view that is adequate to the queries that are foreseen. This will most likely require NoSQL-specific talent to write target queries and conversion scripts. Moreover, query capabilities in NoSQL systems will remain largely unused, as only simple filters and projections are pushed down, meaning the bulk of data processing would need to be performed client-side.

Our proposal is a compromise between these two extreme approaches, that can be summed up as: support for nested data and its manipulation in the abstractions shown to the low-code developer, along with the ability to push aggregation operations down to NoSQL stores from a mediator query engine, will account for the vast majority of use cases. In addition, the ability to embed native query fragments in queries will allow fully using the NoSQL store when talent is available, without disrupting the overall integration. The result is a polyglot query engine, where SQL statements are combined with multiple foreign languages for different NoSQL systems.

The proposed architecture is summarized in Fig. 1, highlighting the proposed NoSQL data access layer. To the existing OutSystems platform, encompassing development tools and runtime components, we add a new *Polyglot connector*, using the Database Integration API to connect to the *Polyglot Query Engine (QE)* through standard platform APIs. The Polyglot QE acts as a mediator.

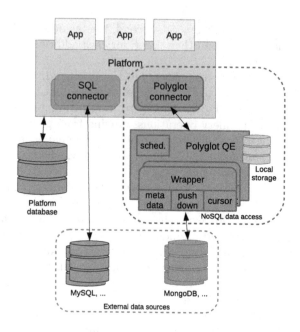

Fig. 1. Architecture overview

It exposes an extended relational database schema for connected NoSQL stores and is able to handle SQL and polyglot queries.

For each NoSQL Store, there is a *Wrapper*, composed of three sub-components: *metadata* extraction, responsible for determining the structure of data in the corresponding store using an appropriate method and mapping it to the extended SQL data model of the Polyglot QE; a query *push-down* component, able to translate a subset of SQL query expressions, to relay native query fragments, or produce a combination of both in a store-specific way; and finally, the *cursor*, able to iterate on result data and to translate and convert it as required to fit the common extended SQL data model.

The Polyglot QE makes use of *Local storage* for the configuration of NoSQL store adapters and for holding materialized views of data to improve response times. The *Job Scheduler* enables periodically refreshing materialized views by re-executing their corresponding queries.

2.1 Implementation

We base our proof-of-concept implementation on open source components. The main component to select is the SQL query engine used as the mediator. Besides its features as a query engine, we focus on: the availability of wrappers for different NoSQL systems and the talent needed to implement additional features; the compatibility of the open source license with commercial distribution;

the maturity of the code-base and supporting open source community; and
finally, on its compatibility with the OutSystems low-code platform. We consider two options.

PostgreSQL with FDW[7]. It is an option as it supports foreign data wrappers according to the SQL/MED standard (ISO/IEC 9075-9:2008). The main
attractive for PostgreSQL is that it is a very mature open source product, with
a business friendly license, a long history of deployment in production, and an
unparalleled developer and user community. There is also support for .NET and
Java client application platforms. In terms of features, PostgreSQL provides a
robust optimizer and an efficient query engine, that has recently added parallel
execution, with excellent support for SQL standards and multiple useful extensions. It supports nested data structures both with the `json`/`jsonb` data types,
as well as by natively supporting arrays and composite types. It has extensive
support for traversing and unnesting them. Regarding support for foreign data
sources, besides simple filters and projections, the PostgreSQL Foreign Data
Wrapper (FDW) interface can interact with the optimizer to push down joins
and post-join operations such as aggregations. With PostgreSQL FDW, it is
possible to declare tables for which query and manipulation operations are del-
egated on adapters. The wrapper interface includes the ability to either impose
or import a schema for the foreign tables. Imposing a schema requires the user
to declare data types and structure and it is up to the wrapper to make it fit
by using automatic type conversions as possible. If this automatic process is
not successful the user will need to change the specified data type to provide
a closer type match. The wrapper can also (optionally) advertise the possibility of importing a schema. In this case, the user simply instructs PostgreSQL
to import meta-data from the wrapper and use it for further operations. This
capability is provided by the wrapper and currently, this is only supported for
SQL databases, for which the schema can be easily queried. Furthermore, PostgreSQL FDW can export the schema of the created foreign tables. In addition to
already existing wrappers for many NoSQL data sources, with variable features
and maturity, the Multicorn[1] framework allows exposing the Python scripting
language to the developer, to complement SQL and express NoSQL data manipulation operations.

In terms of our goals, PostgreSQL falls short on automatically using existing materialized views in queries. The common workaround is to design queries
based on views and later decide whether to materialize them, which is usable
in our scenario. Another issue is that schema inference is currently offered for
relational data sources only. The workaround is for the developer to explicitly
provide the foreign table definition.

Calcite[2] **(in Dremio OSS**[3]**).** The Calcite SQL compiler, featuring an extensible optimizer, is used in a variety of modern data processing systems. We
focus on Dremio OSS as its feature list most closely matches our goal. Calcite

---

[1] https://github.com/Kozea/Multicorn.

is designed from scratch for data integration and focuses on the ability to use the optimizer itself to translate parts of the query plan to different back end languages and APIs. It also supports nested data types and corresponding operators. Dremio OSS performs schema inference, but treats nested structures as opaque and, therefore, does not completely support low-code construction of unnesting operations, in the sense that the user still needs to explicitly handle these. Still, it provides the ability to impose a table schema ad-hoc or flexibly adapt data types which is a desirable feature for overriding incorrect schema inference. Also, Dremio OSS adds a distributed parallel execution engine, based on the Arrow columnar format, and a convenient way to manage materialized views (a.k.a., "reflections"), that are automatically used in queries. Unfortunately, one cannot define or use indexes on theses views, which reduces their usefulness in our target application scenarios.

Although Calcite has a growing user and developer community, its maturity is still far behind PostgreSQL. The variety of adapters for different NoSQL systems is also lagging behind PostgreSQL FDW, although some are highly developed. For instance, the MongoDB adapter in Dremio OSS is able to extensively translate SQL queries to MongoDB's aggregation pipeline syntax, thus being able to push down much of the computation and reduce data transfer. The talent and effort needed for exploiting this in additional data wrappers is, however, substantial. Both for Dremio and PostgreSQL, limitations in schema imposition/inference do not impact querying capabilities, only the required talent to use the system. For PostgreSQL FDW, this can be mitigated by extending adapters to improve support for nested data structures, integrating schema inference/extraction techniques. Finally, the main drawback of this option is that, as we observed in preliminary tests, resource usage and response time for simple queries is much higher than for PostgreSQL.

Choosing PostgreSQL with FDW. In the end, we found that our focus on interactive operational applications and the maturity of the PostgreSQL option, outweigh, for now, the potential advantages from Calcite's extensibility.

Additional Development Completing a proof-of-concept implementation based on PostgreSQL as a mediator requires additional development in the low-code platform itself, an external database connector, and in the wrappers. As examples, we describe support for two NoSQL systems. The first is Cassandra, a distributed key-value store that has evolved to include a typed schema and secondary indexes. It has, however, only minimal ad-hoc query processing capabilities, restricted to filtering and projection. The second is MongoDB, a schema-less document store that has evolved to support complex query processing with either MapReduce or the aggregation pipeline. Both are also widely used in a variety of applications.

Schema Conversion. In order to support relational schema introspection, we reuse mongodb-schema[2], extending it to provide a probabilistic schema, with fields and types, for each collection in a MongoDB database. Top-level document fields are mapped as table attributes. When based on probabilistic schemas, all discovered attributes are included, leaving it to the user/developer to decide which attributes to consider. Nested documents' fields are mapped as top-level attributes, named as the field prefixed with its original path. Nested arrays are handled by creating a new table and promoting fields of inner documents to top-level attributes. Documents from a given collection become a line of the corresponding table (or tables). An alternative would be to create a denormalized table. Notice that this is equivalent to the result of a natural join between the corresponding separate tables. However, separate tables fit better what would be expected from a relational database and thus improve the low-code experience. It should be pointed out that viewing the original collection as a set of separate relational tables has no impact on the performance of a query with a join between these tables. The required unnesting directives, using the $unwind pipeline aggregation operator are also generated and added to the table definition. We also provide the option, on by default, of adding a column referencing the _id of the outermost table to all inner tables on schema generation, that can serve as an elementary foreign key.

MongoDB Wrapper. There are multiple FDW implementations for MongoDB. We selected one based on Multicorn,[3] for ease of prototyping, and change it extensively to include schema introspection and, taking advantage of aggregation pipeline query syntax, to allow push-down to work with user supplied queries. This is greatly eased by MongoDB's syntax for the aggregation pipeline being easily manipulated by programs, by adding additional stages.

Cassandra Wrapper. We also use a wrapper based on Multicorn.[4] In this case, we add the ability to use arbitrary Python expressions to compute row keys from arbitrary attributes, as in earlier versions of Cassandra it was usual to manually concatenate several columns. Even if this is no longer necessary in recent versions of Cassandra, it is still common practice in other NoSQL systems such as HBase. The currently preferred interface to Cassandra, CQL, is not the best fit for being manipulated by programs, although, being so simple, it can be done with relatively small amount of text parsing.

Connectors. We implemented custom connectors for each NoSQL store based on the original PostgreSQL connector. This allows the developer to directly pick the target data store from the platform's visual development environment [6]

---

[2] https://github.com/mongodb-js/mongodb-schema.
[3] https://github.com/asya999/yam_fdw.
[4] https://github.com/rankactive/cassandra-fdw.

drop-down menu and provide system specific connection options. It also allows system specific projection and aggregation operators to be handled.

Developer Platform. The changes needed in the platform to fully accommodate the integration are the ability to express nesting and unnesting operators in the data manipulation UI, and to generate SQL queries that contain them when using the NoSQL integration connectors. It is, however, possible to workaround this by configuring multiple flattened views of data, as needed, when the schema is introspected and imported.

3   Lessons Learned

We discussed the challenges in integrating a variety of NoSQL data stores with the OutSystems low-code platform. This is achieved by a SQL query engine that federates multiple NoSQL sources and complements their functionality, using PostgreSQL with Foreign Data Wrappers as a proof-of-concept implementation. It allowed us to learn some lessons about NoSQL systems and to propose a good trade-off between integration transparency and the ability to take full advantage of each systems' particularities. Lessons target low-code platform providers $(1, 2)$, polyglot developers $(3, 4, 5, 6)$ and NoSQL data store providers $(7, 8)$.

1. Target an extended relational model. The relational data model when extended with nested composite data types such as maps and arrays can successfully map the large majority of NoSQL data models with minimal conversion or conceptual overhead. Moreover, when combined with flatten and unflatten operators, the relational query model can actually operate on such data and represent a large share of target query operations. This is very relevant, as it provides a small set of additional concepts that have to be added to the low-code platform or, preferably, none at all as unnesting is done when importing the schema.

2. A query engine is needed. Due to the varying nature of query capabilities in different data sources, a query engine that can perform various computations is necessary to avoid that developers have to constantly mind these differences. This is true even for querying a single source at a time.

3. Basic schema discovery with overrides is needed. Although Cloud-MdsQl [5] has shown that it is possible to build a polyglot query engine without schema discovery, by imposing ad-hoc schemas on native queries, it severely restricts its usefulness in the context of a low-code platform. However, after getting started with automatically inferred schema, it is useful to allow the developer to impose additional structure such as composite primary keys in key value stores.

4. Embedded scripting is required. Although many data manipulation operations could be done in SQL at the query engine, embedding snippets of a general purpose scripting language allows direct reuse of existing code and reduces the need for talent to translate them. Together with the ability to override automatic discovery, this is key to ensuring that the developer never hits a wall imposed by the platform.

5. Materialized view substitution is desirable. Although our proof-of-concept implementation does not include it, this is the main feature from the Calcite-based alternative that is missing. The ability to define different native queries as materializations of various sub-queries is the best way to encapsulate alternative access paths encoded in a data-store specific language.

6. Combining foreign tables with scripting is surprisingly effective. Although CloudMdsQl [5] proposed its own query engine, a standard SQL engine with federated query capabilities, when combined with a scripting layer for developing wrappers such as Multicorn, is surprisingly effective in expressing queries and supporting optimizations.

7. A NoSQL query interface should be targeted at machines, not only at humans. NoSQL systems such as MongoDB or Elasticsearch, that expose a query model based on an operator pipeline, are very friendly to integration as proposed. In detail, it allows generating native queries from SQL operators or to combine partially hand-written code with generated code. Ironically, systems that expose a simplistic SQL like language that is supposed to be more developer friendly, such as Cassandra, make it harder to integrate as queries in these languages are not as easily composed.

8. Focus on combining query fragments. It might be tempting to overlook some optimizations that are irrelevant when a human is writing a complete query, e.g., as pushing down $match in a MongoDB pipeline. However, these optimizations are fairly easy to achieve and greatly simplify combining partially machine generated queries with developer written queries.

References

1. Alonso, A.N., et al.: Towards a polyglot data access layer for a low-code application development platform. https://arxiv.org/abs/2004.13495 (2020)
2. Apache Calcite - Documentation. https://calcite.apache.org/docs/. Accessed 27 Feb 2020
3. Dremio - The Data Lake Engine. https://docs.dremio.com. Accessed 27 Feb 2020
4. ISO/IEC: Information technology - Database languages - SQL - Part 9: Management of External Data (SQL/MED). ISO/IEC standard (2016)
5. Kolev, B., Valduriez, P., Bondiombouy, C., Jiménez-Peris, R., Pau, R., Pereira, J.: CloudMdsQL: querying heterogeneous cloud data stores with a common language. Distrib. Parallel Databases **34**(4), 463–503 (2015). https://doi.org/10.1007/s10619-015-7185-y
6. Development and Deployment Environments. https://www.outsystems.com/evaluation-guide/outsystems-tools-and-components/#1. Accessed 02 Mar 2020
7. PostgreSQL Foreign Data Wrappers. https://wiki.postgresql.org/wiki/Foreign_data_wrappers. Accessed 27 Feb 2020

A Comparison of Message Exchange Patterns in BFT Protocols
(Experience Report)

Fábio Silva[✉], Ana Alonso, José Pereira, and Rui Oliveira

INESC TEC and U. Minho, Braga, Portugal
{fabio.l.silva,ana.n.alonso}@inesctec.pt, {jop,rco}@di.uminho.pt

Abstract. The performance and scalability of byzantine fault-tolerant (BFT) protocols for state machine replication (SMR) have recently come under scrutiny due to their application in the consensus mechanism of blockchain implementations. This led to a proliferation of proposals that provide different trade-offs that are not easily compared as, even if these are all based on message passing, multiple design and implementation factors besides the message exchange pattern differ between each of them. In this paper we focus on the impact of different combinations of cryptographic primitives and the message exchange pattern used to collect and disseminate votes, a key aspect for performance and scalability. By measuring this aspect in isolation and in a common framework, we characterise the design space and point out research directions for adaptive protocols that provide the best trade-off for each environment and workload combination.

1 Introduction

The popularization of cryptocurrencies backed by blockchain implementations such as Bitcoin has led to a renewed interest in consensus protocols, particularly in protocols that can tolerate Byzantine faults to prevent malicious participants from taking fraudulent economic advantage from the system. Instead of using established BFT protocols such as PBFT [7] to totally order transactions, permissionless blockchains such as Bitcoin's [14] and Ethereum [6] currently use protocols based on Proof-of-Work [14], as scalability in the number of processes is known to be an issue for classic BFT consensus protocols. This, however, represents a trade-off: the ability to scale to large numbers of processes with a possibly very dynamic membership comes at the cost of increased transaction latency and probabilistic transaction finality.

An alternative path is taken by permissioned blockchains such as Hyperledger Fabric [1], which use classical consensus protocols to totally order transactions, motivating the need for higher scalability in BFT protocols. The result has been

ⓒ IFIP International Federation for Information Processing 2020
Published by Springer Nature Switzerland AG 2020
A. Remke and V. Schiavoni (Eds.): DAIS 2020, LNCS 12135, pp. 104–120, 2020.
https://doi.org/10.1007/978-3-030-50323-9_7

that a variety of BFT protocols have been proposed, which, having identified the number and/or size of the messages to be exchanged as the bottleneck for scalability, take advantage of different message exchange patterns combined with different cryptographic primitives [2,4,8,9,12,17].

The proposed protocols might be generally compared through decision latency and throughput measurements in a common experimental setup, and relative scalability evaluated by varying only the number of processes. There are however a number of implementation factors that can affect performance and hide the impact of the abstract protocol, including the programming language, concurrency control strategy, and networking and cryptographic libraries.

We argue that a more interesting result for the proposal and implementation of future protocols can come from assessing the impact of the selected message exchange patterns and cryptographic primitives, in isolation of other implementation factors, as these are key aspects for protocol performance and strongly impact scalability to a large number of processes.

This work makes the following contributions:

- We propose an experimental harness for reliably reproducing the performance and scalability characteristics of the vote dissemination and collection phases in a BFT protocol, including the message exchange pattern and the cryptographic primitive.
- We run experiments for four message exchange patterns and three cryptographic primitives, thus characterizing the design space for these protocols in terms of resource usage (CPU and network) and potential parallelism. We use these results to draw lessons for future research and development.

The rest of this paper is structured as follows. Section 2 briefly describes existing protocols in terms of the message exchange patterns and cryptographic primitives used. Section 3 proposes a model for reproducing and measuring the impact of these protocol features, Sect. 4 presents the results obtained, which are discussed in Sect. 5. Finally, Sect. 6 presents the main lessons learned and outlines future work.

2   Background

A practical BFT protocol for state machine replication was initially proposed by Castro and Liskov [7]. It allows clients to submit requests to a set of processes that order and execute them. The challenge lies in ensuring that all correct processes execute the same sequence of requests, regardless of crash faults, where processes forget what has not yet been saved to a persistent log and byzantine faults, where malicious processes behave arbitrarily, possibly generating messages that do not comply with the protocol. The number of tolerated faults is bound to the number of processes in such a way that it requires $3t + 1$ processes to provide safety and liveness in the presence of t faults.

The challenge is addressed with a three phase message exchange protocol. In a first stage, *pre-prepare* the current leader proposes a sequence number for a pending request. In a second stage, *prepare*, all processes that recognize the sender of the message as the leader acknowledge it to all others. This is however not enough for agreement, as malicious processes might be sending different messages to different destinations. Therefore, in the third phase, *commit*, processes that got $2t$ acknowledgments will then confirm the outcome to all others. Upon reception of $2t + 1$ confirmations, the request can be executed. Note that messages need to be authenticated to prevent malicious processes from forging messages by impersonating other processes.

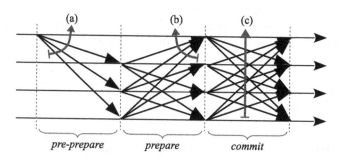

Fig. 1. Message exchange pattern in BFT agreement in three phases. It includes (a) sending a message to all others; (b) receiving a message from all others; and (c) quadratic number of messages being transmitted in the network.

The resulting message exchange pattern (*broadcast*) is depicted in Fig. 1. Even if these messages do not convey the requests themselves and are restricted to protocol information, it is problematic for performance in various ways. First, (a) it requires each process to send a message to all others, which without a true broadcast medium consumes CPU time in transport and network layers. Second, each process has to receive and handle messages from all others (b). In fact, even if only $2t + 1$ replies are needed for progress, in the normal case where no process is faulty, $3t + 1$ messages will have to be delivered and decoded, thus consuming CPU time. Finally, as all-to-all messages are exchanged, the network bandwidth used grows quadratically with the number of processes. These issues are bound to become scalability bottlenecks.

The typical answer to these issues is to design a message exchange pattern that trades latency for bandwidth and exploits parallelism. For instance, instead of directly sending a message to all destinations, it is first sent to a selected subset that then relays it to some other subset. This avoids any of the processes having to deal directly with all destinations and enables message exchange to be done in parallel by the various intermediate processes. A similar strategy can be used when collecting acknowledgments.

An option used in agreement protocols in the crash-stop model [11], is to employ a *centralized* pattern, i.e., to rely on the central coordinator to collect messages from all processes and then re-broadcast to all, making the number of messages grow linearly with the number of processes at the expense of an additional communication step. Another option is to organize processes in a logical ring and have each of them add to and forward the message to the next (*ring pattern*). This is the option taken in Ring Paxos [13] and in the Chain configuration of the Aliph protocol [2]. Gossiping is a well known efficient distributed information dissemination and aggregation strategy, hence it has also been proposed in this context [12]. In this case, each bit of information is routed to a small random subset of destinations, where it can be combined and forwarded (*gossip* pattern).

Unfortunately, the assumption of byzantine faults makes this harder to achieve than in the variants of Paxos for the crash-stop fault model, as a process cannot trust others to correctly forward the information contained in messages from others unless the original (*simple*) cryptographic signature is included verbatim. This works when disseminating information but is less useful when collecting information from other processes, as the agreement protocol needs to do in *prepare* and *commit* phases, as multiple signatures need to be included (*set*), making message size grow with the number of processes. It is nonetheless viable and is used in the Chain configuration of Aliph [2].

Some protocols employ cryptographic techniques that enable signatures to be combined to mitigate this increase in message size. Designating specific processes to act as collectors, which combine a pre-defined number of signatures into a single one (*threshold signatures*), can be used in protocol phases that require the collection of a minimum number of replies/confirmations [9,17]. Alternatively, other protocols leverage techniques that allow signatures to be aggregated at each step (*aggregate signatures*), thus eschewing the need to define specific processes to carry out this operation but, in turn, verification requires knowing exactly which signatures have been aggregated [4,12].

Table 1. Representative protocols for different message exchange patterns (rows) and cryptographic primitive combinations (columns).

	Simple/set	Threshold	Aggregate
Broadcast	PBFT [7]	n/a	n/a
Centralized		SBFT [9], HotStuff [17]	LibraBFT [4]
Ring	Chain [2]		
Gossip			Multi-level [12]

Table 1 lists representative combinations of message exchange patterns and cryptographic primitives for creating digital signatures used in BFT protocols. Notice that for the broadcast message pattern used in the original PBFT protocol [7] there is no need to use a cryptographic primitive to combine message signatures, as these are sent directly. The other options might lead to useful combinations, as the computational effort required by different cryptographic primitives needs to be weighed against savings in the amount of data that is transmitted.

3   Model

To assess the impact of each combination of message exchange pattern and cryptographic primitive we built a cycle-based simulation of the core phases of a byzantine fault tolerant protocol. This allows us to highlight the impact of these two factors without the experimental noise that would result from implementation details such as language, concurrency, networking, serialization and cryptographic libraries. This also allows us to exhaustively experiment with all combinations, including those that haven't been tried before.

The protocol model is as follows. It reproduces only the common path of the replication protocol, namely, the *pre-prepare*, *prepare*, and *commit* phases of PBFT [7] as shown in Fig. 1. A designated process (the coordinator) starts a protocol instance by disseminating a proposal. Each process, upon receiving that proposal, disseminates a first phase vote. Upon collecting first phase votes from two thirds of processes (a first phase certificate), a process disseminates a second phase vote. Agreement is reached when one third of processes collect a second phase certificate (second phase votes from two thirds of processes). The model thus omits request execution, interaction with clients, and the view change protocol, needed to deal with failure of the coordinator.

The key to achieving different message exchange patterns is to allow each process to forward information. In this case, the relevant information consists of the votes for each phase of the protocol: instead of a process having to send a vote directly to all others, as in the original PBFT protocol, it is possible for the vote to be forwarded by intermediate processes, thus avoiding the need for direct communication. We do this in a simple fashion: each process is able to send all votes collected so far in each phase instead of just sending out its own. The decision for when these votes are sent and to whom depends on a strategy parameter, which leads to different message exchange patterns. Based on the protocols described in Sect. 2, the considered message exchange patterns are:

Broadcast: The coordinator broadcasts the proposal and each process broadcasts its own votes.
Centralized: The coordinator broadcasts the proposal and each process sends its own votes only to the coordinator. Upon collecting a certificate, the coordinator forwards it to the remaining processes.
Ring: Processes are disposed in a logical ring. The coordinator sends the proposal to its successor. A process forwards the proposal and collected votes to its successor until it forwards a second phase certificate.
Gossip: The coordinator sends the proposal to *fanout* processes. A process forwards the proposal and collected votes to *fanout* processes every time it receives a set that contains messages (either proposal or votes) it does not

know about, until it forwards a second phase certificate. The destinations are picked from a random permutation of all possible destinations, in a cyclic order, to ensure deterministic termination [15].

All patterns except Broadcast require processes to forward collected votes. Votes must be authenticated and same phase votes from distinct processes, if correct, differ only in their signature. These signatures can be sent individually, as a set, or make use of cryptographic techniques to reduce the size of messages as follows:

Set: A simple approach is to forward a set containing known signatures. However, this entails that message size will be proportional to the number of signatures.

Threshold: Threshold signatures allow any process to convert a set of signatures into a single signature. However, this can only happen when the set contains a pre-defined number of signatures – the threshold value. Up until that point the whole set must be forwarded. In this context, the threshold value should be two thirds of the number of processes (the size of certificates).

Aggregation: With signature aggregation, processes can aggregate any number of signatures into a single signature at any moment, but forwards must include information about which processes' signatures have been aggregated. Additionally, for the gossip pattern, forwarded information must also include how many times each signature has been aggregated, as these may, in turn, be further aggregated.

Regarding the simulator, in each cycle, each active process runs to completion, sequentially processing all pending messages. In detail, a process is active if it is the coordinator at the start of the protocol or if there is an incoming message, ready to be received. Each process can thus receive and send multiple messages per cycle. Messages sent in a cycle are made available at the destination in the next cycle. This allows us to obtain several interesting metrics:

Number of Cycles to Reach a Decision: The number of cycles required to reach a decision is the primary metric, as it provides a measurement of how many communication steps are required.

Number of Messages Sent and Received: The number of messages sent and received provide a measurement of network bandwidth used. By recording these metrics individually for each process, we are also able to point out the cases where the load is asymmetrically distributed.

Message Size in Bytes: The overhead that the message exchange pattern combined with the cryptographic primitive entails in bytes. The space taken by view, sequence number, requests, among others, are not regarded. This metric is calculated from the content of the messages exchanged and is key to assess the impact of collecting multiple votes in each forwarded message.

Number of Active Processes: The number of active processes is a measure of parallelism, pointing out how many processes are able to make progress in parallel and how evenly computational load is distributed.

Actual CPU Time: Since the implementation used to process each message is complete, i.e., includes de-serialization of the input signatures, protocol state changes, cryptographic operations, and serialization of output signatures, and would be usable in a real implementation, we measure the used CPU time using hardware counters, and consider this as a measure of computational effort.

The protocol model and cycle-based simulators have been implemented in C++ and executed in a Linux server with dual *AMD Opteron 6172* processors (2100 MHz and 24 cores/hardware threads) with 128 GB RAM. All cryptography is provided by the *Chia-Network BLS signatures library*.[1]

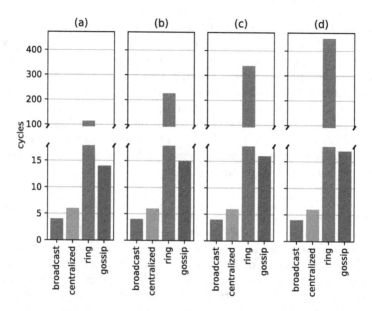

Fig. 2. Number of cycles needed to reach a decision in an agreement instance, by each process, per message exchange pattern for: (a) 49 processes; (b) 97 processes; (c) 145 processes; and (d) 193 processes.

4   Results

The cycle-based simulator and protocol model are now used to obtain results for each relevant message exchange pattern and cryptographic primitive. It should be pointed out that the broadcast pattern uses only simple message signatures, as each process only sends its own vote and sends it directly to every other process. On the other hand, in centralized, ring and gossip patterns, processes forward collected votes and thus are evaluated with all cryptographic primitive

---

[1] https://github.com/Chia-Network/bls-signatures.

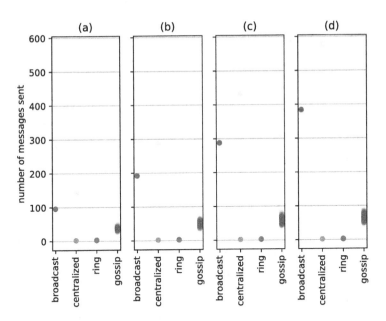

Fig. 3. Number of messages sent in an agreement instance, by each process, per message exchange pattern for: (a) 49 processes; (b) 97 processes; (c) 145 processes; and (d) 193 processes.

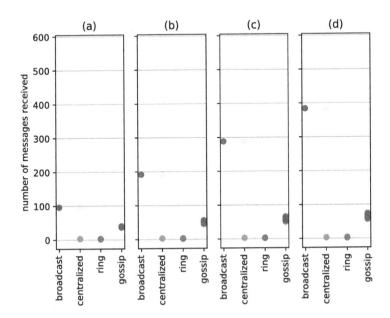

Fig. 4. Number of messages received in an agreement instance, by each process, per message exchange pattern for: (a) 49 processes; (b) 97 processes; (c) 145 processes; and (d) 193 processes.

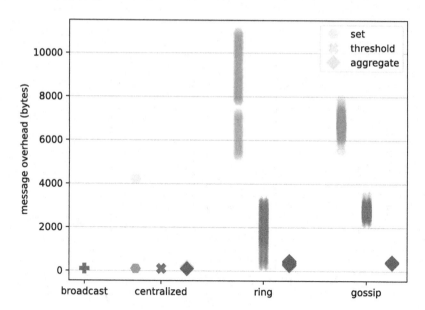

Fig. 5. Message overhead due to signatures (in bytes), averaged per process, for each combination of message exchange pattern and cryptographic primitive, for 97 processes.

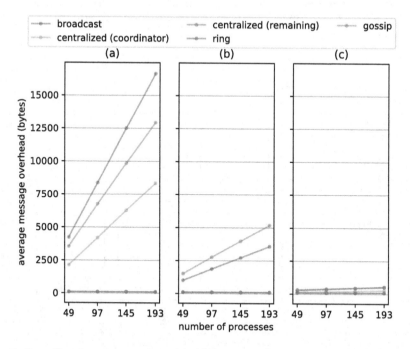

Fig. 6. Overall average message overhead due to signatures (in bytes) for an increasing number of processes, per cryptographic primitive: set of signatures (a), threshold signatures (b) and signature aggregation (c). Values for the Broadcast pattern are also presented for comparison.

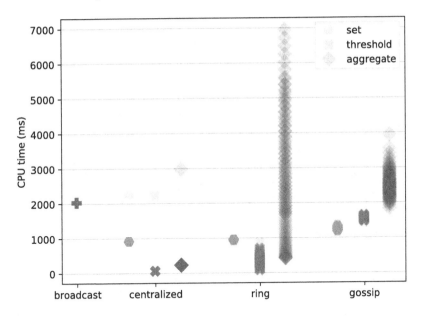

Fig. 7. Total CPU usage (in ms) for each process, per combination of message exchange pattern and cryptographic primitive, for 97 processes.

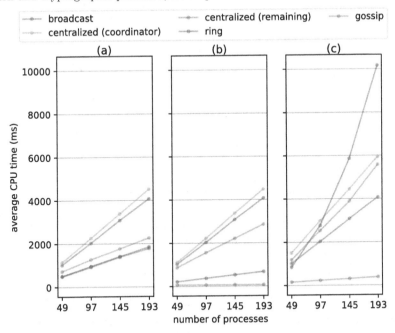

Fig. 8. Average CPU usage (in ms) per process, for an increasing number of processes, per cryptographic primitive: set of signatures (a), threshold signatures (b) and signature aggregation (c). Values for the Broadcast pattern are also presented for comparison.

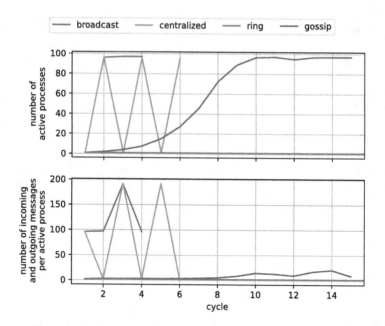

Fig. 9. Number of active processes in each cycle (a) and the average number of incoming and outgoing messages processed by each active process (b), per message exchange pattern, for 193 processes. Ring continues past 400 cycles (cropped).

options. In addition, the number of destinations in the gossip pattern is set as *fanout* = 2, the lowest value that can still define the pattern. These experiments don't account for either network or process faults, so there is no need for retransmissions, no messages are lost and messages are always correct. All experiments are repeated with 49, 97, 145 and 193 processes, the number of processes required to tolerate 16, 32, 48 and 64 malicious processes, respectively.

Because the gossip message pattern includes an element of randomness, the results of several runs were analysed. In order to consolidate the results of those runs, we first ranked the measurements for each metric per run. Then we calculated the average value per rank. An alternative could be to use the identity of each process to calculate average measurements. However, the identity of processes in different runs is ultimately unrelated. Thus, the ranking method provides better predictive ability, allowing us to provide, for example, an estimate for how long it will take for the first process to decide and also for the last to decide.

Figure 2 shows the number of simulation cycles needed for deciding an instance of the protocol, with each of the message exchange patterns. This is the number of communication steps needed for processes to agree on the next command to execute. For instance, with the broadcast pattern processes agree in four communication steps: first the coordinator broadcasts a proposal; processes then receive the proposal and broadcast its first phase vote; afterwards processes receive all first phase vote and broadcast a second phase votes; and finally processes receive all second phase votes.

Results shown in Figs. 3, 4, 5, 6, 7 and 8 focus on resource usage. Note that Figs. 3, 4, 5 and 7 plot a dot for the result observed in each process, showing where appropriate the dispersion of results depicted by the level of color saturation: the more overlap, the higher the color saturation. This is evident in the centralized pattern, as measurements regarding the coordinator are depicted as mostly transparent and color saturation reveals the overlap regarding remaining processes.

In detail, Figs. 3 and 4 show, respectively, the number of messages sent and received for an agreement instance, for each message exchange pattern and for a growing number of processes. Figure 5 shows the message overhead in bytes due to votes carried, including the signatures in a run with 97 processes. A dot is plotted for each process, showing the average message size for that process, which in some configurations is variable. Figure 6 then shows how the average message size varies with the number of processes in the system. Likewise, Fig. 7 shows the CPU time consumed by each process. A dot is plotted for each of them, showing that in some cases the load is variable. Figure 8 then shows how the average CPU time used varies with the number of processes in the system.

Finally, Fig. 9 describes how the load is distributed across different processes and across time, during the run of an agreement instance. In detail, Fig. 9(a) shows the number of active processes (i.e., those that receive and send messages in that cycle) as time progresses. Figure 9(b) shows the average number of incoming and outgoing messages that are processed by each of the active processes.

5 Discussion

The considerations put forth in this section are based on the analysis of the results presented in Sect. 4.

Broadcast. We start by discussing the results for the broadcast pattern as a baseline, as it matches the original PBFT protocol [7]. In this pattern, each process sends and receives messages directly to and from all others. Therefore, all processes work in parallel sending and receiving n messages in each phase. Messages contain only one signature, thus the message overhead due to signatures is always the same and does not change with the total number of processes. The total CPU time is the same for all processes and increases linearly with the number of processes, corresponding to the number of messages processed. As a consequence, a decision is achieved in a small number of cycles.

Centralized. For the centralized pattern we need to make a distinction between the coordinator and the remaining processes since they behave differently. The coordinator sends $3n$ messages and receives $2n$ messages while the remaining processes always send 2 messages and receive 3 messages. The coordinator and the remaining processes alternate executions, with the latter computing in parallel. The coordinator sends and receives n messages in each cycle (high load) while the remaining processes only send and receive 1 message per cycle (low load). The overhead due to signatures in messages received by the coordinator, sent by the remaining processes, is always the same, since the messages only contain one signature regardless of the cryptographic primitive.

Initially, regardless of the cryptographic primitive used the coordinator sends proposals, which are always the same size (one signature). However, with the set of signatures it forwards $2n/3$ signatures in each phase. The total CPU time for the coordinator is slightly higher than in the broadcast primitive because of the certificates being forwarded. On the other hand, the remaining processes verify the signatures from each certificate in batch, which is faster than verifying them one by one as they do in the broadcast pattern. The total CPU time increases linearly with the number of processes for both the coordinator and the remaining processes.

With threshold signatures, all messages sent by the coordinator contain only one signature, so the overhead due to signatures per message does not change with the total number of processes. The coordinator's total CPU time is roughly the same as in the set of signatures primitive since the benefit of creating smaller messages mitigates the drawback of computing threshold signatures. As with the baseline set of signatures option, it also increases linearly with the number of processes. The remaining processes only have to make a single signature verification thus its total CPU time is the lowest overall and remains constant irrespective of the number of processes.

Finally, with the aggregate signatures primitive, the certificates the coordinator forwards contain one signature plus info detailing which signatures have been aggregated. Aggregating signatures is a more expensive operation than creating a threshold signature thus the total CPU time for the coordinator is the highest among the centralized alternatives and it also increases linearly. The remaining processes have to compute the info to verify the aggregated signature which is slower than verifying a threshold signature but faster than verifying a set of signatures.

Ring. With the ring pattern, the protocol completes after $2+1/3$ laps around the ring which results in two thirds of the processes to send and receive 2 messages while one third sends and receives 3 messages. Processes compute sequentially which results in no parallel processing. Process load is small as each process only sends and receives 1 message per cycle.

With the set of signatures, message sizes range from 1 up to $4n/3$ signatures (two certificates) resulting in a big variation in the average size of messages among processes. The total CPU time is the same for all processes, lower than in broadcast and increases linearly with the number of processes.

Using threshold signatures, messages are smaller than if using the set primitive because when the number of signatures for a phase reaches $2n/3$, a threshold signature is created, replacing those individual signatures. The total CPU time varies per process since some processes only verify the computed threshold signatures. Despite the variation, it is lower than when using the set of signatures and also increases linearly with the number of processes, although at a slower rate.

Using aggregate signatures, messages contain up to 3 signatures plus related information, namely the processes for which signatures have been aggregated. Regarding total CPU time, there is a large variation between processes because the computational effort of the processes that send and receive 3 messages is considerably larger than that of processes that only send and receive 2 messages. Still, even among processes that exchange the same number of messages some variation occurs as those that receive a certificate from their predecessor are not required to aggregate their signatures. This makes it the worst combination of message exchange pattern and cryptographic primitive for the total CPU time since it also grows exponentially with the number of processes.

Gossip. The number of messages each process sends and receives with the gossip pattern is lower than with the broadcast message pattern and increases only logarithmically with the number of processes. The number of active processes in each cycle increases exponentially with base *fanout*. After $\log_F n$ cycles, all processes execute in parallel and each process sends and receives a small number of messages in each cycle (low load).

With the set of signatures, message sizes can grow up to $4n/3$ signatures (two certificates). Since each process sends and receives more messages, the variation of the average size of messages is smaller than in the ring pattern. The total CPU time shows a small variation between processes but is always lower than for the broadcast pattern, increasing linearly with the number of processes.

Using threshold signatures, messages are smaller because, again, when the number of signatures for a phase reaches $2n/3$, a threshold signature is created replacing these. The total CPU time also shows a small variation among different processes, being higher overall than if using the set of signatures. The reason is that it is likely that by the time some process is able to generate a threshold signature and send it to others, most of the processes will have also collected enough messages to generate a certificate themselves. This means that most processes will use CPU time to generate threshold signatures but few processes will actually make use of the threshold signatures generated by others. Nevertheless, it is still lower than with the broadcast pattern and increases linearly with the number of processes.

Using aggregate signatures, messages contain up to 3 signatures plus information on aggregation. There is a big variation among different processes regarding the total CPU time, with the average being higher than with the broadcast pattern. It increases linearly with the number of processes.

6 Lessons Learned and Future Work

Considering the results obtained with our simulation model of the core part of the protocol needed for a byzantine fault tolerant replicated state machine, we can now draw some important lessons to steer future research and development effort:

There is No Absolute Best Message Exchange Pattern. The first interesting conclusion is that none of the tested message exchange patterns performs optimally in all scenarios. In fact, if processes can handle sending and receiving as many messages as the number of processes (i.e., small clusters of powerful servers), then the centralized pattern combined with threshold signatures should be the best option, since it requires exchanging the least messages and results in lower computational effort for the majority of processes, when compared to the broadcast pattern. This is the approach of SBFT [9] and HotStuff [17]. However, as the number of processes grows it becomes harder to sustain such loads. In this case, the gossip pattern with signature aggregation might be the best choice since it evenly distributes the load across servers, without the overhead of the broadcast pattern. The ring pattern induces very high latency since there is no parallel processing. However, it might allow for high throughput if multiple protocol instances run in parallel. Moreover, there are also other patterns not included in this work, such as the communication trees employed by ByzCoin [10].

Cryptographic Primitives Provide a Range of CPU vs Network Bandwidth Trade-Offs. The threshold signatures primitive requires a set of signatures to be forwarded until the threshold value is reached, which is a disadvantage when combined with either the ring or the gossip patterns. Moreover, if the set of processes changes, new private keys must be generated for each process to create a new master public key with which threshold signatures can be verified. In terms of computation, the signature aggregation primitive is always the slowest. This is partly due to the operations necessary for aggregating signatures and for verifying them. This means that we get a range of trade-offs between computational effort and network bandwidth, that suit different environments. Finally, we also believe that the cryptographic library is not optimized to re-aggregate existing aggregate signatures, which affects ring and gossip but not the centralized pattern [5].

Overall Conclusion: The Case for Adaptive Protocols. The results obtained thus make a strong case for adaptive protocols that can be configured to use different message exchange patterns and a choice of cryptographic primitives to suit different environment and application scenarios. Moreover, these results make a strong case for automated selection of the best message pattern and cryptographic primitive combination by monitoring the current environment. Current proposals addressing these issues are Aliph [2] and ADAPT [3] which, however, don't cover the full spectrum of options. Other optimizations can also be included in such a protocol, like recent work on distributed pipelining [16], since they are orthogonal to this proposal.

Future Work. First, the proposed simulation model can be used to obtain additional results and as a test bed for the optimization of the various patterns. For instance, message size in the gossip pattern, for any cryptographic primitive, might be further reduced if one takes into consideration the destination process. For example, if a second phase vote from the destination is already known, there is no point in sending it the first phase certificate. We can also collect results for a wider range of protocol parameters (e.g., varying the fanout in the gossip pattern) and, also, assess the behavior or each combination in the presence of faults, by implementing the view change protocol. Finally, these results also pave the way for research, namely, by providing data that can be used to train and test adaptation policies.

Acknowledgment. This work is financed by National Funds through the Portuguese funding agency, FCT - Fundação para a Ciência e a Tecnologia within project UIDB/50014/2020.

References

1. Androulaki, E., et al.: Hyperledger fabric: a distributed operating system for permissioned blockchains. In: Proceedings of the Thirteenth EuroSys Conference EuroSys 2018. Association for Computing Machinery, New York (2018). https://doi.org/10.1145/3190508.3190538
2. Aublin, P.L., Guerraoui, R., Knežević, N., Quéma, V., Vukolić, M.: The next 700 BFT protocols. ACM Trans. Comput. Syst. **32**(4), 12:1–12:45 (2015). https://doi.org/10.1145/2658994
3. Bahsoun, J.P., Guerraoui, R., Shoker, A.: Making BFT protocols really adaptive. In: Proceedings of the 29th IEEE International Parallel & Distributed Processing Symposium, May 2015
4. Baudet, M., et al.: State machine replication in the libra blockchain (2019)
5. Boneh, D., Drijvers, M., Neven, G.: Compact multi-signatures for smaller blockchains. In: Peyrin, T., Galbraith, S. (eds.) ASIACRYPT 2018. LNCS, vol. 11273, pp. 435–464. Springer, Cham (2018). https://doi.org/10.1007/978-3-030-03329-3_15
6. Buterin, V.: Ethereum: a next-generation smart contract and decentralized application platform (2014). https://github.com/ethereum/wiki/wiki/White-Paper
7. Castro, M., Liskov, B.: Practical byzantine fault tolerance. In: Proceedings of the Third Symposium on Operating Systems Design and Implementation OSDI 1999, pp. 173–186. USENIX Association, Berkeley (1999). http://dl.acm.org/citation.cfm?id=296806.296824
8. Gilad, Y., Hemo, R., Micali, S., Vlachos, G., Zeldovich, N.: Algorand: Scaling byzantine agreements for cryptocurrencies. In: Proceedings of the 26th Symposium on Operating Systems Principles SOSP 2017, pp. 51–68. ACM, New York (2017). https://doi.org/10.1145/3132747.3132757
9. Gueta, G.G., et al.: SBFT: a scalable and decentralized trust infrastructure. In: IEEE International Conference Dependable Systems and Networks (DSN) (2019)
10. Kogias, E.K., Jovanovic, P., Gailly, N., Khoffi, I., Gasser, L., Ford, B.: Enhancing bitcoin security and performance with strong consistency via collective signing. In: 25th {usenix} Security Symposium ({usenix} Security 16), pp. 279–296 (2016)

11. Lamport, L., et al.: Paxos made simple. ACM Sigact News **32**(4), 18–25 (2001)
12. Long, J., Wei, R.: Scalable BFT consensus mechanism through aggregated signature gossip. In: 2019 IEEE International Conference on Blockchain and Cryptocurrency (ICBC), pp. 360–367, May 2019. https://doi.org/10.1109/BLOC.2019. 8751327
13. Marandi, P.J., Primi, M., Schiper, N., Pedone, F.: Ring Paxos: a high-throughput atomic broadcast protocol. In: 2010 IEEE/IFIP International Conference on Dependable Systems & Networks (DSN), pp. 527–536. IEEE (2010)
14. Nakamoto, S.: Bitcoin: a peer-to-peer electronic cash system (2009). http://www. bitcoin.org/bitcoin.pdf
15. Pereira, J., Oliveira, R.: The mutable consensus protocol, pp. 218–227 (2004). https://doi.org/10.1109/RELDIS.2004.1353023
16. Voron, G., Gramoli, V.: Dispel: byzantine SMR with distributed pipelining. arXiv preprint arXiv:1912.10367 (2019)
17. Yin, M., Malkhi, D., Reiter, M.K., Gueta, G.G., Abraham, I.: Hotstuff: BFT consensus with linearity and responsiveness. In: Proceedings of the 2019 ACM Symposium on Principles of Distributed Computing, pp. 347–356 (2019)

Kollaps/Thunderstorm: Reproducible Evaluation of Distributed Systems
Tutorial Paper

Miguel Matos[(✉)] [iD]

U. Lisboa & INESC-ID, Lisbon, Portugal
miguel.marques.matos@tecnico.ulisboa.pt
https://www.gsd.inesc-id.pt/~mm/

Abstract. Reproducing experimental results is nowadays seen as one of the greatest impairments for the progress of science in general and distributed systems in particular. This stems from the increasing complexity of the systems under study and the inherent complexity of capturing and controlling all variables that can potentially affect experimental results. We argue that this can only be addressed with a systematic approach to all the stages and aspects of the evaluation process, such as the environment in which the experiment is run, the configuration and software versions used, and the network characteristics among others. In this tutorial paper, we focus on the networking aspect, and discuss our ongoing research efforts and tools to contribute to a more systematic and reproducible evaluation of large scale distributed systems.

1 Introduction

Evaluating distributed systems is hard. The underlying network topology, in particular, can have a drastic impact on key performance metrics, such as throughput and latency but also on correctness depending, for instance, on the asynchrony assumptions made by the system designer. With the increasingly popular deployment of geographically distributed applications operating at a global scale [5], assessing the impact of geo-distribution, and hence network topology, is fundamental to build and tune systems that perform correctly and meet the desired Service Level Objectives. Unfortunately, there is still an important gap between the easiness of deploying a distributed system and its evaluation.

On the one hand, the deployment of geographically distributed systems was made simpler thanks to the increasing popularity of container technology (*e.g.*, Docker [13], Linux LXC [8]). Big IT players introduced such technologies in their commercial offering (*e.g.*, Amazon Elastic Container Service [1], Microsoft Azure Kubernetes Service [2] or Google Cloud Kubernetes Engine [7]), and they are an attractive mechanism to deploy large-scale applications.

On the other hand network properties such jitter, packet loss, failures of middle-boxes (*i.e.*, switches, routers) are by definition difficult, if not impossible, to predict from the standpoint of a system developer, who has no control over the underlying network infrastructure. Moreover, such conditions are the

© IFIP International Federation for Information Processing 2020
Published by Springer Nature Switzerland AG 2020
A. Remke and V. Schiavoni (Eds.): DAIS 2020, LNCS 12135, pp. 121–128, 2020.
https://doi.org/10.1007/978-3-030-50323-9_8

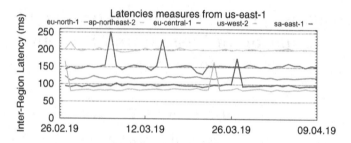

Fig. 1. Latency variability between five different AWS regions across the world over 45 days. Latencies vary on average between 90 ms and 250 ms, while spikes occur across all regions.

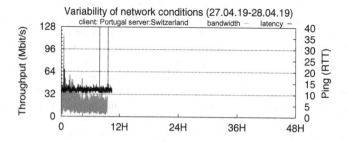

Fig. 2. Dynamic network conditions between two university campuses in Europe, in Portugal and Switzerland respectively.

norm rather than the exception, in particular when considering large-scale wide-area networks that might cross several distinct administrative domains. As a motivating example, consider Fig. 1 which shows the average latency between six AWS [1] regions over 45 days measured by https://www.cloudping.info. We observe that even in the infrastructure of a major cloud provider, there are significant and unpredictable variations in latency.

Variability is not limited to latency. We demonstrates this with a measurement experiment for two different cases. The first set of measures are taken between two stable endpoints inside university networks, respectively in Portugal and Switzerland, shown in Fig. 2. The second case measures the network conditions between a remote AWS instance in the `ap-northeast-1a` zone (in Tokyo) and a server node in Switzerland (Fig. 3). As we can observe, there are important variations both for bandwidth and latency. Such variability can have a dramatic effect not only on a system's performance but also on reliability as shown by recent post-mortem analysis of major cloud providers [4]. The challenge, therefore, is how to equip engineers and researchers with the tools that allow to systematically understand and evaluate how this variability affects system's performance and behavior.

In our ongoing work, we are conducting research and developing tools to precisely enable these experiments. In this tutorial paper, we briefly introduce

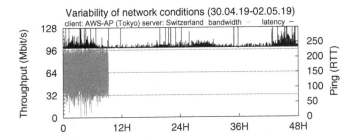

Fig. 3. Dynamic network conditions between a university node in Switzerland and a node in AWS `ap-northeast-1a` (Tokyo).

KOLLAPS [10], a decentralized and scalable topology emulator (Sect. 2), and THUNDERSTORM [12], a compact domain specific language to describe dynamic experiments on top of KOLLAPS (Sect. 3). Then we present some experiments enabled by KOLLAPS and THUNDERSTORM in Sect. 4 and conclude in Sect. 5.

2   Kollaps

In this section, we briefly describe the architecture and workflow KOLLAPS, depicted in Fig. 4.

First, the user must describe the topology in the THUNDERSTORM Description Language (TDL), discussed in the next section. This includes the network topology, network dynamics, if any, and the Docker images of the distributed application being evaluated (Fig. 4, *define* step). These images can come from either private repositories or public ones such as Docker Hub [3].

With the experiment defined, the user invokes the *deployment generator*, a tool shipped with KOLLAPS that transforms the TDL into a Kubernetes Manifest file, or a Docker compose file. This file is ready to be deployed using Kubernetes or Docker Swarm, but the user can manually fine-tune it if needed.

The user can then use this file to deploy the experiment in any Kubernetes cluster (Fig. 4, *deploy* step). This deploys not only the target application under evaluation but also an Emulation Manager component per physical machine (Fig. 4, *execute* step). The Emulation Manager is a key component of KOLLAPS responsible for maintaining and enforcing the emulation model in a distributed fashion. More details on the design and implementation of KOLLAPS can be found in [10].

3   Thunderstorm

In this section, we describe the THUNDERSTORM Description Language (TDL). The TDL abstracts the low level details of KOLLAPS and allows to succinctly express dynamic experiments. An example of the TDL, illustrating the main features of the language can be found in Listing 1.1.

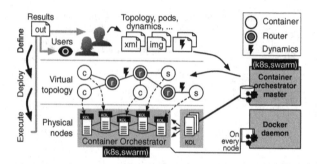

Fig. 4. KOLLAPS architecture and workflow. We assume the existence of an existing cluster and a working Docker Swarm or Kubernetes environment.

The language describes the services (lines 3–6), the static topology (lines 10–14) and the dynamics in the topology (lines 16–26). The service, bridge and link elements can get an arbitrary number of tags. In the example, the api and db services belong to the backend, while the server belongs to the frontend. These three are grouped into the same application together, expressed by the app tag. The client is not part of the application. We use tags to group services and links together based on real-world criteria. For example, one of the most common causes for network "failures" is the distributed roll-out of software upgrades [14], *e.g.* for routers. Tags help to capture groups of devices sharing network status-relevant characteristics, *e.g.*, driver versions that could be updated at the same time. Tags could also be used to map services to data centers (*i.e.*, what if one's connection suddenly changes?) or to logical parts of a distributed system (frontend, backend). Bridges (line 8) must have unique names. Links must specify the source, destination and the properties (*e.g.*, latency, bandwidth, jitter, etc.). The symmetric keyword allow to easily create bidirectional links with the same specified properties.

The dynamic events can be expressed in a concise yet rich manner. In our example, we first start all application services (3 replicas for the api and the db, and 5 replicas for the server, lines 16–19), and after 30 s the clients (line 19). After 30 min, we inject several faults into the topology. The churn keyword crashes either an absolute number of services, or a certain share of all instances of that service. The replace keyword then specifies the probability of such a service to immediately re-join the cluster. At line 20, we specify that the server replicas will be subject to churn over a 3 h period. In particular, 40% of the servers will crash uniformly at random over this period, and of those, 50% will be replaced immediately. Although the language allows to define events with a degree of randomness, such as the churn event above, it is possible to systematically reproduce the same order of events by setting a fixed random seed. We can also specify the dynamic behavior for a specific container. In the example, one server instance leaves the system at four hours and twenty, and joins 5 min later (lines 21–22).

```
 1 bootstrapper thunderstorm:2.0
 2
 3 service server img=nginx:latest tags=frontend;app
 4 service api img=api:latest tags=backend;app
 5 service client img=client:1.0 command=['80']
 6 service db img=postgres:latest tags=backend;app
 7
 8 bridges s1 s2
 9
10 link server—s1 latency=9.1 up=1Gb down=800Mb
11 link api—s1 latency=5.1 up=1Gb symmetric
12 link s1—s2 latency=0.11 up=1Gb symmetric
13 link client—s1 latency=23.4 up=50Mb down=1Gb
14 link db—s2 latency=8.0 up=1Gb symmetric
15
16 at 0s api join 3
17 at 0s db join 3
18 at 0s server join 5
19 at 30s client join
20 from 30m to 3h30m server churn 40% replace 50%
21 at 4h20m server—s1 leave
22 at 4h25m server—s1 join
23 from 10h2m to 10h6m api—s1 flap 0.93s
24 from 12h to 24h tags=be leave 60%
25 from 15h to 15h20s server disconnect 1
26 at 18h20m api—s1 set latency=10.2 jitter=1.2
```

Listing 1.1. Example of experiment descriptor using the THUNDERSTORM description language. Link rates are given in 'per second'.

The language supports *link flapping*, where a single link connects and disconnects in quick succession [14]. In the experiment, the link between service api and bridge s1 flaps every 0.93 s during a period of 4 min (line 23). The leave action, used to define which entities should leave the emulation, takes as a parameter an absolute number or a share of all selected instances. At line 24, 60% of all nodes with the *backend* tag, chosen uniformly at random, will leave the experiment. Internally, when the language is translated into the lower level format used by the KOLLAPS engine, we keep track of all nodes that have joined, left, connected, or disconnected. Thus, if a percentage rather than an absolute number is provided, that is always relative to the amount of legal targets in the cluster *at that moment*.

The output of the parser is a XML file, ready to be consumed by the deployment generator and starting the experiment workflow discussed in the previous section. Further details about the design and implementation of THUNDERSTORM can be found in [12].

4   Experiments

In this section, we illustrate the capabilities of KOLLAPS and THUNDERSTORM. The goals are two-fold: show that the emulation is accurate, and also that it allows to easily evaluate a system under network dynamics.

The evaluation cluster is composed of 4 Dell PowerEdge R330 servers where each machine has an Intel Xeon E3-1270 v6 CPU and 64 GB of RAM. All nodes run Ubuntu Linux 18.04.2 LTS, kernel v4.15.0-47-generic. The tests conducted on Amazon EC2 use `r4.16xlarge` instances, the closest type in terms of hardware-specs to the machines in our cluster.

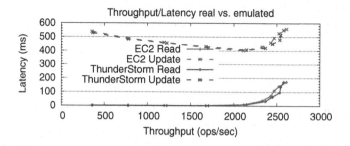

Fig. 5. Throughput/latency of a geo-replicated Cassandra deployment on Amazon EC2 and KOLLAPS

We start by comparing the results of benchmarking a geo-replicated Apache Cassandra [6,11] deployment on Amazon EC2 and on KOLLAPS. The deployment consists of 4 replicas in Frankfurt, 4 replicas in Sydney and 4 YCSB [9] clients in Frankfurt. Cassandra is set up to active replication with a replication factor of 2. In order to model the network topology in KOLLAPS, we collected the average latency and jitter between all the Amazon EC2 instances used, prior to executing the experiment. Figure 5 shows the throughput-latency curve obtained from the benchmark on both the real deployment on Amazon and on KOLLAPS. The curves for both reads and updates are a close match, showing only slight differences after the turning point where response latencies climb fast, as Cassandra replicas are under high stress. This experiment demonstrates how such issues can be identified, debugged and eliminated with KOLLAPS before expensive real-life deployments.

We now highlight the unique support for dynamic topologies through the use of the TDL. This allows to easily evaluate the behaviour of complex systems in a variety of scenarios. In this experiment, the intercontinental link from EU to AP used for the Cassandra experiment in Fig. 5 suddenly changes its latency to half (at 240 s), and later on (at 480 s) the original latency is restored. In Fig. 6 we report the update latency observed by YCSB. Note that read operations do not use the intercontinental link and hence are not affected (not shown). This shows that the network dynamics imposed by KOLLAPS have a direct impact in

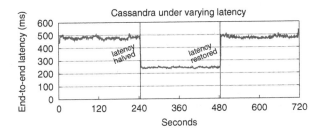

Fig. 6. Latency variations measured by YCSB during a transitory period: one of the replicas is moved to a far away region.

client-facing metrics. Engineers and researchers can therefore use KOLLAPS and THUNDERSTORM to conduct controlled and reproducible experiments to assess the behavior of real system under a wide range of network dynamics and devise the best strategies to adopt when such events happen in production.

5 Discussion

In this tutorial paper we illustrated the main features of KOLLAPS and THUNDERSTORM, in particular the accuracy of the emulation with respect to a real system deployed in a real environment, and also the dynamic experiments that THUNDERSTORM enables. Both tools are available as open source at https://github.com/miguelammmatos/Kollaps.

We believe the ability to systematically reproduce experiments in a controlled environment, and the ability to subject a system to a wide range of dynamic scenarios provided by KOLLAPS and THUNDERSTORM are a step towards building more robust and dependable distributed systems.

Acknowledgments. The work presented in this tutorial paper is the joint effort of researchers at the University of Lisbon, Portugal, and researchers at the Univerité de Neuchâtel, Switzerland, namely: Paulo Gouveia, João Neves, Carlos Segarra, Luca Lietchi, Shady Issa, Valerio Schiavoni and Miguel Matos. This work was partially supported by national funds through FCT, Fundação para a Ciência e a Tecnologia, under project UIDB/50021/2020 and project Lisboa-01-0145- FEDER- 031456 (Angainor).

References

1. Amazon elastic container service. https://aws.amazon.com/ecs/
2. Azure kubernetes service. https://azure.microsoft.com/en-us/services/kubernetes-service/
3. Docker hub. https://hub.docker.com/
4. Google cloud post-mortem analysis. https://status.cloud.google.com/incident/cloud-networking/18012?m=1
5. Containers: real adoption and use cases in 2017. Technical report, Forrester, March 2017

6. Apache Cassandra (2019). https://cassandra.apache.org/. Accessed 12 Mar 2020
7. Google cloud kubernetes engine (2019). https://cloud.google.com/kubernetes-engine/. Accessed 12 Mar 2020
8. Linux LXC (2019). https://linuxcontainers.org/. Accessed 12 Mar 2020
9. Cooper, B.F., Silberstein, A., Tam, E., Ramakrishnan, R., Sears, R.: Benchmarking cloud serving systems with YCSB. In: Proceedings of the 1st ACM Symposium on Cloud Computing SoCC 2010, pp. 143–154. ACM, New York (2010). https://doi.org/10.1145/1807128.1807152
10. Gouveia, P., et al.: Kollaps: decentralized and dynamic topology emulation. In: Proceedings of the Fifteenth European Conference on Computer Systems EuroSys 2020. Association for Computing Machinery, New York (2020). https://doi.org/10.1145/3342195.3387540
11. Lakshman, A., Malik, P.: Cassandra: a decentralized structured storage system. ACM SIGOPS Oper. Syst. Rev. **44**(2), 35–40 (2010). https://doi.org/10.1145/1773912.1773922
12. Liechti, L., Gouveia, P., Neves, J., Kropf, P., Matos, M., Schiavoni, V.: THUNDER-STORM: a tool to evaluate dynamic network topologies on distributed systems. In: 2019 IEEE 38th International Symposium on Reliable Distributed Systems SRDS2019 (2019)
13. Merkel, D.: Docker: lightweight Linux containers for consistent development and deployment (2014). https://doi.org/10.1097/01.NND.0000320699.47006.a3. https://bit.ly/2IuhKBv
14. Potharaju, R., Jain, N.: When the network crumbles: an empirical study of cloud network failures and their impact on services. In: Proceedings of the 4th Annual Symposium on Cloud Computing SOCC 2013, pp. 15:1–15:17. ACM, New York (2013). https://doi.org/10.1145/2523616.2523638

Machine Learning for Systems

Self-tunable DBMS Replication
with Reinforcement Learning

Luís Ferreira[ID], Fábio Coelho[(✉)][ID], and José Pereira[ID]

INESC TEC and Universidade do Minho, Braga, Portugal
{luis.m.ferreira,fabio.a.coelho}@inesctec.pt, jop@di.uminho.pt

Abstract. Fault-tolerance is a core feature in distributed database systems, particularly the ones deployed in cloud environments. The dependability of these systems often relies in middleware components that abstract the DBMS logic from the replication itself. The highly configurable nature of these systems makes their throughput very dependent on the correct tuning for a given workload. Given the high complexity involved, machine learning techniques are often considered to guide the tuning process and decompose the relations established between tuning variables.

This paper presents a machine learning mechanism based on reinforcement learning that attaches to a hybrid replication middleware connected to a DBMS to dynamically live-tune the configuration of the middleware according to the workload being processed. Along with the vision for the system, we present a study conducted over a prototype of the self-tuned replication middleware, showcasing the achieved performance improvements and showing that we were able to achieve an improvement of 370.99% on some of the considered metrics.

Keywords: Reinforcement learning · Dependability · Replication

1 Introduction

Distributed systems, namely scalable cloud-based Database Management Systems (DBMS), encompass a growing number of tunable criteria that may deeply affect the system's performance [5]. This is particularly true for replicated DBMS as replication capabilities are often tightly connected with the overall system design, and the lack of proper tuning may impact on the system dependability, degrading quality of service. Moreover, the inner characteristics of each workload also directly affect how the DBMS engine performs.

The number and type of adjustable criteria available in each DBMS [4,16,18] varies, but generally, they allow to configure a common set of properties, such as memory space available, the number of parallel workers allowed, together with

© IFIP International Federation for Information Processing 2020
Published by Springer Nature Switzerland AG 2020
A. Remke and V. Schiavoni (Eds.): DAIS 2020, LNCS 12135, pp. 131–147, 2020.
https://doi.org/10.1007/978-3-030-50323-9_9

the dimension of execution pools for specific tasks. In what regards replication, usually systems allow to tune the type of replication mechanism considered, the number of active instances, the acknowledgement of delays admissible and how far can a given replica drift on data consistency before the system's dependability is compromised.

The perceived performance of the system is usually measured through the number of executed operations in a time frame, which is often collected as an exogenous property provided by external benchmarking tools, and not as an intrinsic system property. Ultimately, achieving the best possible configuration is the result of a multi-stage process where trial and error plays an important role, attributing to the database administrator (DBA) the tuning responsibility and centring on him/her the intuition of former adjustments and their consequences. Even when considering this approach, the DBA is faced with a daunting task as the recommendations instruct configurations to be changed one-a-time, but it is clear that tunable configurations are not independent [5].

The rapid expansion of autonomous and machine learning techniques is currently pushing these approaches to be considered in the optimization of systems, namely for pattern discovery and recognition, and for self-tuning of systems.

Classical supervised learning approaches split the process into distinct stages, encompassing a period strictly for learning based on previous feedback and a second one for making predictions. The decoupling of these stages is restrictive as they are disjoint, and typically incorporating new data patterns into the model implies a new training period. The use of techniques that merge both stages, learning and making predictions in unison *e.g.,* Reinforcement Learning (RL) [20] promises to overcome that limitation.

This paper presents a self-tunable mechanism based on Reinforcement Learning, to configure and adjust in real time a hybrid replication middleware, paired together with a DBMS system. In a nutshell, when requests arrive at the replication middleware, they are split into shards, *i.e.,* a set of logical partitions based on the workload, which are then assigned to distinct DBMS replicas. The system is able to probe the middleware configuration and tune it to an ideal configuration in real-time, without having to incur in the cost of restarting the middleware or the underlying DBMS. Moreover, it does so in a dynamic manner, the configuration is constantly adjusted to reflect the best values for the current workload.

We deployed and evaluated the system, considering the TPC-C benchmark to inject a workload into PostgreSQL [17], the underlying DBMS system attached. Results show that for some of the metrics considered, the gains were of 370.99%.

The rest of this paper is organized as follows: Sect. 2 provides the core concepts and motivation for the system, while Sect. 3 goes over the design of the architecture. The use of reinforcement learning is detailed in Subsect. 3.3 and the system's evaluation in Subsect. 3.5. Finally, related work is presented in Sect. 4 and Sect. 5 concludes this paper, highlighting the major takeaways and future work.

2   Motivation

Nowadays, there is a plethora of DBMS, each focusing on a particular workload type, namely: OnLine Transactional Processing (OLTP), OnLine Analytical Processing (OLAP) and even newer Hybrid Transactional and Analytical Processing (HTAP) workloads. Even though there are guidelines on how to assess and tune a DBMS, the configurations are not universal and each vendor decides on which tunable configurations to expose. Moreover, workload types are very distinct to allow a common configuration across systems. This is so as optimizing an OLTP targeted operation would intrinsically degrade OLAP performance and vice-versa [6]. Therefore, as the type of configurations available for tuning is increasing, and, most importantly, the fact that the challenges associated with a given workload type are different for each vendor, renders the DBA with most of the know-how and responsibility to assess and fine tune a workload in a particular DBMS.

This is particularly true for replication mechanisms and for the provision of fault-tolerance and high-availability, as such features are usually deeply connected with the way each DBMS handles data, particularly in OLTP systems. Database systems typically provide fault-tolerance capabilities through replication at the cost of lowering the throughput, where the algorithms are intricately deployed as part of the DBMS's kernel. When pairing a DBMS engine with the provision of fault-tolerance guarantees through external middleware systems, the number of tunable configurations considered increases. The advantages that come with the decoupling such as modularity and pluggability, come at the expense of higher complexity and a possible detachment between the design consequences of the replication middleware and their impacts on the underlying DBMS considered. Moreover, the logical detachment is typically achieved through standard interfaces such as the Java DataBase Connector (JDBC), which also imposes new concerns.

As to reduce the complexity and automate the decision and tuning process associated, particularly with the provision of fault-tolerance, we envision a system architecture aided through the use of machine forecasting, via reinforcement learning techniques.

Therefore, successfully joining the configurability and detachment of a replication middleware, with the capabilities of RL techniques to self-adjust the system, would reduce the key features undermining the current solution.

3   System Design

On the basis of the previously described vision, the proposed architecture is depicted in Fig. 1.

3.1   Overview

The system is abstracted in three distinct components, namely: *(i)* the middleware replica nodes holding the metric Monitor and the Update Handler, *(ii)* the reinforcement learning system holding the metric Monitor Handler, the Update Dispatcher and the Reinforcement Learning Agent itself and *(iii)* the underlying DBMS. The replication middleware is built around the Apache Bookkeeper Distributed Log (DL) [1].

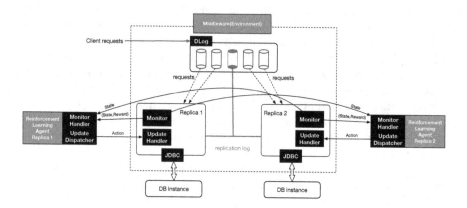

Fig. 1. System architecture.

In a nutshell, the replication middleware receives incoming JDBC requests from clients, which are then fed into a group of distributed log instances. The distributed log is an efficient and high-performance solution to enable replication and replica communication. Its interface considers two roles in its architecture, namely: writers and readers; holding the responsibility to push and read records from the incoming events received through the log stream, *i.e.,* incoming database requests. The requests undergo a sharding procedure [8], splitting them in slots according to a configurable number of DataBase (DB) instances and mapping each distributed log instance to a group of shards. The replica nodes execute the client requests assigned to them, while also writing the resulting state changes to the replication log. They also receive the replicated state changes from other replicas and update their records accordingly. The replication middleware is based on the active replication protocol [24], with a semi-active variant [13]. On one hand, as shards are assigned to a replica, that replica becomes the primary, handling requests for that shard. On the other hand, the same replica acts as backup, incorporating updates of other primary replicas in charge of other shards.

The Reinforcement Learning system is built from a set of subcomponents: the Monitor and Update Handler, that act as probes in each replica, and, the Monitor Handler, the Update Dispatcher and the Learning Agent. The architecture comprehends an instance for each one of these components per replica. The Monitor probes and aggregates metrics (Sect. 3.3) about each replica that are afterwards pushed to the Monitor Handler. The results are then fed into the Reinforcement Learning Agent that adjusts a base configuration and instructs replicas to modify their configurations via the Update Dispatcher and the replica's local

Update Handler probe. Changes are applied on-line, without having to restart the middleware or the underlying DB instances.

In this paper we considered for adjustment all the tuning variables that are made available by the middleware, as depicted in Table 1. The set of possible actions for the reinforcement learner is composed by incremental changes to these variables. Also, it should be noted that each replica has an independent reinforcement learning agent controlling its tuning variables, which can be deployed in a different machine. This allows us to add new replicas to the cluster without having to retrain the model for the already existing replicas. Also, since different replicas process different shards, the workload may vary between them. By tuning each one individually, we get a configuration that is optimized for the workload of each replica.

Table 1. Adjustable configurations considered for on-line adjustment.

Configuration	Description
db.pool	Size of the connection pool
dlog.reader.threads	Number of worker threads
db.writeset.transactions	Max batch size
db.writeset.delay	Delay between writes to replication log

3.2 Components

In order to feed the Reinforcement Learning mechanism, the design comprehends a set of custom components to observe and collect metrics, but also, to trigger the required configuration changes. The components are split into two groups, the ones pertaining to the replica, the probes, and the ones that pertain to the reinforcement learning agent.

Monitor. The monitor component is deployed in each replica of the replication middleware. It probes a set of local properties that are then fed into the learning mechanism. The cornerstone of this component is a publish-subscribe queueing service [9], that periodically pushes readings into the Monitor Handler component. In practice, this component feeds the reinforcement learning algorithm with state and reward updates. Updates are sent every 15 s.

Update Handler. The Update Handler component is deployed in each replica of the replication middleware. It receives asynchronous actions from the Update Dispatcher and applies them directly in each node of the middleware (our environment), allowing a dynamic change without having to restart the middleware or the DB engine.

Monitor Handler. The Monitor Handler component is deployed outside the replica nodes, in each of the Reinforcement Learning Agents. It collects the metrics sent by the Monitor agents in each replica by subscribing their updates through the publish-subscribe service. This data will be used to determine the current state of the environment and the reward associated with an action.

Update Dispatcher. The Update dispatcher component is also deployed on each of the Reinforcement Learning Agents. It considers a set of actions dictated by the RL component and triggers the Update Handlers to impose the changes into the new configurations.

3.3 Reinforcement Learning Agent

Each replica is controlled by a distinct Reinforcement Learning agent. The RL component is responsible for analysing data arriving from the Monitor via the Monitor Handler. At each step, the RL algorithm characterizes incoming raw data from the Monitor component into the *state* to be fed to the RL algorithm, which will be translated by the agent's policy to an *action*. That action is then applied to the environment, the middleware replica. The reward derived from an action is also obtained from the data retrieved by the Monitor Handler.

The tuning of the configuration variables is done dynamically, meaning that configuration values are constantly being fine-tuned, in response to changes in the workload.

The search space associated to these strategies is characterized by a combinatorial set built from all possible states and actions. The data that is collected, the state, is characterized by the variables identified in Table 2, a set of discrete variables, with a large search space associated. The algorithm chosen was the *Deep Q-learning* algorithm, as it can accommodate larger search spaces. This mechanism incorporates a complex neural network on top of the *Q-learning* algorithm [23]. Given this choice, the action space was sampled into a subset of 10 possible choices, depicted in Table 3.

States. The states taken into account by the RL method are a composition of the current values of the variables depicted in Table 1, which are then complemented by a set of metrics that characterize the overall performance of the system in each replica. These metrics represent an average value over the period comprehended between two consecutive metric readings. The complete set of elements that compose the state of our Reinforcement Learning model are depicted in Table 2.

The metrics allow to establish a relationship between the number of requests received in a given replica and the number of requests executed in that same replica. Moreover, the number of received and executed transactions on other replicas of the system (which will not be optimised) are also part of the state.

This allows to establish a ratio between the number of replicated requests executed and the total number of requests that other replicas have already sent to the distributed log for persistence. Thus, it allows the system to know whether or not a lower throughput of replicated transactions is due to a lack of performance from the replica itself or from the replica that is sending the updates.

Table 2. Set of elements that compose the state in the RL process.

Configuration	Description
db.pool	Current size of the connection pool
dlog.reader.threads	Current number of worker threads
db.writeset.transactions	Current max batch size
db.writeset.delay	Current delay between writes to replication log
ClientRequests	Executed transactions
Txn Written	Transactions' (Txn) state updates sent to replication log
Replicated Txn	Replicated transactions' state updates applied to the DBMS
ClientRequests	Nr. of new client requests for this replica
rep_Txn in DL	Transactions sent to replication log by other replicas

The current values for the variables that are being adjusted is made part of the state so that relations between the variables' values and between them and the collected metrics can be established by the neural network, since the possible actions, the outputs of our neural network, do not reflect actual values for the variables, but rather incremental changes to them.

Actions. The actions decided by the neural network build the possible changes that can be made on each step to the environment. While using Deep Q-Learning, variables were sampled in the form of incremental changes. The possible set of actions is depicted in Table 3. In order to prevent system crashes, an upper and lower limit was set for each tuning variable. The increment and decrement values were chosen by trial and error. The objective was to choose increments that wouldn't be so small that they wouldn't have a significant effect on the performance of the system, but not so large that the number of possible values for each variable became very low (taking into account the boundaries set).
In summary, with each step of the algorithm, only one of the above mentioned actions is executed. This means that only one variable is changed in each step, and its value is only changed by a small amount, as described in Table 3.

The configuration variable *db.writeset.transactions* can be set to a special value, 0. When this value is set, the limit on how many transactions can be written on each batch is removed.

Table 3. Actions considered in the RL process.

Actions	Description
No action	Nothing is changed
Increment db.pool	Incremented by 1
Decrement db.pool	Decremented by 1
Increment dlog.reader.threads	Incremented by 1
Decrement dlog.reader.threads	Decremented by 1
Increment db.writeset.transactions	Increment by 100
Decrement db.writeset.transactions	Decrement by 100
Set db.writeset.transactions special	Set to 0
Increment db.writeset.delay	Increment by 100
Decrement db.writeset.delay	Decrement by 100

Reward Function. As the environment being considered is bounded to database replication and overall database execution, the impact can be directly associated with the overall throughput. A higher throughput represents a better outcome. Consequently, the reward function is associated with the throughput, being defined as the sum of all latest metric averages that refer to replica throughput. Since all the averages are in transactions per second, there is no need for any normalization or transformation to be applied to the values. In this case, all reward components have the same weight towards the computed reward.

$$reward = ClientRequests + TxnWritten + ReplicatedTxn \qquad (1)$$

3.4   Reinforcement Learning Mechanism

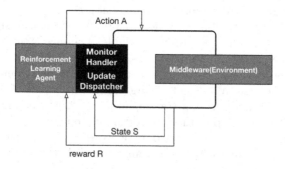

Fig. 2. Reinforcement Learning in the environment

The mechanism proposed considers RL based on Deep Q-Learning. Within a RL approach, the Agent monitors a certain Environment. For a given State the agent decides on an Action, by means of its Policy. A Policy maps States to Actions. The objective of the agent is to find the best possible Policy, the one that maximizes the considered Reward. Reward values are calculated after an Action is applied to the Environment using the Reward Function considered. The system is depicted in Fig. 2.

The Deep Q-Learning algorithm sets an evolution over Q-Learning. The latter establishes a table that defines the agent's policy. It cross-matches the possible actions and states, attributing to each combination a q-value.

At the beginning of the training process, all q-values are equal to zero. The policy defines that for each state we should choose the action with the highest q-value, corresponding to the biggest reward. However, always choosing the action with the highest q-value could prevent the discovery of alternative plausible actions, which could become exacerbated as the number of states increases. So, a small percentage of actions are chosen at random.

Introducing a neural network in place of a state table, enables Deep Q-Learning to consider a larger combinatorial set of states. Each output node represents a possible action and the value calculated by the network for that node will be the q-value of the action. The neural network considered is depicted in Fig. 3. It holds two hidden layers of 16 neurons each. In each step, the selected action will be the one with the highest q-value. Rewards are used to adjust the weights of the neural network by back-propagation. According to Fig. 3, the chosen action would be incrementing *dlog.reader.threads*, because it's the one with the highest q-value, in the step depicted.

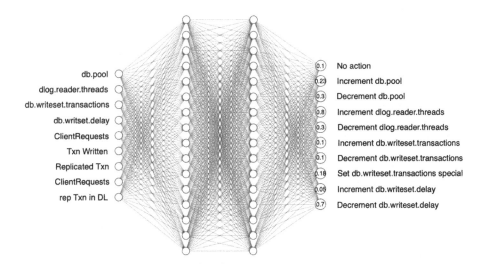

Fig. 3. Neural Network used in the Reinforcement Learning agents. Computed q-values are depicted on the right hand side, paired with the respective action.

3.5   Preliminary Evaluation

The evaluation of the system was built considering the TPC-C benchmark, designed specifically for the evaluation of OLTP database systems. The TPC-C specification models a real-world scenario where a company, comprised of several warehouses and districts, processes orders placed by clients. The workload is defined over 9 tables operated by a transaction mix comprised of five different transactions, namely: New Order, Payment, Order-Status, Delivery and Stock-Level. Each transaction is composed of several read and update operations, where 92% are update operations, which characterizes this as a write heavy workload.

Table 4. Configuration tuned with reinforcement learning from base configuration. Baseline and cycle results in transactions per second (Txn/sec).

Metric	Baseline	RL#1	Gain	RL#2	Gain
ClientRequests-R1	80.80	94.07	+16.42%	91.87	+13.70%
Replicated Txn-R1	35.24	55.56	+57.64%	55.00	+56.05%
Txn Written-R1	27.57	61.73	+123.92%	91.87	+233.25%
ClientRequests-R2	178.20	129.51	−27.32%	157.82	−11.44%
Replicated Txn-R2	27.16	61.75	+127.40%	91.56	+237.18%
Txn Written-R2	31.86	129.51	+306.44%	150.08	+370.99%
Avg Reward-R1	143.61	211.35	+47.17%	238.74	+66.24%
Avg Reward-R2	237.22	320.78	+35.22%	399.46	+68.39%
Metric	Baseline	RL#4	Gain	RL#6	Gain
ClientRequests-R1	80.80	99.96	+23.71%	86.04	+6.49%
Replicated Txn-R1	35.24	52.57	+49.15%	52.09	+47.79%
Txn Written-R1	27.57	99.96	+262.59%	86.04	+212.11%
ClientRequests-R2	178.20	142.30	−20.15%	207.00	+16.16%
Replicated Txn-R2	27.16	99.96	+268.09%	68.21	+151.16%
Txn Written-R2	31.86	142.30	+346.57%	111.55	+250.09%
Avg Reward-R1	143.61	252.48	+75.81%	224.17	+56.09%
Avg Reward-R2	237.22	384.55	+62.11%	386.75	+63.03%
Metric	Baseline	RL#8	Gain	RL#10	Gain
ClientRequests-R1	80.80	111.92	+38.52%	112.95	+39.79%
Replicated Txn-R1	35.24	30.45	−13.59%	69.08	+96.01%
Txn Written-R1	27.57	75.46	+173.74%	112.95	+309.73%
ClientRequests-R2	178.20	220.57	+23.77%	205.47	+15.30%
Replicated Txn-R2	27.16	68.20	+151.15%	98.25	+261.81%
Txn Written-R2	31.86	96.73	+203.57%	94.26	+195.82%
Avg Reward-R1	143.61	217.84	+51.69%	294.99	+105.41%
Avg Reward-R2	237.22	385.50	+62.51%	397.99	+67.77%

Setup. TPC-C was set up in a configuration comprising 150 warehouses with a load of 50 client connections per warehouse. Moreover, the middleware replication component was set up to accommodate 25 warehouses per distributed log instance. Tests were conducted on a local server built from a Ryzen 3700 CPU, 16 GB of RAM and 2 SSDs (with one of them being NVME), hosting all services. Replica 1 (R1) and two distributed log bookies used the NVME driver, while replica 2 (R2) and one other bookie used the other SSD drive.

Overall, the evaluation was achieved by running the TPC-C benchmark and while it was sending transactions to be committed on the underlying database through the replication middleware, the reinforcement learning agent was deployed on a separate machine.

A total of 10 learning cycles were run, all starting from the same baseline configuration. The initial baseline configuration was built from the researchers assumptions of a reasonable configuration for the system being used. The initial baseline configuration is the same for all learning cycles so that the initial state of the middleware doesn't differ between them.

The first 5 cycles were adjusted for a faster learning process, leaning more towards exploration. This series of cycles was comprised by 100 steps each, updating the Neural Network's weights every 15 steps, and with a probability for the action taken being chosen randomly of 20%.

On the final 5 cycles, weights were updated every 20 steps and actions were chosen at random only 10% of the time. The number of steps was also increased to 120 steps. The number of steps was chosen so that the reinforcement learning agent is active for about the same time that the benchmark takes to conclude. Each step involves taking one of the actions described in Table 3. The final weights of the neural network on each cycle were transferred to the next, in order to incrementally refine the Neural Network used by the Reinforcement Learning agent.

It is worth noting that the learning mechanism benefits from environment state updates within short intervals, which would otherwise induce large delays in the learning process, hence the custom monitoring system implemented.

Results. Table 4 depicts the results for a subset of the learning cycles of the reinforcement learning agent. The average results reported are the average results for each evaluation cycle. The results show the impact on both deployed replicas, depicted as R1 and R2. We can see that on all learning cycles, the performance was better than for the baseline case. We can also see that the average reward value tends to increase in the case of R1, while in the case of R2, the maximum gain seems to have been achieved, at around 68%.

The actions that were taken in each RL adjustment are depicted in Fig. 4 and 5. The figures depict 6 of the 10 cycles, detailing the evolution of each considered configuration.

It is possible to observe that the pattern for each configuration variable evolved over the learning cycles, and that those patterns differ for each replica.

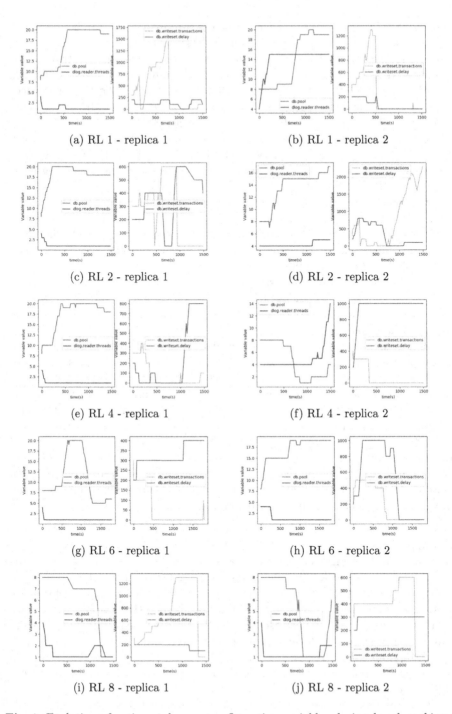

Fig. 4. Evolution of actions taken on configuration variables during benchmarking, Cycle 1, 2, 4, 6 and 8.

It's also worth noting that there is a distributed component, and therefore, a dependency between. The value for the Replicated Txn metric (Table 2) of one replica can only be as high as the value for the TxnWritten metric of the other replica. This means that the performance of a replica is partly influenced by the performance of the other.

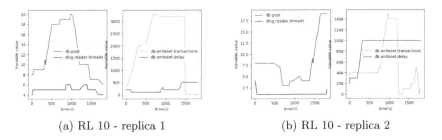

(a) RL 10 - replica 1   (b) RL 10 - replica 2

Fig. 5. Evolution of actions taken on configuration variables during benchmarking. Cycle 10.

Moreover, a deeper look into the results depicted, allows complementary conclusions, namely the fact that across all observed cycles in both replicas, the *db.writeset.transactions* is set to 0 at some point. This implies that the replicas were running with no limits for batching operations. Moreover, the *dlog.reader.threads*, which guides the thread pool associated with the distributed log read handler (in charge of acquiring data) was mostly reset to minimum values, which highlights the intense write profile of the considered benchmark.

Table 5 overviews the final results, extracted from Table 4. Overall, comparing the baseline results to the last tuning cycle, the state metrics directly associated with the replication mechanism registered a significant improvement, an order of magnitude higher for some of the state parameters.

Table 5. Results overview.

Metric	Baseline (Txn/sec)	RL#10 (Txn/sec)	Gain
ClientRequests-R1	80.80	112.95	**+39.79%**
Replicated Txn-R1	35.24	69.08	**+96.01%**
Txn Written-R1	27.57	112.95	**+309.73%**
ClientRequests-R2	178.20	205.47	**+15.30%**
Replicated Txn-R2	27.16	98.25	**+261.81%**
Txn Written-R2	31.86	94.26	**+195.82%**

This scenario holds a limited number of tuning variables, so a neural network with two 16 hidden layers was enough to capture the complexity of the problem.

Furthermore, our state contains information limited to the replication middleware action, holding no variables associated with the underlying hardware, for instance. These characteristics allowed us to train our model in a very short time, but deny the possibility of applying the trained model from one machine to another. We defer to future work the problem of inter-machine compatibility of the models.

4   Related Work

Prominent related work is generally focused in providing optimisations towards the physical deployment and data layouts of database systems. The linkage with the physical data layout allow self-adjustment systems to expedite index [22] creation, data partitions [3] or materialized views [2]. However, these approaches are unable to capture the details behind the DBMS, where the adjustment of specific tuning requirements impact on the DBMS internals. Most database products like IBM BD2, Microsoft SQL Server or MySQL include tools for tuning their respective systems in respect to the server performance [4,15]. Broadly speaking, these systems test alternative configurations in off-production deployments and assess their outcome. However, this solutions are bound to the discretion of the DBA in selecting the strategies to apply and what subsequent actions are taken in the DBMS.

The set of tools described also (indirectly) cover tunable criteria that strictly concerns the adjustment of the replication techniques, as part of the tunable configuration variables that are made available in each system. However, the consideration of tunable variables is generally absent [5], although some systems specialize in selecting the most meaningful configurations [19]. Even so, this is usually an independent process.

Although not a novelty in the machine and autonomous learning interest groups, Reinforcement Learning strategies are currently trendy techniques to be applied in distinct realms of computation. This class of techniques encompass an agent that tries to acquire state changes in their respective environment while aiming to maximize a balance of long-term and short-term return of a reward function [7]. Specifically in the field of database systems, such strategies have started to be applied in the internals of DBMSs to aid query optimisers to outperform baseline optimisation strategies for join ordering [21] and overall query planning [11]. The outcome is usually a sequential set of decisions based on Markov Decision Chains [12,14]. The considered RL technique does not change the optimisation criterion, but rather the how the exploration process is conducted.

These techniques enable the agent to search for actions during a *learning stage* where it deliberately takes actions to learn how the environment responds, or to come closer to the optimisation goal. Moreover, these techniques are commonly powered through heuristic-based exploration methods, built on statistics collected from the environment.

More recently, RL based solutions specific to single instance database self configuration have been presented, they leverage either metrics made available by the database [25], or information from the DBMS's query optimizer and the type of queries that compose the workload of the database [10]. In this paper we try to demonstrate that this is also possible at the level of the replication middleware. Moreover, we introduce the idea of dynamic configuration, meaning that tuning variables are seen as constantly changing, adapting their values in real time to changes in the workload.

We also show that although Deep Q-Learning can't work with continuous action spaces without them being sampled, contrary to some more recent algorithms like Deep Deterministic Policy Gradient (DDPG), it still manages to achieve very good results. The use of Deep Q-Learning versus DDPG might be advantageous in resource limited contexts, since it uses only one neural network, instead of two (one for the actor and one for the critic).

5   Conclusion

This paper details a reinforcement learning mechanism that attaches to a JDBC replication middleware, optimising its tunable configurations. An architecture was introduced, showcasing the components that are part of the design. Afterwards, we test a prototype of the system and evaluate its performance, relying on the industry standard TPC-C Benchmark as a workload injector.

The main focus of this paper shows that it is possible to consider self-learning mechanisms that are able to tune a replication middleware system, as so far, optimisation efforts consider the database engines as a whole, and do not focus in specific internal components such as the replication controllers. Moreover, they do not consider external pluggable dependability mechanisms.

The evaluation allowed us to confirm the effectiveness of these techniques, but also, the major impact that adjustable tuning variables have on the overall performance of the system. The results validate the approach, highlighting maximum improvements of around 370.99% for some of the considered metrics of the replication middleware.

Future work will guide us to improve the learning mechanism to go beyond the number of tunable criteria considered, and perhaps to recognize which ones may have more impact by analysing the system's performance.

Acknowledgements. The authors would like to thank Claudio Mezzina and the anonymous reviews for their helpful comments. The research leading to these results has received funding from the European Union's Horizon 2020 - The EU Framework Programme for Research and Innovation 2014–2020, under grant agreement No. 731218.

References

1. Apache Distributed Log (2018). http://bookkeeper.apache.org/distributedlog/. Accessed 19 July 2019
2. Agrawal, S., Chaudhuri, S., Narasayya, V.R.: Automated selection of materialized views and indexes in SQL databases. In: VLDB, pp. 496–505 (2000)

3. Curino, C., Jones, E., Zhang, Y., Madden, S.: Schism: a workload-driven approach to database replication and partitioning. Proc. VLDB Endow. **3**(1–2), 48–57 (2010)
4. Dias, K., Ramacher, M., Shaft, U., Venkataramani, V., Wood, G.: Automatic performance diagnosis and tuning in oracle. In: CIDR, pp. 84–94. CIDR (2005)
5. Duan, S., Thummala, V., Babu, S.: Tuning database configuration parameters with ituned. Proc. VLDB Endow. **2**(1), 1246–1257 (2009)
6. French, C.D.: "One size fits all" database architectures do not work for DSS. In: Proceedings of the 1995 ACM SIGMOD International Conference on Management of Data, SIGMOD 1995, pp. 449–450. ACM, New York (1995). https://doi.org/10.1145/223784.223871
7. García, J., Fernández, F.: A comprehensive survey on safe reinforcement learning. J. Mach. Learn. Res. **16**(1), 1437–1480 (2015)
8. George, L.: HBase: The Definitive Guide: Random Access to your Planet-Size Data. O'Reilly Media Inc., Sebastopol (2011)
9. Hintjens, P.: ZeroMQ: Messaging for many Applications. O'Reilly Media Inc., Sebastopol (2013)
10. Li, G., Zhou, X., Li, S., Gao, B.: Qtune: a query-aware database tuning system with deep reinforcement learning. Proc. VLDB Endow. **12**(12), 2118–2130 (2019)
11. Marcus, R., Papaemmanouil, O.: Deep reinforcement learning for join order enumeration. In: Proceedings of the First International Workshop on Exploiting Artificial Intelligence Techniques for Data Management, aiDM 2018, pp. 3:1–3:4. ACM, New York (2018). https://doi.org/10.1145/3211954.3211957
12. Morff, A.R., Paz, D.R., Hing, M.M., González, L.M.G.: A reinforcement learning solution for allocating replicated fragments in a distributed database. Computación y Sistemas **11**(2), 117–128 (2007)
13. Powell, D.: Delta-4: A Generic Architecture for Dependable Distributed Computing, vol. 1. Springer, Cham (2012). https://doi.org/10.1007/978-3-642-84696-0
14. Puterman, M.L.: Markov Decision Processes: Discrete Stochastic Dynamic Programming. Wiley, Hoboken (2014)
15. Schiefer, K.B., Valentin, G.: Db2 universal database performance tuning. IEEE Data Eng. Bull. **22**(2), 12–19 (1999)
16. Schnaitter, K., Abiteboul, S., Milo, T., Polyzotis, N.: Colt: continuous on-line tuning. In: Proceedings of the 2006 ACM SIGMOD International Conference on Management of Data, SIGMOD 2006, pp. 793–795. ACM, New York (2006). https://doi.org/10.1145/1142473.1142592
17. Stonebraker, M., Rowe, L.A.: The Design of Postgres, vol. 15. ACM, New York (1986)
18. Storm, A.J., Garcia-Arellano, C., Lightstone, S.S., Diao, Y., Surendra, M.: Adaptive self-tuning memory in db2. In: Proceedings of the 32nd International Conference on Very Large Data Bases, pp. 1081–1092. VLDB Endowment (2006)
19. Sullivan, D.G., Seltzer, M.I., Pfeffer, A.: Using Probabilistic Reasoning to Automate Software Tuning, vol. 32. ACM, New York (2004)
20. Sutton, R.S., Barto, A.G.: Reinforcement Learning: An Introduction. MIT Press, Cambridge (2018)
21. Trummer, I., Moseley, S., Maram, D., Jo, S., Antonakakis, J.: Skinnerdb: regret-bounded query evaluation via reinforcement learning. Proc. VLDB Endow. **11**(12), 2074–2077 (2018). https://doi.org/10.14778/3229863.3236263
22. Valentin, G., Zuliani, M., Zilio, D.C., Lohman, G., Skelley, A.: Db2 advisor: an optimizer smart enough to recommend its own indexes. In: Proceedings of 16th International Conference on Data Engineering (Cat. no. 00CB37073), pp. 101–110. IEEE (2000)

23. Watkins, C.J., Dayan, P.: Q-learning. Mach. Learn. **8**(3–4), 279–292 (1992)
24. Wiesmann, M., Pedone, F., Schiper, A., Kemme, B., Alonso, G.: Understanding replication in databases and distributed systems. In: Proceedings 20th IEEE International Conference on Distributed Computing Systems, pp. 464–474. IEEE (2000)
25. Zhang, J., et al.: An end-to-end automatic cloud database tuning system using deep reinforcement learning. In: Proceedings of the 2019 International Conference on Management of Data, pp. 415–432 (2019)

DroidAutoML: A Microservice Architecture to Automate the Evaluation of Android Machine Learning Detection Systems

Yérom-David Bromberg[✉] and Louison Gitzinger[✉]

Université de Rennes 1, Rennes, France
{david.bromberg,louison.gitzinger}@irisa.fr

Abstract. The mobile ecosystem is witnessing an unprecedented increase in the number of malware in the wild. To fight this threat, actors from both research and industry are constantly innovating to bring concrete solutions to improve security and malware protection. Traditional solutions such as signature-based anti viruses have shown their limits in front of massive proliferation of new malware, which are most often only variants specifically designed to bypass signature-based detection. Accordingly, it paves the way to the emergence of new approaches based on Machine Learning (ML) technics to boost the detection of unknown malware variants. Unfortunately, these solutions are most often under-exploited due to the time and resource costs required to adequately fine tune machine learning algorithms. In reality, in the Android community, state-of-the-art studies do not focus on model training, and most often go through an empirical study with a manual process to choose the learning strategy, and/or use default values as parameters to configure ML algorithms. However, in the ML domain, it is well known admitted that to solve efficiently a ML problem, the tunability of hyper-parameters is of the utmost importance. Nevertheless, as soon as the targeted ML problem involves a massive amount of data, there is a strong tension between feasibility of exploring all combinations and accuracy. This tension imposes to automate the search for optimal hyper-parameters applied to ML algorithms, that is not anymore possible to achieve manually. To this end, we propose a generic and scalable solution to automatically both configure and evaluate ML algorithms to efficiently detect Android malware detection systems. Our approach is based on devOps principles and a microservice architecture deployed over a set of nodes to scale and exhaustively test a large number of ML algorithms and hyper-parameters combinations. With our approach, we are able to systematically find the best fit to increase up to 11% the accuracy of two state-of-the-art Android malware detection systems.

Keywords: Machine learning · Android · Malware · AutoML

© IFIP International Federation for Information Processing 2020
Published by Springer Nature Switzerland AG 2020
A. Remke and V. Schiavoni (Eds.): DAIS 2020, LNCS 12135, pp. 148–165, 2020.
https://doi.org/10.1007/978-3-030-50323-9_10

1   Introduction

Smartphones are currently generating more than half of the global internet traffic [1], and its related market surpasses by far computer sales. The Android operating system is one of the most important market players. It owns 70% of market shares, and accounts for 2.5 billion active devices worldwide [6]. Unfortunately, this boundless adoption opens a lucrative business for attackers and ill-intentioned people. The number of Android malware peaks in 2020 [10]. Malicious applications spread across the Android ecosystem at an alarming rate [3,4,7]. Attackers leverage on various techniques such as *dynamic code loading, reflection* and/or *encryption* to design ever more complex malwares [22,48] that systematically bypass existing scanners. To counter this phenomenon, Android security actors, from both research and industry, massively adopt machine learning techniques to improve malware detection accuracy [11,15,16,39]. Although it is a first step towards improving detection, unfortunately, most of related studies neglect the search for fine tuned learning algorithms.

We argue that there are still rooms for improvements unexplored. In particular, it is commonly admitted in the machine learning domain, that performances of trained machine learning models depend strongly on several key aspects: (i) training datasets [25], (ii) learning algorithms [20], and (iii) parameters (i.e. hyper-parameters) used to tune learning algorithms [19,21,23,46]. Accordingly, the key underlying problem, usually referred as *Automated Machine Learning* (AutoML) [29], is how to automate the process of finding the best suitable configuration to solve a given machine learning problem. As far as our knowledge, no attempts have been done towards improving Android malware detection systems based on machine learning algorithms. Whether one [11,16] or several algorithms [17,39,50] are evaluated, the evaluations are always carried out empirically, implying a manual process with few and/or default hyper-parameter combinations. Testing various algorithms along with a large set of hyper-parameters is a daunting task that costs a lot both in terms of time and resources [36].

In this paper, we present DroidAutoML, a new approach that automatically performs an extensive and exhaustive search by training various learning algorithms with thousand of hyper-parameter combinations to find the highest possible malware detection rate given the incoming dataset. DroidAutoML is both generic and scalable. Its genericity comes from its ability to be agnostic to underlying machine learning algorithms used, and its scalability comes from its ability to scale infinitely horizontally by adding as much as machines as required to speed up the processing. To achieve this aim, and leveraging our expertise in the field of Android malware detection, we have defined and deployed a dedicated microservices architecture.

Our contributions are as follow:

– We propose the very first *AutoML* approach, named DroidAutoML, to improve the accuracy of technics based on machine learning algorithms to detect malware on Android. With DroidAutoML, there is no need anymore to manually perform empirical study to configure machine learning algorithms.

- We provide a dedicated microservices architecture specifically designed to fulfill the needs for genericity and flexibility as required by the Android malware detection domain.
- We thoroughly evaluate our approach, and applied it to the state of the art solutions such as Drebin [16] and MaMaDroid [39]. We demonstrated that DroidAutoML enables to improve significantly their performances: detection accuracy has been increased up to 11% for Drebin and 10% for MaMaDroid.

The remainder of this paper is organized as follows: Sect. 2 explains the context of the study. Section 3 presents in details our microservices architecture, and Sect. 4 details our thorough evaluation. We make a review of the state of the art in Sect. 5, and finally conclude the paper in Sect. 6.

2   Background

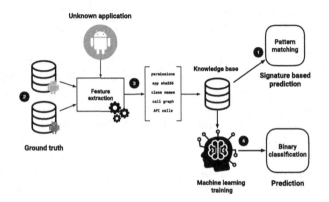

Fig. 1. Overview of the malware detection process on Android

2.1   Emergence of Machine Learning Algorithms to Detect Android Malware

Traditional anti-viruses heavily rely upon signatures to identify malware [8,9] (see Fig. 1, ❶). As soon as new malware are discovered in the wild, antivirus software companies put their hands on, and compute their related signatures. The latter are added to the ground truth database (see Fig. 1, ❷) of the antivirus software. In this way, anti-viruses calculate the signatures of files to be analyzed (see Fig. 1, ❸), and compare them with previously stored signatures to perform the detection of malware. While signature based detection is efficient to catch old and already seen malware, they struggle to deal with new malware generations [22,45]. Indeed, malware authors use various techniques, such as *polymorphism* [31], to generate malware variants that inherently have unforeseen signatures to bypass anti-viruses. These new attacks emphases the need for more intelligent systems to detect proactively unseen malware variants, commonly known as 0-day threats.

In this aforementioned perspective, the last decade, strong efforts have been achieved to generalize the problem, and to develop new approaches based on machine learning (ML) [11,16,17,39,50] (see Fig. 1, ❹). In contrast to signature based anti-viruses, ML anti-viruses rely on sets of meticulously chosen heuristics, or features (see Fig. 1, ❸) to train learning models from a ground truth (see Fig. 1, ❷) dataset that includes both benign and malicious applications. Once trained, models are thereafter able to make predictions on unseen files. They give either a confidence score [32] or take a binary decision to decide whether a file is benign or potentially harmful.

2.2   Importance of Features in ML Malware Classification Problem

Feature extraction, selection and encoding are essential steps towards building an efficient classification system based on ML. Features must be chosen in such a way that they help ML algorithms to generalize the classification problem and help them to adequately classify them. When badly chosen, algorithms may be unable to generalize the problem or suffer from *overfitting*. More importantly, the number of used features can drastically slow down model training time.

Table 1. Examples of basic and behavioral features that can be extracted from an Android application

Type	Features	Static analysis	Dynamic analysis	Location
Basic	Permissions	✓	✗	manifest
	Intent-filters	✓	✗	manifest
	Components	✓	✗	manifest
	File signatures	✓	✗	apk level
	Protected method calls	✓	✓	bytecode
	Suspicious method calls	✓	✓	bytecode
Behavioural	Call graph	✓	✓	bytecode
	Dynamic code loading	✗	✓	apk level
	Network traffic	✗	✓	OS level
	Intent messages	✗	✓	OS level

Feature Selection. Feature selection is a widely studied area regarding ML malware detection in the Android ecosystem [11,16,39]. Mainly, we distinguish two types of features: (i) basic, and (ii) behavioral features, as illustrated in Table 1. Basic features qualify information inherent in an application, but by themselves do not directly encode its corresponding behavior [16]. It is the correlation of the features altogether that allows machine learning models to differentiate a benign application from a malicious one. For instance, the basic *permission* feature READ_CONTACTS can be used by both benign and malicious applications. As such, it does not give any information about intentions of the application. However, when correlated with the basic *method call* feature `url.openConnection()`, it may highlight the intentions of a malicious application to steal user's contacts. Contrariwise, behavioral features are information about an application that allows to extract both intentions and actions of an application [39]. These features can be extracted by statically extracting the call graph of an application or by monitoring the application during its execution.

Feature Extraction. Mainly two approaches can be used to extract features from an Android application: (i) static, and (ii) dynamic analysis. A static analysis allows to quickly analyze binaries of Android applications without having to execute it. In the Android ecosystem, static analysis is a widely used approach [28,35,38,47] as they allow to analyze applications at scale without having an impact on resources, and in particular on the reactiveness of applications being scanned. However, static analysis are limited to the analysis of the visible part of the application's bytecode. Malware authors may use advanced obfuscations techniques such as *dynamic code loading* or *encryption* to try to defeat static analysis.

Due to the weaknesses of static analysis, dynamic analysis are often explored as an alternative in Android malware detection systems [27,49,51]. Dynamic analysis consists of executing malware to monitor their behaviors at runtime. Most often, to make it scales and for isolation purposes, such analyses are typically executed in *sandboxed* environments. However, malware may implement *evasion* techniques such as *logic bombs*, and *time bombs*, which allow them to bypass runtime surveillance. A *logic bomb* is the ability of a malware to detect its runtime environment (i.e. a sandboxed environment such as a virtual machine), and to prevent itself to trigger its own malicious behavior in such conditions [44]. A *time bomb* enables malware to trigger their malicious actions only after a certain amount of time or periodically, at specific hours. Accordingly, dynamic analysis suffer from scalability issues, and are rarely used due to their inherent strong requirements in terms of both time and resources.

Feature Encoding. Feature vectors are used to represent the characteristics of studied items in a numerical way to simplify their analysis and comparison. Most of ML classification algorithms such as neural networks, nearest neighbor classification or statistical classification use feature vectors as input to train their model. While it is easy to use pixels of an image as a numerical feature vector, it is harder to numerically encode more complex features such as basic or behavioral features of Android applications. For that reason, many studies [11,16,26,39] provide new alternatives for feature encoding. Authors of Drebin [16] embed *basic* extracted features into a feature vector using *one-hot encoding* to code the presence, or the absence of a given feature. Contrariwise, MaMaDroid [39] encodes *behavioral* extracted features using a Markov chain algorithm, which calculates the probability for a method to be called by another in a call graph.

2.3   Choosing and Training the Classification Algorithm

While feature selection and encoding remain important in machine learning based malware detection, the problem of training an accurate model also needs to be addressed. On one side, Android application vendors must ensure that no malicious applications bypass their security barriers. On the other side, discarding too many applications, to stay conservative, may lead to profit losses, as many benign applications can be flagged as false positive. Hence, training a binary classifier with good performances in terms of precision and recall is essential. While features selection can be very helpful to solve this, choosing the best classification algorithm with the best training parameters can greatly improve classification.

Classification Algorithms. In machine learning, and especially on binary classification problems, it is admitted that choosing the right learning algorithm depends on many factors such as the available resources, the algorithm complexity or the input data. As there is no silver bullet to always find the best algorithm, researchers often go through an empirical process to find a good fit. Regarding the Android ecosystem, various algorithms to train models, mostly Random Forest (RF), Support Vector Machine (SVM), and k-nearest neighbors (KNN), have already been tested depending on type of data extracted from applications, and the number of applications used for training ML models [16,33,39,50]. Although all these studies show good evaluation performances, all of them have been empirically evaluated with a manual trial and error strategy. As it is a very time consuming task, it is a safe bet to say that these studies did not found the best learning algorithm to solve the classification problem. Therefore, we claim that automating such a task would be a great help for the research community.

Hyperparameter Optimization. Another important aspect are parameters used to train chosen learning algorithms (most often set to default values). Usually, the number of *hyper-parameters* for a given algorithm is small (≤ 5), but may take both continuous and discrete values leading to a very high number of different values and so of combinations. For instance, common hyper-parameters include the *learning rate* for a neural network, the C and *sigma* for SVM, or the K parameter for KNN algorithms. The choice of hyper-parameters can have a strong impact on performances, learning time and resource consumption. As a result, *Automated hyper-parameter search* is a trending topic in the machine learning community [37,52]. Currently, grid search and brute force approaches remain a widely used strategy for hyper-parameter optimization [18] but can require time and computational resources to test all possibilities. To deal with this issue, several frameworks are able to efficiently parallelize grid-searching tasks on a single machine, but this does not scale with the ever growing search space [12,41].

3   A Microservice Architecture for ML

DroidAutoML relies on a microservice architecture that separates concerns between data processing (feature *selection, extraction* and *encoding*) and training optimization ML models. Such a design enables DroidAutoML to scale and stay agnostic to the evaluated scanner.

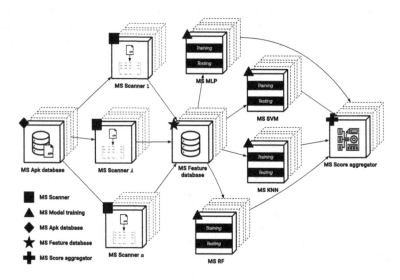

Fig. 2. Overview of DROIDAUTOML

Microservices Dedicated to Features Operations. Feature extraction and *encoding* are both operations specifics to each scanner. As such, each scanner has its own dedicated microservice for performing these operations (Fig. 2, ■). We define k as the number of applications to process for a given dataset. For n different scanners, $n * k$ instances of ■$_{(i,j)}$ microservices with $i \in \{1..n\} \wedge j \in \{1..k\}$ will be deployed. Each ■$_{(i,j)}$ instance takes as input an *apk* to generate its corresponding features vector, interpretable by any machine learning algorithms. The generated *feature vector* is then stored into the *feature database* microservice (See Fig. 2,★).

Microservices Dedicated to Model Training. ML model training operations are specific to a classification algorithm and the set of *hyper-parameter* used to parametrize it. Therefore, each algorithm has its own dedicated microservice to perform the training and testing of a model for one *hyper-parameter combination* (see Fig. 2, ▲). For l different algorithms, l different kinds of m instances of ▲$_{(i,j)}$ with $i \in \{1..l\} \wedge j \in \{1..m\}$ will be deployed where m is equals to the number of *hyper-parameter combinations* to test for a given algorithm. This allows to scale horizontally by spreading the workload across the available nodes in the cluster. A ▲ microservice takes two inputs: (i) a feature vector matrix from the feature database ★, and (ii) a set of hyper-parameter values. ▲ microservices leverage *Scikit-learn* to perform both training, and testing steps. Afterwards, each ▲ instance parametrizes its ML algorithm according to the input hyper-parameter combination. All ML models are trained with a 10-cross fold validation process to avoid *overfitting* problems. The input data is split according to machine learning ratio standards: 60% of the data is used to fit the model and 40% to test it. Performances of each model are assessed in terms of *accuracy* and *F1 score*. Finally, trained models are stored within the database along with the configured hyper-parameter settings so that they can further be used by the end-user. The obtained results on the testing set are then communicated to *score aggregator* microservices (see Fig. 2, ✚).

Microservices Dedicated to Score Aggregation. A third set of microservices are the ones dedicated to the collecting of results from ▲ mircroservices to identify the pair {*algorithm,hyper-parameters*} that gives the best performances for a given scanner. Each score aggregator microservice is dedicated to a couple {*scanner, algorithm*} so that it collects only results related to it for all hyper-parameter combinations tested. Accordingly, for n scanners and l algorithms, there will be at least $n * l$ instances of aggregators. Once the best predictive model have been found for a given scanner, the corresponding algorithm and hyper-parameters are communicated to the end-user.

Efficient Microservice Scheduling. DroidAutoML is a system designed to run on top of a cluster of hardware machines. To optimize resources and efficiently schedule tasks on such a cluster, DroidAutoML leverages on a bin packing algorithm [24]. As such, by splitting scanner benchmarking operations into smaller tasks, DroidAutoML can capitalize on properties offered by microservice architectures. Firstly, DroidAutoML fully takes advantage of multi node clusters as each microservice can be scheduled independently on any node in the cluster. Secondly, as scanner benchmarks are parallelized, ▲ microservices can run side by side with ■ microservices as long as they do not work for the same scanner. Thirdly, if a microservice fails during its execution, only its workload is lost and it can be automatically rescheduled.

4   Evaluation

4.1   Implementation

DroidAutoML is built on *Nomad*, an open-source workload orchestrator developed by *HashiCorp* [5], which provides a flexible environment to deploy applications on top of an abstracted infrastructure. More precisely our Nomad instance federates a cluster of 6 nodes (see Fig. 3, ❶) that accounts for 600 GB of RAM and 124 cores at 3.0 Ghz. We use the bin packing algorithm implemented in *Nomad* to schedule (see Fig. 3, ❷) DroidAutoML microservices instances across available nodes in the cluster as schematized in Fig. 3. Each microservice instance is represented as a *job* managed by the *Nomad* scheduler. Hardware resources

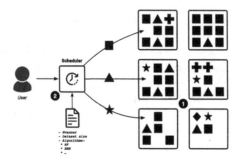

Fig. 3. Overview of DroidAutoML implementation

allocated to each microservice depend on its type: scanner specific instances take 2 cores and 4 GB of RAM each, model training instances take 1 core and 2 GB of RAM, and score aggregator instances take 1 CPU and 1 GB or RAM. The time required for a scanner instance to build a feature vector depends on the size of the input apk as well as its operating time. It ranges from 6 s for a 2 MB application to 61 s for a 100 MB application on average. The apk database of DroidAutoML is currently composed of 11561 applications, 5285 malware and 6276 benign applications and the average size of an application is 20.25 MB with a standard deviation of 21.48.

Given the resources required for one instance, our infrastructure can run 61 ■ microservice instances in parallel, therefore the entire apk database can be processed in 24 min with our current cluster. The time required to train and test a ML model depends on the algorithm, the set *hyper-parameters* used, and the size of the input vector matrix. We provide in Table 4 the minimum, average and maximum time required to train and test a model according to an algorithm. As we use a grid-search approach to perform *hyper-parameter tuning*, the number of ML models train to evaluate a scanner depends on the number of hyper-parameter combinations to test. The Table 4 summarizes the values tested for each *hyper-parameter* according to an algorithm as well as the number of combinations to test them all. For example, given the resource constraints of a ML model microservice, our cluster can run 123 ▲ microservice instances in parallel, thus testing all 3120 hyper-parameter combinations for the Random Forest takes on average 9 min for an input feature vector matrix of 11561 items.

4.2 Evaluation of Two State of the Art Scanners

To evaluate our approach, we propose to apply our microservice architecture to two state-of-the-art machine learning based malware detection systems in order to improve learning algorithm selection and training. More precisely, we conduct our experiments on approaches proposed by Drebin [16] and MaMaDroid [39]. We benchmark our approach against the ground truth of the related work by reusing the same ML algorithms used by the two approaches: Support Vector

Machine (SVM) for Drebin and Random Forest, SVM and K-Nearest Neighbors for MaMaDroid.

We build a dataset of 11561 applications composed of 5285 benign and 6276 malware samples. Malicious samples are collected from three malware datasets: the Drebin dataset [16], the `Contagio` dataset [2] and a dataset of 200 verified ransomware from `Androzoo` [13]. Concerning benign applications, we collect samples from the top 200 of most downloaded applications for each app category in the Google Play Store. To ensure that collected samples are really benigns, we upload them to VirusTotal, an online platform that makes it possible to have a file analyzed by more than 60 commercial antivirus products. According to the literature [40], applications can be safely labeled as benign if less than 5 antivirus detect it as malware, as several antivirus consider *adwares* as potentially dangerous. Among the 6276 applications downloaded, 95, 04% (5965 samples) have not been detected as malware at all and 99, 18% (6225 samples) by less than 5 antivirus. To guarantee the overall dataset quality, we remove all samples with a detection rate over this threshold.

Table 2. Baseline results for Drebin and MaMaDroid models trained with original *hyper-parameters* settings.

Scanner	Algorithm	Accuracy	F1-Score	Precision	Recall	TP	TN	FP	FN
Drebin	**SVM**	88.91	88.23	84.43	92.39	1833	2087	338	151
MaMaDroid	**KNN**	82.35	81.76	83.25	80.33	1744	1887	427	351
	Random Forest	80.54	83.08	72.65	97.01	2106	1445	65	793
	SVM	79.22	81.97	71.57	95.90	2082	1411	89	827

Ground Truth Results. As original experiments by Drebin and MaMaDroid authors were made on older data, both approaches may suffer from *temporal bias* [14,43]. *Temporal bias* refers to inconsistent machine learning evaluations with data that do not correctly represent the reality over time. To take this bias into account, we start our experiment by measuring ground truth results for both Drebin and MaMaDroid approaches using our own dataset. These results will serve as a baseline to evaluate DroidAutoML performances and compare further results against it. Authors from Drebin use a SVM algorithm to perform the binary classification of malware and benign applications. As the original source code of their approach is not available, we develop our own implementation of their solution using available information in the original paper. While our implementation of Drebin may slightly differ from the original one, the approach and the algorithm used (SVM) remain conceptually the same. As no details are given about *hyper-parameters* used to parametrize the algorithm, we take common default values suggested by machine learning frameworks to train the algorithm. Regarding MaMaDroid, authors tested three learning algorithms: Random Forest, SVM and KNN. We calculate the baseline by using the MaMadroid's approach source code, and the same *hyper-parameters* set by the authors.

The Table 3 reports the grid of *hyper-parameter* values used to train and test each learning models for both approaches. The Table 2 reports the baseline results for each trained model. We observe that the accuracy and F1 scores for both approaches decrease compared to the original results. The accuracy score for the Drebin SVM drops by 5.09% from 94% to 88.91%. Considering MaMaDroid, F1-Scores are below 84% for all studied algorithms, with a false-positive rate over 5%, which is more than 15% lower than best results presented originally in terms of F1-Score. As samples in our dataset are more recent than those used in original experiments, these results confirm that both Drebin and MaMaDroid approaches are suffering from *temporal bias*.

Table 3. Default hyper-parameters used to parametrize evaluated algorithms

	Parameters	Mamadroid	Drebin
Random Forest	n_estimators	101	
	max_depth	32	
	min_samples_split	2	
	min_samples_leaf	1	
	max_features	auto	
SVM	C	1	1
	kernel	rbf	linear
	degree	3	3
	gamma	auto	auto
KNN	n_neighbors	[1, 3]	
	weights	uniform	
	leaf_size	30	
	p	2	

Model Evaluation with DroidAutoML. In the following of this experiment, we aim at answering the following questions:

– **RQ1**: Is DroidAutoML able to find a learning algorithm that performs better than default algorithms used for studied scanners?
– **RQ2**: Can DroidAutoML improve the prediction results of studied scanners by finding an optimal set of *hyper-parameters*?

We answer these questions by running DroidAutoML for each studied scanner with a large grid of *hyper-parameters* (see Table 4) and 4 different learning algorithms for each scanner: Random Forest, SVM, KNN, and a multi layer perceptron (Neural Network).

Table 4. Grid hyper-parameters used to train models with DroidAutoML

	Parameters	Hyperparameters	# of combinations to test	Time for a single run (in seconds for 11 238 apks)		
				min	avg	max
Random Forest	n_estimators	[200, 400, 600, 800, 1000, 1200, 1400, 1600, 1800, 2000]	10 * 13 * 3 * 4 * 2 = 3120	15	21	35
	max_depth	[10, 20, 30, 40, 50, 60, 70, 80, 90, 100, 500, 1000,None]				
	min_samples_split	[2, 4, 6, 10]				
	min_samples_leaf	[2,5,10,20]				
	max_features	[auto,sqrt]				
SVM	C	[0.0001,0.001,0.01,0.1, 1,10,100,1000,10000]	9* 4* 7 = 252	23	25	31
	kernel	[linear,rbf,sigmoid,poly]				
	gamma	[0.0001,0.001,0.01,0.1, 1,auto,scale]				
KNN	n_neighbors	[1,3,4,5,6,7,8,9,10]	9 *2 *8 *2 = 288	23	42	56
	weights	uniform,distance				
	leaf_size	[1,3,5,10,20,30,50,100]				
	p	[1,2]				
MLP	hidden_layer_sizes	[(50, 50, 50), (50, 100, 50), (100,)]	3 *2 *3* 2* 2 = 72	123	164	250
	activation	[tanh, relu]				
	solver	[sgd, adam, lbfgs]				
	alpha	[0.0001, 0.05]				
	learning_rate	[constant, adaptative]				

Table 5. Best results after model training on DroidAutoML

Scanner	Algorithm	Accuracy	F1-Score	Precision	Recall	TP	TN	FP	FN
Drebin	**KNN**	98.82	98.82	99.91	97.75	2169	2188	2	50
	Random Forest	98.57	98.56	99.63	97.52	2163	2183	8	55
	SVM	99.50	99.50	99.86	99.13	2168	2219	3	19
	MLP	99.61	99.60	99.68	99.54	2164	2228	7	10
MaMaDroid	**KNN**	85.48	86.41	93.69	80.17	2034	1735	137	503
	Random Forest	87.93	88.57	94.98	82.98	2062	1815	109	423
	SVM	88.97	88.49	86.09	91.03	1869	2054	302	184
	MLP	84.71	85.36	90.55	80.73	1966	1769	205	469

The Table 5 reports the best results obtained for both Drebin and MaMaDroid. For the Drebin approach, accuracy and F1 scores of the model trained with SVM increase by 10.59% and 11.27% respectively compared to the baseline. Moreover, we observe that the multi layer perceptron algorithm performs slightly better than the SVM algorithm with +0.11% in accuracy and +0.10% in F1-Score, thus reducing the number of false negative from 19 to 10. DroidAutoML also succeeds to improve MaMaDroid baseline results for all three studied algorithms. In details, DroidAutoML increases MaMaDroid's SVM

Table 6. Hyper-parameters found for best case performance

	Parameters	Mamadroid	Drebin
Random Forest	n_estimators	1600	1500
	max_depth	50	30
	min_samples_split	2	4
	min_samples_leaf	2	10
	max_features	sqrt	auto
SVM	C	1000	1000
	kernel	linear	rbf
	degree	3	3
	gamma	auto	scale
KNN	n_neighbors	3	5
	weights	uniform	uniform
	leaf_size	30	20
	p	2	2
MLP	hidden_layer_sizes	100	50, 100, 50
	activation	tanh	tanh
	solver	adam	lbfgs
	alpha	0.05	0, 0001
	learning_rate	adaptative	constant

baseline accuracy by 9.75%, KNN by 3.13% and RF by 7.39%. These accuracy improvements are accompanied by a significant increase of F1-scores for all algorithms. It represents a significant decrease of the number of false positives and false negatives. In their paper, MaMaDroid's authors discard the SVM algorithm due to poor performance compared to other algorithms tested. We show here that SVM is actually better than other algorithms tested by authors when it is parametrized with the adequate *hyper-parameter* values as shown in Table 6. Notice that in machine learning, optimal *hyper-parameters* values depends on the problem to solve [23]. Therefore, as the feature vectors are encoded differently for Drebin and MaMaDroid, optimal *hyper-parameter* values may slighlty differ from one approach to the other.

We answer **RQ1** by showing that DroidAutoML has been able to find a ML algorithm that performs better than those tested empirically with studied scanners. More precisely, the Multi Layer Perceptron outperforms the SVM algorithm used by Drebin originally and the MaMaDroid SVM originally discarded by the authors due to poor results performs better than other algorithms initially retained (i.e. RF and KNN).

Furthermore, we answer **RQ2** by showing that DroidAutoML has been able to find a combination of *hyper-parameters* in a reasonable amount of time (less than 30 min) that enables to significantly improve prediction results for all machine learning models trained for studied scanners.

5   Related Work

Machine Learning Based Malware Detection on Android. As of today, many studies [11,16,33,39,42,50,53] use machine learning to improve malware detection in the Android ecosystem. Over time, trained models become more and more accurate thanks to the heavy work on feature extraction and feature selection. Among studies published on the subject, several of them [11,16,42] use basic semantic feature to model application's behavior. Particularly, in 2014, authors of DREBIN [16] use various features such as permissions, application components, calls to hardware components, intent filters, etc. to train a support vector machine on more than 5000 malware and 123 000 benign applications. Other studies [39,53] model and encode the application control flow to increase the robustness against adversarial attacks [22,48] that modify the application's byte code without touching its behavior. Unfortunately, the great majority of these studies do not focus on model training, and most often go through a manual process to choose the learning strategy. Only a few studies [39,50] are actually testing more than one learning algorithms. However, the process is still done manually and *hyper-parameters* are empirically chosen or left by default.

Automated Machine Learning Frameworks. Several works already studied *automated machine learning* as a research problem [30,34]. These works have mainly paved the way to make machine learning available to non-experts from the domain. Frameworks such as *Auto-Sklearn* and *Auto-WEKA* related to these studies are actually responding to a demand for machine learning methods that automatically works without expert knowledge. With *Auto-Sklearn* [30], authors leverage on Bayesian optimization and past performance on similar datasets to automate classifier selection and increase trained model *efficiency*. However as stated before, the quality of a model training depends on the input data. While an *AutoML* framework may find an acceptable solution for a given problem, it is not sufficient in many expert domains, especially Android security and malware detection where the best possible efficiency is required. It is a big assumption to trust an *AutoML* framework to choose the best fit for the problem to solve. Especially in Android malware detection, input data can vary a lot depending on the feature selection and encoding approach. Moreover, while *Auto-Sklearn* can efficiently parallelize on a single machine, it is not designed to horizontally scale on a multi-node cluster. For that reason, we consider frameworks such as *Auto-Sklearn* as another option to test along with others classical classifiers such as Random Forest or SVM in DroidAutoML.

6   Conclusion

We have identified that machine learning solutions are underexploited in the Android ecosystem and proposed a novel approach to address this issue. We have built DroidAutoML, a microservice architecture to test malware detection scanners on a large number of machine learning algorithms and hyper-parameter combinations. We have shown that DroidAutoML can significantly improve scanners detection rate while optimizing used resources. DroidAutoML becomes a cornerstone to correctly benchmark both existing and novel ML approaches on existing ML algorithms.

As a future work we plan to integrate new machine learning algorithms in our framework and potentially more efficient approaches to speed up the hyper-parameter optimization process such as *Bayesian optimization*. We also plan to release DroidAutoML as an open-source framework, as the Android security community could greatly benefit from it.

References

1. Cisco visual networking index: Global mobile data traffic forecast update, 2017–2022. https://s3.amazonaws.com/media.mediapost.com/uploads/CiscoForecast.pdf. Accessed 20 042020
2. Contagio dataset. http://contagiodump.blogspot.com/. Accessed 12 Sept 2019
3. Cyber attacks on android devices on the rise. https://www.gdatasoftware.com/blog/2018/11/31255-cyber-attacks-on-android-devices-on-the-rise. Accessed 30 Jan 2020
4. Mcafee mobile threat report q1 (2018). https://www.mcafee.com/enterprise/en-us/assets/reports/rp-mobile-threat-report-2018.pdf. Accessed 30 Jan 2020
5. Nomad by hashicorp. https://www.nomadproject.io/. Accessed 10 Feb 2020
6. There are now 2.5 billion active android devices - the verge. https://www.theverge.com/2019/5/7/18528297/google-io-2019-android-devices-play-store-total-number-statistic-keynote. Accessed 30 Jan 2020
7. Threat intelligence report 2019. https://networks.nokia.com/solutions/threat-intelligence/infographic. Accessed 30 Jan 2020
8. Virustotal. https://www.virustotal.com/gui/home/upload. Accessed 04 Feb 2020
9. Yara. https://virustotal.github.io/yara/. Accessed 04 Feb 2020
10. Malware statistics & trends report — av-test (2020). https://www.av-test.org/en/statistics/malware/. Accessed 20 Apr 2020
11. Aafer, Y., Du, W., Yin, H.: Droidapiminer: mining API-level features for robust malware detection in android. In: Security and Privacy in Communication Networks (SecureCom) (2013)
12. Abadi, M., et al.: Tensorflow: a system for large-scale machine learning. In: Symposium on Operating Systems Design and Implementation (OSDI) (2016)
13. Allix, K., Bissyandé, T.F., Klein, J., Le Traon, Y.: Androzoo: collecting millions of android apps for the research community. In: Working Conference on Mining Software Repositories (MSR)
14. Allix, K., Bissyandé, T.F., Klein, J., Le Traon, Y.: Are your training datasets yet relevant? In: International Symposium on Engineering Secure Software and Systems (2015)

15. Amos, B., Turner, H., White, J.: Applying machine learning classifiers to dynamic android malware detection at scale. In: International Wireless Communications and Mobile Computing Conference (IWCMC) (2013)
16. Arp, D., Spreitzenbarth, M., Hübner, M., Gascon, H., Rieck, K.: Drebin: Effective and explainable detection of android malware in your pocket. In: Annual Network and Distributed System Security Symposium (NDSS) (2014)
17. Bedford, A., et al.: Andrana: Quick and Accurate Malware Detection for Android (2017)
18. Bergstra, J., Bengio, Y.: Random search for hyper-parameter optimization. J. Mach. Learn. Res. **13**, 281–305 (2012)
19. Bergstra, J.S., Bardenet, R., Bengio, Y., Kégl, B.: Algorithms for hyper-parameter optimization (2011)
20. Bottou, L., Bousquet, O.: The tradeoffs of large scale learning (2008)
21. Chapelle, O., Vapnik, V., Bousquet, O., Mukherjee, S.: Choosing multiple parameters for support vector machines. arXiv preprint arXiv:1502.02127 (2002)
22. Chen, X., et al.: Android HIV: a study of repackaging malware for evading machine-learning detection. Trans. Inf. Forens. Secur. (TIFS) **15**, 987–1001 (2019)
23. Claesen, M., De Moor, B.: Hyperparameter search in machine learning. arXiv preprint arXiv:1502.02127 (2015)
24. Coffman Jr., E.G., Garey, M.R., Johnson, D.S.: An application of bin-packing to multiprocessor scheduling. SIAM J. Comput. **7**(1), 1–17 (1978)
25. Cortes, C., Jackel, L.D., Chiang, W.P.: Limits on learning machine accuracy imposed by data quality. In: Advances in Neural Information Processing Systems (NIPS) (1995)
26. Dai, S., Tongaonkar, A., Wang, X., Nucci, A., Song, D.: Networkprofiler: towards automatic fingerprinting of android apps. In: 2013 Proceedings IEEE INFOCOM (2013)
27. Enck, W., et al.: Taintdroid: an information-flow tracking system for realtime privacy monitoring on smartphones. Trans. Comput. Syst. (TOCS) **32**(2), 5 (2014)
28. Feng, Y., Anand, S., Dillig, I., Aiken, A.: Apposcopy: semantics-based detection of android malware through static analysis. In: International Symposium on Foundations of Software Engineering (FSE) (2014)
29. Feurer, M., Eggensperger, K., Falkner, S., Lindauer, M., Hutter, F.: Practical automated machine learning for the AUTOML challenge 2018. In: International Workshop on Automatic Machine Learning at ICML (2018)
30. Feurer, M., Klein, A., Eggensperger, K., Springenberg, J.T., Blum, M., Hutter, F.: Auto-sklearn: efficient and robust automated machine learning. In: Hutter, F., Kotthoff, L., Vanschoren, J. (eds.) Automated Machine Learning. TSSCML, pp. 113–134. Springer, Cham (2019). https://doi.org/10.1007/978-3-030-05318-5_6
31. Fogla, P., Sharif, M.I., Perdisci, R., Kolesnikov, O.M., Lee, W.: Polymorphic blending attacks. In: USENIX Security Symposium (2006)
32. Grace, M., Zhou, Y., Zhang, Q., Zou, H., Jiang, X.: Riskranker: scalable and accurate zero-day android malware detection. In: International Conference on Mobile Systems, Applications, and Services (MobiSys) (2012)
33. Hou, S., Saas, A., Chen, L., Ye, Y.: Deep4maldroid: a deep learning framework for android malware detection based on Linux kernel system call graphs. In: International Conference on Web Intelligence Workshops (WIW) (2016)
34. Kotthoff, L., Thornton, C., Hoos, H.H., Hutter, F., Leyton-Brown, K.: Auto-weka 2.0: automatic model selection and hyperparameter optimization in Weka. J. Mach. Learn. Res. **18**, 826–830 (2017)

35. Li, L., et al.: Static analysis of android apps: a systematic literature review. Inf. Software Technol. **88**, 67–95 (2017)
36. Li, L., Jamieson, K., DeSalvo, G., Rostamizadeh, A., Talwalkar, A.: Hyperband: a novel bandit-based approach to hyperparameter optimization. J. Mach. Learn. Res. **18**(1), 6765–6816 (2017)
37. Lin, S.W., Ying, K.C., Chen, S.C., Lee, Z.J.: Particle swarm optimization for parameter determination and feature selection of support vector machines. Expert Syst. Appl. **35**(4), 1817–1824 (2008)
38. Lu, L., Li, Z., Wu, Z., Lee, W., Jiang, G.: Chex: statically vetting android apps for component hijacking vulnerabilities. In: Conference on Computer and Communications Security (CCS) (2012)
39. Mariconti, E., Onwuzurike, L., Andriotis, P., De Cristofaro, E., Ross, G., Stringhini, G.: Mamadroid: detecting android malware by building Markov chains of behavioral models. In: Annual Network and Distributed System Security Symposium (NDSS) (2017)
40. Miller, B., et al.: Reviewer integration and performance measurement for malware detection. In: Caballero, J., Zurutuza, U., Rodríguez, R.J. (eds.) DIMVA 2016. LNCS, vol. 9721, pp. 122–141. Springer, Cham (2016). https://doi.org/10.1007/978-3-319-40667-1_7
41. Pedregosa, F., et al.: Scikit-learn: machine learning in python. J. Mach. Learn. Res. **12**, 2825–2830 (2011)
42. Peiravian, N., Zhu, X.: Machine learning for android malware detection using permission and API calls. In: International Conference on Tools with Artificial Intelligence (2013)
43. Pendlebury, F., Pierazzi, F., Jordaney, R., Kinder, J., Cavallaro, L.: Tesseract: eliminating experimental bias in malware classification across space and time. In: USENIX Security Symposium (2019)
44. Petsas, T., Voyatzis, G., Athanasopoulos, E., Polychronakis, M., Ioannidis, S.: Rage against the virtual machine: hindering dynamic analysis of android malware. In: Proceedings of the Seventh European Workshop on System Security (2014)
45. Preda, M.D., Christodorescu, M., Jha, S., Debray, S.: A semantics-based approach to malware detection. ACM Trans. Program. Lang. Syst. (TOPLAS) **30**(5), 1–54 (2008)
46. Probst, P., Bischl, B., Boulesteix, A.L.: Tunability: importance of hyperparameters of machine learning algorithms. arXiv preprint arXiv:1802.09596 (2018)
47. Rasthofer, S., Arzt, S., Lovat, E., Bodden, E.: Droidforce: enforcing complex, data-centric, system-wide policies in android. In: International Conference on Availability, Reliability and Security (2014)
48. Rastogi, V., Chen, Y., Jiang, X.: Droidchameleon: evaluating android anti-malware against transformation attacks. In: Symposium on Information, Computer and Communications Security - ASIA CCS 2013 (2013)
49. Saracino, A., Sgandurra, D., Dini, G., Martinelli, F.: Madam: effective and efficient behavior-based android malware detection and prevention. Trans. Depend. Secur. Comput. **15**(1), 83–97 (2016)
50. Shabtai, A., Kanonov, U., Elovici, Y., Glezer, C., Weiss, Y.: "andromaly": a behavioral malware detection framework for android devices. J. Intell. Inf. Syst. **38**(1), 161–190 (2012)
51. Sun, M., Wei, T., Lui, J.C.: Taintart: a practical multi-level information-flow tracking system for android runtime. In: Conference on Computer and Communications Security (CCS) (2016)

52. Tsai, J.T., Chou, J.H., Liu, T.K.: Tuning the structure and parameters of a neural network by using hybrid Taguchi-genetic algorithm. Trans. Neural Netw. **17**(1), 69–80 (2006)
53. Zhang, M., Duan, Y., Yin, H., Zhao, Z.: Semantics-aware android malware classification using weighted contextual API dependency graphs. In: Conference on Computer and Communications Security (SIGSAC) (2014)

Distributed Algorithms

A Resource Usage Efficient Distributed Allocation Algorithm for 5G Service Function Chains

Guillaume Fraysse[1,2]($\boxtimes$) ⓘ, Jonathan Lejeune[2] ⓘ, Julien Sopena[2], and Pierre Sens[2] ⓘ

[1] Orange, Paris, France
guillaume.fraysse@orange.com
[2] Sorbonne Université, CNRS, Inria, LIP6, 75005 Paris, France
{jonathan.lejeune,julien.sopena,pierre.sens}@lip6.fr

Abstract. Recent evolution of networks introduce new challenges for the allocation of resources. Slicing in 5G networks allows multiple users to share a common infrastructure and the chaining of Network Function (NFs) introduces constraints on the order in which NFs are allocated. We first model the allocation of resources for Chains of NFs in 5G Slices. Then we introduce a distributed mutual exclusion algorithm to address the problem of the allocation of resources. We show with selected metrics that choosing an order of allocation of the resources that differs from the order in which resources are used can give better performances. We then show experimental results where we improve the usage rate of resources by more than 20% compared to the baseline algorithm in some cases. The experiments run on our own simulator based on SimGrid.

Keywords: Computer network management · Distributed algorithms · Network slicing · Distributed systems · k-mutex · Drinking philosophers · Deadlock

1 Introduction

The flexibility of 5G networks allows the apparition of new services. Complex services rely on Slices split across multiple Network Service Provider (NSP)s. The allocation of a service is now not only the allocation of a single Network Function (NF) but the chaining of multiple NFs. Chains of NFs introduce a constraint on the order of the allocation.

We argue that in such use cases the system can be modeled as a distributed system. The various NFs from the different NSPs can be abstracted as **resources**. One or more **instances** of these resources can be available for each of these resources. We define the allocation of a chain of NFs as a **request** of a **set of resources** with an associated **request order**. The allocation of a request means allocating all the resources in the set while respecting this request order.

A. Remke and V. Schiavoni (Eds.): DAIS 2020, LNCS 12135, pp. 169–185, 2020.
https://doi.org/10.1007/978-3-030-50323-9_11

In distributed systems, allocation of resources is seen as a **Mutual Exclusion** problem. Several variants of the problem have been defined considering a single resource [14,27] or multiple instances of a single type of resource [25,26]. Very few solutions have been proposed for the problem of Mutual Exclusion for systems with multiple instances of multiple resources [2,15].

We propose here a distributed algorithm to solve the problem of the allocation of resources to create chains of NFs in 5G Slices for Multi-Domain use cases. We address this as a distributed Mutual Exclusion problem. We show that for systems with multiple instances of resources the selection of the instances to allocate has an influence on performances. Our algorithm extends the LASS algorithm [15] for systems with N instances of M resources. We introduce a subroutine to select the instance of the resource based on the orders of the requests as the LASS algorithm does not address this constraint. The algorithm is based on the transmission of a token that contains the permissions to use the resources. In a Network Functions Virtualization (NFV) network the resources are the nodes themselves, and they can't be transferred from one node to another. In such system each node is the manager of its own resource. We propose an extension to manage systems where the decisions to allocate the resources are made locally by each node.

We introduce a broader description of these use cases as well as some related work and background in Sect. 2. We describe our problem in Sect. 3. In Sect. 4 we introduce our algorithm, and define the allocation order as distinct from the order in the requests. We then introduce the methodology used to evaluate the algorithm with the SimGrid [3] simulator and show the experimental results in Sect. 5. We finally present our conclusions and future works in Sect. 6.

2   Related Work

The architecture of Telecom Networks is rapidly evolving. Operators have launched the NFV [10] initiative at the European Telecommunications Standards Institute (ETSI) to move the NFs from dedicated hardware to virtualized infrastructures based on Cloud and Software-Defined Networking (SDN) technologies.

Allocation of a single NF is rarely sufficient. More complex services require multiple NFs to inter-operate while respecting an order. To this end ETSI defined the **VNF Forwarding Graph (VNF FG)s** [9] as the analogue to the connection of physical appliances with cables. Following the description of the VNF FG use case in 2013, RFC7665 [22] introduced in 2015 Service Function Chaining (SFC) to allow the allocation of a chain of NFs. In 2017, RFC8402 [23] introduced Segment Routing to allow a node to send a list of instructions to be run by subsequent nodes. problem of resources allocation for multiple NFs in the correct order.

5G is the first generation of mobile networks to include NFV as an enabler for new types of services. 3GPP has introduced **Network Slices** [28,29] that enables multiple virtual end-to-end networks to share the same NFV infrastructures.

A service offered by a Slice can rely on the infrastructures of multiple NSPs, it is then called **Multi-Domain**. This can be the case when a large operator has split its network in multiple subdomains (e.g. datacenters) or when a use case may require the infrastructures of multiple operators. The European 5G Public Private Partnership (5G PPP) initiative launched projects that defined several use cases based on Slices and Multi-Domain. The SLICENET project's eHealth use case [29] requires multiple NSPs to provide Slices that are chained together to provide the service.

Multiple centralized solutions exist for the allocation of resources such as Virtual Network Function (VNF) in networks or the placement of Virtual Machines in Cloud infrastructure [11, 20, 24, 31]. These approaches focus on finding an optimal placement depending on a set of constraints. Some papers focus on finding heuristics to respect Service Level Agreement (SLA)s [17] or security rules [12]. These problems are mostly addressed with Integer Linear Programming (ILP) formulations. This centralized method may not be adequate for Multi-Domain use cases when it is not be possible to have a centralized manager or when the cost of building a global view of the system has a high cost. A centralized method also often requires an a priori knowledge of the requests.

We propose to address such systems as distributed systems, and propose a solution where there is no centralized manager. In such systems resources all execute the algorithms locally and get (resp. send) information from (resp. to) other resources by the passing of messages.

The allocation of resources in distributed systems can be handled as a Mutual Exclusion problem on these resources. The Mutual Exclusion is a fundamental problem in distributed systems and was first described by E. W. Dijkstra in 1965 [7] for systems where multiple processes try to allocate concurrently a single shared resource. Allocating this resource allows them to execute a portion of code known as **Critical Section (CS)** allowing processes to use the resource exclusively. Multiple solutions [14, 21, 27, 30] have been proposed.

The mutual exclusion problem was later generalized in two ways:

- for systems with **one instance of** M **resources** known as the dining philosophers problem, when the requests are static, and **drinking philosophers problem**, when the requests are dynamic. It was defined by K. M. Chandy and J. Misra in 1984 [4].
- for systems with k **instances of a single resource**, known as the k-mutex problem [25]. A variant of this problem is known as the k-out of-M resources allocation problem [26] when one process tries to allocate multiple instances of a single type of resource.

Algorithms to solve drinking philosophers problems, need to address potential **conflicts** between two requests. A conflict occurs when two requests try to allocate a common resource. If two requests don't conflict, they are allowed to enter their CS simultaneously.

The Dining/Drinking philosophers problem was generalized in 1990 by Awerbuch and Saks [1] as the *Dynamic Job Scheduling problem* where processes require resources that can be used by a single process at a time. A job can only be executed when all its required resources are available for exclusive use by the process. The problem is also related to the *job-shop* scheduling optimization problem, in which n jobs have to be scheduled on m machines with the shortest-length schedule. This problem is NP-hard [16].

Algorithms addressing the mutual exclusion for systems with M resources can be divided into two groups: **incremental** algorithms and **simultaneous** algorithms. Algorithms in the first group incrementally allocate resources according to a static total order on the resources. They are using consecutive mutexes on each of the M resources. E. W. Dijkstra's algorithm from this group [6] is the baseline algorithm for our comparison and is detailed in Sect. 5.2. Algorithms in the second group do not set a predefined total order on the resources but try to simultaneously allocate resources for multiple requests. To achieve this multiple mechanisms have been proposed. Some require a knowledge of the conflict graph [4,8]. Others rely on a broadcast mechanism with high messages complexity [18] or a global lock that is not efficient when the concurrency of requests is high [2]. All the simultaneous algorithms have in common to build a total order of the requests to schedule them.

Finally, it is possible to extend drinking philosopher and k-mutex problems by considering systems with N instances of M types of resources and requests for k instances of 1 or more types, we call it *the $k - M - N$ problem*.

In a system with N instances of M resources, it is necessary to decide which instance to allocate for a given request. Once an instance has been selected, we have a simplification of the $k - M - N$ problem to the drinking philosophers problem, where each instance is uniquely identified by its location. To the best of our knowledge this problem has not been specifically addressed. Some papers address the drinking philosophers problems and mentioned possible extension of their algorithms to systems with N instances [2,15] but did not consider the selection of the instances as a specific constraint.

Algorithms from the state of the art don't consider the latency of the network links. They also do not address that the nodes selected for a chain of NFs need to respect a specific request order. In our model we add a weight to the edges of the graph to take this latency into consideration and be able to compute a path that respects the order in which resources are used. They also do not take into consideration that network links are not First In First Out (FIFO) channels. Our algorithm makes no assumption on the order in which messages are received.

The LASS algorithm [15] is a simultaneous algorithm that addresses systems with a single instance of M resources. It has been shown that its performance are better than those of incremental algorithms. It builds **allocation vectors** for all requests. These vectors are then used to compute a total order on requests, as detailed in Sect. 3. Our algorithm extends it and includes a preemption mechanism that is used when messages are received in an order that is different from the total order of the requests.

3   Problem Statement

The allocation of resources for VNF Forwarding Graph (VNF FG) in Multi-Domain 5G slices is addressed as a Mutual Exclusion problem for systems with N instances of M resources. In an example of VNF FG described in [9], packets need to traverse an Intrusion Detection Systems (IDS), a Firewall (FW) and a Load-Balancer (LB). The left part of Fig. 1 shows this example with three NSPs. The figure shows the cases where there are three instances of each resource distributed across the three NSPs.

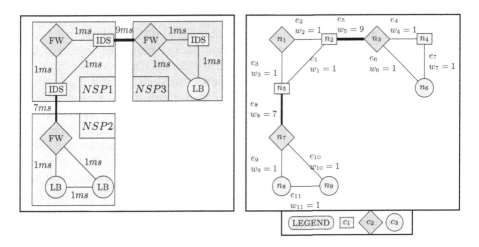

Fig. 1. A system with 3 types of resources: c_1 (IDS), c_2 (FW), and c_3 (LB)

We model our system as a non-directed connected static graph $G = (\mathcal{N}, \mathcal{E})$ where $\mathcal{N}$ is the set of **nodes** and $\mathcal{E}$ the set of **edges**. A node contains at most one resource. Edges have positive **weights** that allow to model the latency of the links between nodes. A weight of 0 on an edge allows to model a system with multiple resources on a single node. A node with 2 resources can be modeled in the graph as two nodes holding one resource each and connected by a zero-weight edge. We note $\mathcal{C}$ the set of **types of resources**.

Each node in the graph can issue an allocation request. A request is modeled as a couple $Req(n, \{c_1, ..., c_s\})$here:

- n is the **requesting node**,
- $\{c_1, ..., c_s\}$ where $c_r \in \mathcal{C}, \forall r$ is an ordered set of types of resources needed. The **request order** gives the order of the resources in the request. The order of resources can be different across requests.

The right side of Fig. 1 shows a model of the use case introduced above. We pose a request $Req_1 = Req(n_1, \{c_3, c_2, c_1\})$ in this system.

n_1 is the requesting node, 3 types of resources c_1, c_2 and c_3 are requested. The request order is $c_3 \le c_2 \le c_1$, i.e. first c_3, then c_2 and finally c_1.

Our algorithm does not require a knowledge of the conflict graph like [4,8]. It requires that each node has knowledge of its neighbors and knows where to find each type of resource so that each node can send messages to others.

The first subroutine of the algorithm presented in Sect. 4 computes a **path** in the graph. A path contains all the nodes from, and including, the requesting node, to the last resource requested, respecting the request order. The path contains the nodes holding the requested resources as well as the nodes connecting those, e.g. a valid path for Req_1 is the ordered set of nodes $(n_1, n_5, n_7, n_8, n_7, n_5)$. The originating node is n_1, the first type of resource requested is c_3 and n_8 holds an instance of it. It is necessary to go through n_5 and n_7 to reach n_8 from n_1. Then n_7 and n_5 hold the two other requested resources.

A request is **satisfied** when the path contains nodes that hold all the types of resources in the correct request order and all the requested resources are allocated to it, allowing the requesting node to enter its CS.

The algorithm builds an **allocation vector** for each request. Each entry of an allocation vector is a pair $(n, value)$, called a **counter**, where $n \in \mathcal{N}$ is the node having the requested resource and $value$ is a positive integer incremented by the node upon reception of the request, as detailed in Sect. 4. It is not possible for two requests to get the same counter value for a node n in their allocation vectors. The allocation vector for request Req_r is noted $V_{Req_r} = ((n_1^r, counter_{n_1}^r), \ldots, (n_s^r, counter_{n_s}^r))$ where r is the identifier of the request and s is the size of request Req_r, e.g. a valid allocation vector for Req_1 is $V_{Req_1} = ((n_8, 3), (n_7, 2), (n_5, 4))$. The allocation vectors allow the algorithm to compute a **total order of the requests**.

To sort the requests according to the global order we define the **precedence** of a request Req as its rank in the total order. Req_i precedes Req_j if the average of the counters of the allocation vector V_{Req_i} is less than the average of the counters of the allocation vector V_{Req_j}. For instance, if we consider $Req_2 = Req(n_4, \{c_3, c_2, c_1\})$ and $Req_3 = Req(n_6, \{c_1, c_2, c_3\})$ with $V_{Req_2} = ((n_6, 3), (n_3, 3), (n_4, 1))$ and $V_{Req_3} = ((n_4, 2), (n_3, 2), (n_6, 1))$ their respective allocation vectors, Req_3 will be allocated before Req_2 since $\frac{3+3+1}{3} > \frac{2+2+1}{3}$.

If two allocation vectors have the same average value, it is necessary to add a way to break the tie. No generic method is proposed here since it can be implementation-specific, but the method used in our experimental platform is detailed in Sect. 5.3.

4   Algorithms

Our algorithm consists of two consecutive subroutines:

- the **path computation** subroutine, in which the algorithm selects the resources instances to be allocated and computes a routing path between them that respects the allocation order present in the request,
- the **allocation** subroutine in which the algorithm allocates the resources selected during the path computation subroutine.

4.1 Path Computation Subroutine

This subroutine assumes that each node of the system has some local knowledge on how to reach each type of resource. Each node keeps an up-to-date local routing table containing the name of the neighbor node that is the closest to each type of resource as well as the distance to this node. The entry in the routing table can be the node itself for the type of resource it is holding. How these routing tables are built is out of scope of this paper. The solution used in our simulation is described in Sect. 5. Table 1 gives some routing tables for the system in Fig. 1.

Table 1. Routing tables for n_1, n_5 and n_7. D is for Distance.

(a) n_1

Type	Node	D
c_1	n_2	1
c_2	n_1	0
c_3	n_5	9

(b) n_5

Type	Node	D
c_1	n_5	0
c_2	n_1	1
c_3	n_8	8

(c) n_7

Type	Node	D
c_1	n_5	7
c_2	n_7	0
c_3	n_7	1

In this example, node n_1's shortest path to the type of resource c_3 is of length 9 and starts at n_5: (n_1, n_5, n_7, n_8), and node n_5's shortest path to the type of resource c_3 is of length 8 and starts at n_7: (n_5, n_7, n_8).

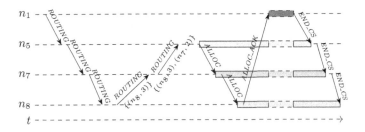

Fig. 2. Algorithm execution for Req_1

Path computation relies on the *ROUTING* message. A first *ROUTING* message is sent by the requesting node to the node holding the first resource requested, according to its routing table. This node then sends a *ROUTING* message to the next node on the path to the node holding the next resource. The operation is repeated on each node until a complete path with all the requested resources in the correct order has been found. Figure 2 shows the messages sent during the execution of the algorithm in the sample system.

This subroutine computes a valid path with the selected instances of all the requested resources in the order given in the request. It does not check that the resources are available nor does it guarantee that the path computed is the shortest path containing all the resources.

Once the algorithm has reached the node holding the last resource requested, the allocation subroutine described below starts from the last node of the path.

Building the Allocation Vector. We compute a total order of the requests to preserve the **liveness** property, i.e. it guarantees that all requests are satisfied in a finite time. We use the method from the LASS algorithm to compute this order based on vectors build for each request.

The first step is to build the allocation vector for the request. The vector is built by each of the node on the computed path. Each node has a local counter that is initialized to 0. This counter acts as a logical clock, but contrary to Lamport's logical clocks [14] it is local and only incremented by the node when it receives a new request. As such it is then not possible for two requests to get the same counter value for a node in their allocation vector. The first request receives the value 1, the second receives the value 2, and so on. Upon reception of a request a node increments its local counter. It then updates the allocation vector with the value of its counter. The updated allocation vector is inserted in the request message when it is forwarded to the next node in the path. As a simplification this has been merged in our implementation with the *ROUTING* messages. Thus, the allocation vector is built during the forwarding of the *ROUTING* messages as shown in Fig. 2.

4.2   The Allocation Subroutine

The allocation subroutine allocates the instances of resources selected during the path computation subroutine. Nodes receive allocations messages in an arbitrary order, and it can be completely different from the order computed on the requests. To deal with this situation, the subroutine has a preemption mechanism to enforce the total order of the requests. Simulations show that the **allocation order** within a request has a strong impact on the performance of the algorithm, we compare here two allocation orders. All this is detailed below.

The Allocation. The core of the allocation subroutine is based on the *ALLOC* messages. In a system where all the resources are initially in the **IDLE** state, this message is sent to the first node in the *allocation order*, detailed below. This node enters the **ALLOCATED** state and sends an *ALLOC* message to the next node. The operation is then repeated until the last node in the *allocation order* is reached. Then the last node send an *ALLOC_ACK* message to the requesting node to inform it that the allocation of all resources has been made. It then enters its CS and starts using the resources. Upon leaving its CS it sends a *END_CS* message that is forwarded along the path to all the nodes holding the requested resources. The messages sent for the allocation of Req_1 are shown on Fig. 2.

The Allocation Order. Each request has an associated partial **request order** for the resources within the request, i.e. the order in which the resources are used, cf. Sect. 3. We define the **allocation order** as the order used by the algorithm to allocate the resources. There is no relation between the request order and the allocation order and they can be different for a same request. As a mean of comparison, we introduce two different allocation orders that are then evaluated in Sect. 5.

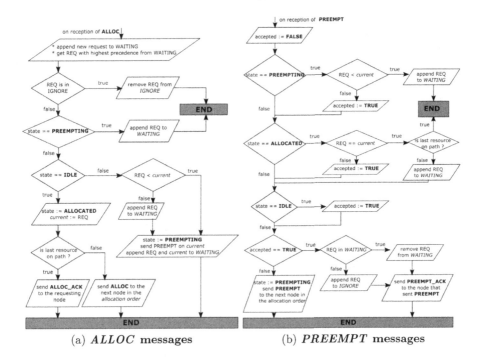

(a) *ALLOC* messages   (b) *PREEMPT* messages

Fig. 3. State diagrams for *ALLOC* and *PREEMPT* messages

The **by values** allocation order sends the *ALLOC* messages according to the values of the counters in the allocation vector. The last node of the path sends a *ROUTING_ACK* message to the requesting node. Upon reception of this message the requesting node sends an *ALLOC* message to the node with the highest counter value in the allocation vector. The allocation then follows the order of the counters in the allocation vector. As an allocation based on this order starts by allocating the node with the highest counter value, it reduces the probability that requests with higher precedence will arrive during the rest of the allocation of the request.

The **reverse order** allocation order sends the *ALLOC* messages in the reverse order of the routing path. The first subroutine follows the path as it selects it. With this *reverse order*, the allocation follows the path backwards to go back to the requesting node.

For Req_1 with the computed path $(n_1, n_5, n_7, n_8, n_7, n_5)$ if the allocation vector is $V_{Req_1} = ((n_8, 3), (n_7, 2), (n_5, 4))$, the allocation for *reverse order* follows the order n_5, n_7, n_8. For *by values* the order is n_5, n_8, n_7.

Preemption of Resources. Since the system is distributed a request can arrive on a node already in the **ALLOCATED** state for a request that has a lower precedence. This can lead to deadlocks. To manage these situations the algorithm preempts the resources to enforce the global order on the requests. This requires an additional state for the nodes, **PREEMPTING**, and two additional messages: *PREEMPT* and *PREEMPT_ACK* . The state diagram in Fig. 3a shows how *ALLOC* messages are handled, Fig. 3b shows how *PREEMPT* messages are handled. Apart from the case where the node is **IDLE** described above there are two other cases to consider. If a node is already **PREEMPTING**, or if it is **ALLOCATED** and the new request has a lower precedence than the request that currently holds the resource, then the request is stored in a local *WAITING* queue. Otherwise, i.e., when the node is **ALLOCATED** and the new request has a higher precedence than the request that currently holds the resource, the algorithm performs a preemption of the resource on the request that currently holds it, named *current*. To perform a preemption a node sends a *PREEMPT* message to the node that received its resource, i.e., the node to which it previously sent an *ALLOC* message for *current*. If the node that received the *PREEMPT* is not the last node in the path of *current*, it continues the preemption to put *current* on hold. For this it sends a *PREEMPT* message to the next node in the *allocation order* of *current*. *current* resumes later when it becomes the request with the highest precedence in the *WAITING* queue.

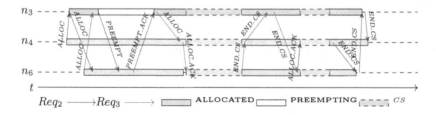

Fig. 4. Allocations for Req_2 and Req_3, preemption of n_6 by Req_2

Figure 4 shows how preemption works in the case of Req_2 and Req_3. When n_3 receives the *ALLOC* message for Req_3, it is already **ALLOCATED** because it has previously received the *ALLOC* message for Req_2. It then sends a *PREEMPT* message along the path of Req_2 to n_6. n_6 accepts the preemption, stores Req_2 in its local *WAITING* queue and sends back a *PREEMPT_ACK* message. Req_3 then sends an *ALLOC* message for its last required resource to n_4. Req_3 is now satisfied and enters its CS. When it leaves its CS, n_6 resumes Req_2.

Further Considerations on Preemptions. When a preemption occurs, the algorithm ensures that the resource is always released. Either the node that receives the *PREEMPT* message decides to release it immediately, either it waits for the current request to leave its CS. As CS have finite durations the algorithm ensures that the resource is released in finite time.

If multiple requests have a higher precedence than the one currently holding its resource, a node can receive a *PREEMPT* message when it is already **PREEMPTING**. In this case, priority is given to the request with the highest precedence.

As the communications channels are not FIFO, even if *PREEMPT* messages are sent along the same path than the *ALLOC* messages, a node may receive a *PREEMPT* before it has received the corresponding *ALLOC* . To deal with such situations, each node maintains an *IGNORE* list. When it receives a *PREEMPT* for a request and it has not yet received the corresponding *ALLOC* , it stores the request in the *IGNORE* list. When it finally receives the *ALLOC* for a request that is present in the *IGNORE* list, it ignores the *ALLOC* and removes the request from the list.

5   Experimental Results

We present an evaluation of the two allocation orders *reverse path* and *by values* of the algorithm detailed above. We compare their performance through metrics that are introduced below to Dijkstra's *Incremental* algorithm detailed in Sect. 5.2 as the baseline.

5.1   Metrics and Evaluation

Several metrics are used to compare the results of the algorithms:

- the **average usage rate** is the average time during which resources are used. It is the sum of the times during which each resource is used divided by the overall duration of the experiment for all resources. 100% means that all resources are used all the time. 50% means that 50% of the resources are used on average. The objective is to maximize this metric,
- the **average waiting time** is the average time spent by requests between the moment at which they are emitted and the moment they are satisfied. The objective is to minimize this metric,
- The **average number of messages per request** is the ratio between the total number of messages sent in the system for the duration of the test and the number of requests. The objective is to minimize this metric.

5.2   Dijkstra's *Incremental* Algorithm

The baseline algorithm for our experiments is Dijkstra's *Incremental* algorithm [6]. It does not require any additional assumption on the system which allows to evaluate it against the same systems as our algorithm described above. This algorithm is selected because it gives the best average usage rate among all the state of the art algorithms evaluated. Other algorithms are not included here for the sake of space. Our implementation of the algorithm relies on the same first subroutine described above for the selection of the path, but does not require the building of the allocation vectors. The second subroutine of the

Incremental algorithm relies on a static **global order** of the nodes. For the test system in Fig. 1, our implementation considers that the global order of nodes is $n_1 < n_2 < \ldots < n_9$ according to the subscript value.

This algorithm has a drawback we call the **domino effect**. It is possible when the number of conflicts is high that nodes wait for each other's requests to be finished. Until these resources become available all the resources from nodes that come after in the order are unavailable. The probability of occurrence of the domino effect increases with the size of the requests.

5.3   Simulating the System with SimGrid

The algorithms have been tested on topologies from the Internet Topology Zoo [13], a dataset of topologies provided by Operators. The topologies are enriched with resources distributed across their nodes. Weights are attributed to the network links between the nodes to simulate the latency. To limit the number of parameters, all experiments in this paper use the same constant weight for all the links.

The results presented here are based on the *Cesnet200706* topology which consists of $N = 44$ nodes. This topology was selected because it has a sufficient enough size to avoid the possible bias in the results from topologies that have few nodes. Larger topologies lead to longer simulation times to get similar results. In this topology, the degrees of the nodes vary from 1 to 18, with an average degree of 2.

The simulator is based on SimGrid 3.23 [3]. SimGrid provides multiple Routing Models for the routing of packets between nodes. The experiments use only the *Full* routing model. This model requires all routes to be explicitly described in the configuration file. It ensures that no routing algorithm is used to connect two nodes that are not explicitly connected by a *Link* to each other. It allows the routing of the packets to be made at the application level and thus allows to simulate the first subroutine of the algorithm.

The routing tables necessary for the first subroutine are built statically by the simulator during the initialization using Dijkstra's Shortest Path algorithm [5]. Routing tables are based on the *Link* and *Hosts* of the configuration.

The system is under maximum load during the tests. To achieve this, the simulation starts as many requests as there are nodes in the system, and a new request is sent as soon as a request ends. The contents of the requests are generated by the node following a linear random function. The size of the requests in a single experiment is constant. As shown by other experimental results not included here for sake of space, using a constant size does not affect the results significantly.

The duration of all experiments is the same. The time spent in CS by the requests is also constant. Empirically we settled for a duration of CS of $300,000$ and a duration of experiment of $500,000,000$ so that time spent in CS is orders of magnitude longer than the time spent to send a message between nodes. These durations are in simulator time unit. This approximately simulates CS of $30\,s$ and a total simulation duration of $14\,h$. Experiments show that this duration is long enough to make the impact of randomness negligible and the results representative.

In this experimental platform, if two allocation vectors have the same average value, the id of the nodes are used to break the tie. Since requests all have the same size, we first compare the id of the first nodes in each allocation vector. If it is the same node for both requests, we compare the id of second nodes and so on. It this comparison also results in a tie, when both requests are for the same nodes, then the internal identifiers of the requests are compared.

Figure 5 shows the results of the evaluation of the metrics defined in Sect. 3 for the *Incremental* and the algorithm detailed in Sect. 4 using two *allocation orders* : *reverse path* and *by values* in two different system configurations detailed below. The x-axis show the size of requests for a given simulation. Both axes of all the figures use a logarithmic scale.

5.4   System with 1 Instance of M Resources

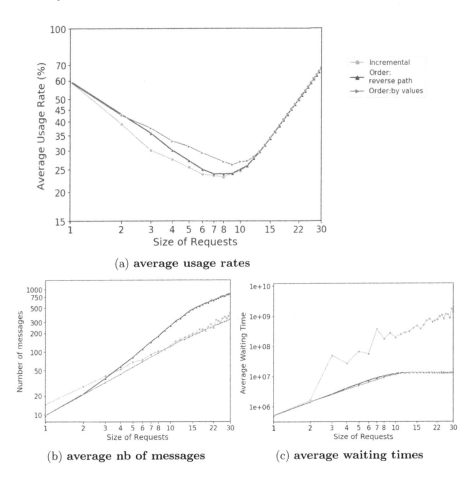

(a) **average usage rates**

(b) **average nb of messages**

(c) **average waiting times**

Fig. 5. Evaluation for one instance of 44 types of resources

This section shows the evaluation on a system with one instance of $C = 44$ types of resources.

For requests of size 1, Figs. 5a and 5b show that the algorithm itself has no influence on the *Average Usage Rate* or the *Average Waiting Time*. In such configuration, no preemption is performed.

For requests of size 2 to 7, we can observe that *Average Usage Rate* decreases for all the algorithms. We reach a minimum between 7 and 9 depending on the algorithms. This can be deduced from Maekawa's proof of his quorum algorithm [19], based on Finite Projective Planes properties, that $\sqrt{N} \approx 6.63$ is the minimum size so that all requests have at least one intersection. Usage rate rises up again after this lowest point because requests become larger and even if there are more conflicts between requests, each request leads to the allocation of a larger number of resources.

If the size of requests is greater than half the size of the system, then it is not possible to allocate concurrently two requests. In such situations the only possibility is to allocate the requests sequentially. The *Average Usage Rate* of the system then grows linearly with the size of the requests. The figure has been truncated at size 30 for the sake of readability. It is almost 100% for requests of size N as each consecutive request allocates all the resources. It is not exactly 100% due to the cost of the algorithm.

Our algorithms show an improvement on the *Incremental* of the *Average Usage Rate* with both allocation orders. The *by values* allocation order gives the best results for all metrics. For the *Average Usage Rate* we can see improvement of up to 20% from the *Incremental*. As shown in Fig. 5b, *by values* does not generate more messages than the *Incremental* whereas *reverse path* shows a larger number of messages for requests of size 4 and more. This is due to the high number of preemptions taking place. The *by values* order limits the number of preemptions by starting with the node that has the highest counter value. This node is the most likely to receive requests with a higher precedence. Once its resource is allocated, the probability that the other nodes are preempted by requests with higher precedence gets lower. Experimental results show in Fig. 5c that the *by values* order does not impact negatively the *Average Waiting Time*. The *Average Waiting Time* for the *Incremental* algorithm is significantly worse than for any of the variants. This is due to the domino effect. For the sake of space a full comparison with a near-optimal allocation is not included here, but results show that even the best results included here are 10 to 20 points lower than a near-optimal solution until requests of size 11, after which the difference starts to decrease.

5.5   System with N Instances of M Resources

Figure 6 shows the *Average Usage Rate* of the same algorithms on the same topology but with a different placement of the resources. Instead of a single instance of each resource, the system holds 4 instances for each of $C = 11$ different types. The figure includes three additional algorithms. Each of this additional algorithm is a variant of one of the three presented above: it uses the same *allocation subroutine* but a different *path computation subroutine*. As the *path computation subroutine* detailed in Sect. 4.1 uses a static routing table, a node always selects the same node for a type of resource. The result is that the load is not well balanced across all the instances, which leads to lower *Average Usage Rate*. For requests of size 4, the lowest *Average Usage Rate* observed, the algorithm with the best result, the *by values*, reaches around 17%. This is lower than the worst result for the configuration with a single instance of M resources in Fig. 5a where the *Incremental* reaches 27%.

As shown in the three additional algorithms, the load balancing improves with a simple round-robin on the different instances of each type of resource during the *path computation subroutine*. For example with 4 instances of c_1, the first request selects the first instance, the second request the second one, and so on. It starts over with the fifth request that selects the first one. The selection of the route has a significant impact when there are more than one instance of the resources and improves the *Average Usage Rate*.

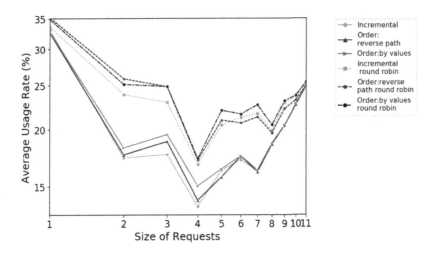

Fig. 6. Evaluation for 4 instances of 11 types of resources

6 Conclusion and Future Works

We introduced in this paper a new algorithm for distributed Mutual Exclusion for systems with N instances of M resources, known as the $k - M - N$ problem. This is applicable to the allocation of Multi-Domain Chains of NFs in 5G Slices. We show an improvement of up to 20% of the *Average Usage Rate* of resources from the baseline *Incremental* algorithm, with an *Average Waiting Time* that can be several orders of magnitude lower and no degradation of the number of messages. The results show the impact of the **allocation order** in which allocation is performed. The presented results focus on a few key parameters.

For the *path allocation subroutine* of the algorithm, the results showed the importance of the selection of the instance when $N > 1$. We plan to study how the performance can be further improved.

Our approach to the allocation of resources in the *allocation subroutine* is pessimistic, i.e., it considers that deadlocks are going to happen. But their probability of occurrence can be low in some situations. We plan to study an optimistic approach that let deadlocks occur and fix them a posteriori.

We also plan to implement the algorithm in the scheduler of a NFV platform, if possible in the live network of an Operator.

References

1. Awerbuch, B., Saks, M.: A dining philosophers algorithm with polynomial response time. In: Proceedings [1990] 31st Annual Symposium on Foundations of Computer Science, vol. 1, pp. 65–74 (1990)
2. Bouabdallah, A., Laforest, C.: A Distributed Token-Based Algorithm for the Dynamic Resource Allocation Problem. SIGOPS Oper. Syst. Rev. **34**(3), 60–68 (2000)
3. Casanova, H., et al.: Versatile, scalable, and accurate simulation of distributed applications and platforms. J. Parallel Distrib. Comput. **74**(10), 2899–2917 (2014)
4. Chandy, K.M., Misra, J.: The drinking philosophers problem. ACM Trans. Program. Lang. Syst. **6**(4), 632–646 (1984)
5. Dijkstra, E.W.: A note on two problems in connexion with graphs. Numer. Math. **1**(1), 269–271 (1959)
6. Dijkstra, E.W.: Hierarchical ordering of sequential processes. Acta Informatica **1**(2), 115–138 (1971)
7. Dijkstra, E.W.: Solution of a problem in concurrent programming control. Commun. ACM **8**(9), 569 (1965)
8. Ginat, D., Shankar, A.U., Agrawala, A.K.: An efficient solution to the drinking philosophers problem and its extensions. In: Bermond, J.-C., Raynal, M. (eds.) WDAG 1989. LNCS, vol. 392, pp. 83–93. Springer, Heidelberg (1989). https://doi.org/10.1007/3-540-51687-5_34
9. ETSI NFV ISG. ETSI GS NFV 001: Network Functions Virtualisation (NFV) Use Cases (2013). https://www.etsi.org/deliver/etsi_gs/NFV/001_099/001/01.01.01_60/gs_NFV001v010101p.pdf
10. ETSI NFV ISG. ETSI GS NFV-MAN 001 V1.1.1 Network Functions Virtualisation (NFV); Management and Orchestration (2014)
11. Jennings, B., Stadler, R.: Resource management in clouds: survey and research challenges. J. Netw. Syst. Manage. **23**(3), 567–619 (2014). https://doi.org/10.1007/s10922-014-9307-7
12. Jhawar, R., et al.: Supporting security requirements for resource management in cloud computing. In: 2012 IEEE 15th International Conference on Computational Science and Engineering, pp. 170–177 (2012)
13. Knight, S., et al.: The internet topology zoo. IEEE J. Sel. Areas Commun. **29**(9), 1765–1775 (2011)
14. Lamport, L.: Time, clocks, and the ordering of events in a distributed system. Commun. ACM **21**(7), 558–565 (1978)

15. Lejeune, J., et al.: Reducing synchronization cost in distributed multi- resource allocation problem. In: 2015 44th International Conference on Parallel Processing, pp. 540–549 (2015)
16. Garey, M.R., et al.: The complexity of flowshop and jobshop scheduling - mathematics of operations research (1976). https://pubsonline.informs.org/doi/abs/10.1287/moor.1.2.117
17. Machida, F., et al.: Redundant virtual machine placement for fault-tolerant consolidated server clusters. In: 2010 IEEE Network Operations and Management Symposium - NOMS 2010, pp. 32–39 (2010)
18. Maddi, A.: Token based solutions to m resources allocation problem. In: Proceedings of the 1997 ACM Symposium on Applied Computing. SAC 1997, pp. 340–344. ACM, New York (1997)
19. Maekawa, M.: A N algorithm for mutual exclusion in decentralized systems. ACM Trans. Comput. Syst. 3(2), 145–159 (1985)
20. Mills, K., et al.: Comparing VM-placement algorithms for on-demand clouds. In: 2011 IEEE Third International Conference on Cloud Computing Technology and Science, pp. 91–98 (2011)
21. Naimi, M., et al.: A log (N) distributed mutual exclusion algorithm based on path reversal. J. Parallel Distrib. Comput. 34(1), 1–13 (1996)
22. Pignataro, C., Halpern, J.: Service Function Chaining (SFC) Architecture (2015). https://tools.ietf.org/html/rfc7665
23. Previdi, S., et al.: Segment Routing Architecture (2018). https://tools.ietf.org/html/rfc8402
24. Rai, A., et al.: Generalized resource allocation for the cloud. In: Proceedings of the Third ACM Symposium on Cloud Computing, SoCC 2012, pp. 15:1–15:12. ACM, New York (2012)
25. Raymond, K.: A tree-based algorithm for distributed mutual exclusion. ACM Trans. Comput. Syst. 7(1), 61–77 (1989)
26. Raynal, M.: A distributed solution to the k-out of-M resources allocation problem. In: Dehne, F., Fiala, F., Koczkodaj, W.W. (eds.) ICCI 1991. LNCS, vol. 497, pp. 599–609. Springer, Heidelberg (1991). https://doi.org/10.1007/3-540-54029-6_209
27. Ricart, G., Agrawala, A.K.: An optimal algorithm for mutual exclusion in computer networks. Commun. ACM 24(1), 9–17 (1981)
28. Rost, P., et al.: Network slicing to enable scalability and flexibility in 5G mobile networks. IEEE Commun. Mag. 55(5), 72–79 (2017)
29. SLICENET. Deliverables - SLICENET (2018). https://slicenet.eu/deliverables/
30. Suzuki, I., Kasami, T.: A distributed mutual exclusion algorithm. ACM Trans. Comput. Syst. 3(4), 344–349 (1985)
31. Widjajarto, A., et al.: Cloud computing reference model: the modelling of service availability based on application profile and resource allocation. In: 2012 International Conference on Cloud Computing and Social Networking (ICCCSN), pp. 1–4 (2012)

A Self-stabilizing One-To-Many Node Disjoint Paths Routing Algorithm in Star Networks

Rachid Hadid[(✉)] and Vincent Villain[(✉)]

MIS, Université de Picardie Jules Vernes, 33 rue Saint Leu, Cedex 1, 80039 Amiens, France
hadid.rashid@gmail.com, vincent.villain@u-picardie.fr

Abstract. The purpose of the paper is to present the first self-stabilizing algorithm for finding $n-1$ *one-to-many node-disjoint* paths in *message passing* model. Two paths in a network are said to be node disjoint if they do not share any nodes except for the endpoints. Our proposed algorithm works on n-dimensional star networks S_n. Given a source node s and a set of $D = \{d_1, d_2, ..., d_{n-1}\}$ of $n-1$ destination nodes in the n-dimensional star network, our algorithm constructs $n-1$ node-disjoints paths $P_1, P_2, ..., P_{n-1}$, where P_i is a path from s to $d_i, 1 \leq i \leq n-1$. Since the proposed solution is self-stabilizing [7], it does not require initialization and withstands transient faults. The stabilization time of our algorithm is $O(n^2)$ rounds.

Keywords: Fault-tolerance · Self-stabilization · Distributed systems · Star networks · Node disjoint paths

1 Introduction

The concept of *self-stabilization* [7] is the most general technique to design a system to tolerate arbitrary transient (in other words, limited in time) faults. A self-stabilizing system, regardless of the initial states of the processors and initial messages in the links, is guaranteed to converge to the intended behaviour in finite time. We view a fault that perturbs the state of the system but not its program as a transient fault. The problem of finding disjoint paths in a network has been given much attention in the literature due to its theoretical as well as practical significance to many applications, such as layout design of integrated circuits [22], communication protocols [10], secure message transmission [24], survivable design of telecommunication networks [23] and reliable routing [15]. Node disjoint paths can be used for secure communication by breaking up data into several shares and sending them along the disjoint paths to make it difficult for an adversary with bounded eavesdropping capability to intercept a transmission or tamper with it. Network survivability reflects the ability of a network to maintain service continuity during and after failures. In practice, it is important to construct node disjoint paths in networks, because they can be used to enhance the transmission reliability. Alternatively, the same crucial message can be sent over multiple node disjoint paths in a network that is prone to message losses to avoid omission failures, or information on the re-routing of traffic along non-faulty disjoint paths can be provided in the

A. Remke and V. Schiavoni (Eds.): DAIS 2020, LNCS 12135, pp. 186–203, 2020.
https://doi.org/10.1007/978-3-030-50323-9_12

presence of faults in some disjoint paths. Routing is a process of transmitting messages among nodes, and its efficiency is crucial to the performance of a network. Efficient routing can be achieved by using internally node disjoint paths, because they can be used to avoid congestion, accelerate transmission rate, and provide alternative trans- mission routes. Moreover, node disjoint paths between two processes present additional benefits such as broadening the network bandwidth and load balancing of the network by allowing communicating pair of processes to distribute the communication load on node disjoint paths without congesting communication channels in the network. There are three paradigms for the study of node disjoint paths in interconnection networks: the *one-to-one*, and the *one-to-many*, and the *many-to-many* node disjoint paths [8]. The one-to-one node disjoint paths constructs the maximum number of node dis- joint paths in the network between two given nodes, and the one-to-many node disjoint paths constructs node disjoint paths in the network from a given node to each of nodes in a given set. The one-to-many node disjoint paths problem are fundamental and exten- sively studied in graph theory. One-to-many node disjoint paths were first presented in [26] where the Information Dispersal Algorithm (IDA) was proposed on the hyper- cube. Some algorithms to find one-to-many node disjoint paths in a variety of networks are proposed in [5,6,8–10,14,17–19,21,25]. Let $G = (V, E)$ be a connected graph, where V and E represent the node set and edge set of G, respectively. Throughout this paper, we use network and graph, processor and node, and link and edge, interchange- ably. The *n-dimensional star* network (*n-star* for short) [1–3] is one of most effi- cient and popular interconnection networks because of its attractive properties, includ- ing regularity, node symmetric, small diameter, and recursive construction. The *n-star* network, denoted as $S_n = (V, E)$, is a bidirected graph consisting of $n!$ nodes, each node is identified with a distinct *permutation* of n symbols $1, 2, \ldots, n$. There is a link between any two permutations (nodes) iff one can be reached from the other by

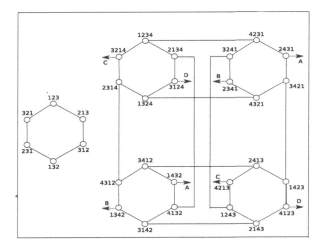

Fig. 1. An example 3-star and 4-star.

interchanging its first symbol with any other symbol. More precisely, the node representing permutation $a_1 a_2 \ldots a_{i-1} a_i a_{i+1} \ldots a_n$ have links to n-1 other permutations (nodes) $a_i a_2 \ldots a_{i-1} a_1 a_{i+1} \ldots a_n$, for some $2 \leq i \leq n$. The node with the permutation $123 \ldots n$ will be called the *identity node*. Figure 1 illustrates the 3-*star* and 4-*star* systems. The construction of the one-to-many node disjoint paths in the n-star has also been considered by researchers in graph theory [5,8,29]. The disjointness of these paths is ensured by using different approaches. In a first approach [29], we can fix a particular symbol j, $1 \leq j \leq n$, at the last position of all the nodes on the path noted P_j. So, all the nodes of the path P_j (except for at most one) have a common symbol j at the last position of their permutations. Hence, each selection of the symbol j, $1 \leq j \leq n$, will make the path P_j node disjoint from the others paths. The following example illustrates the concepts (see example 1).

Example 1. Assume that we have 4-*star* system and let $s = 1234$ and $D = \{4321, 1342, 4123, 2134\}$. We construct 4 node disjoint paths P_1, P_2, P_3 and P_4 from s to each destination process $d_1 = 4321$, $d_2 = 1342$, $d_3 = 4123$, and $d_4 = 2134$, respectively, by fixing the symbols $1, 2, 3$, and 4 at the last position of all the nodes (except for at most one) on P_1, P_2, P_3, and P_4, respectively. The node disjoint paths P_1, P_2, P_3, and P_4 may look as follows. (i) $P_1 = (s = 1234 \rightarrow, 423\underline{1} \rightarrow, 32\underline{4}1 \rightarrow, 2\underline{3}41 \rightarrow, 4\underline{3}21)$. (ii) $P_2 = (s = 1234 \rightarrow, 2\underline{1}34 \rightarrow, 413\underline{2} \rightarrow, 31\underline{4}2 \rightarrow, 1\underline{3}42)$. (iii) $P_3 = (s = 1234 \rightarrow, 32\underline{1}4 \rightarrow, 421\underline{3} \rightarrow, 2\underline{4}13 \rightarrow, 14\underline{2}3 \rightarrow, 4\underline{1}23)$. (iv) $P_4 = (s = 1234 \rightarrow, 2\underline{1}34)$. Where the underlined digit denotes the swapped one.

However, since n-star graphs are node symmetric, the position at which to fix the symbol j does not have to be the last one, as shown in [8]. The position at which we fix our symbols could be i for $2 \leq i \leq n$. Therefore, we have $n - 1$ ways of fixing the symbol j in the path noted P_i^j, where i denotes the position where the symbol j is fixed. So, for each path P_i^j is designed a unique position i, $2 \leq i \leq n$, and a distinct symbol j, $1 \leq j \leq n$, such that i is the position of the symbol j in all the permutations (except for at most one) of the nodes on the path P_i^j. We can illustrate this approach by using the following example (see example 2).

Example 2. Assume that we have 4-*star* system and let $s = 1234$ and $D = \{4321, 1342, 4123\}$. We construct 3 node disjoint paths P_2^1, P_3^2, and P_4^3 by fixing the symbols $1, 2$, and 3 at the second, third, and fourth position for each node on the path P_2^1, P_3^2, and P_4^3, respectively. (i) A path P_2^1 from s to $d_1 = 4321$ that keeps the symbol 1 at position 2 may look as follows: $P_2^1 = (s = 1234 \rightarrow, 2\underline{1}34 \rightarrow, 31\underline{2}4 \rightarrow, 1\underline{3}24 \rightarrow, 4321)$. (ii) A path P_3^2 from s to $d_2 = 1342$ that keeps the symbol 2 at position 3 may look as follows: $P_3^2 = (s = 1234 \rightarrow, 2\underline{1}34 \rightarrow, 31\underline{4}2 \rightarrow, 1\underline{3}42)$. (iii) A path P_4^3 from s to $d_3 = 4123$ that keeps the symbol 3 at position 4 may look as follows: $P_3^2 = (s = 1234 \rightarrow, 32\underline{1}4 \rightarrow, 421\underline{3} \rightarrow, 2\underline{4}13 \rightarrow, 14\underline{2}3 \rightarrow, 4\underline{1}23)$.

However, this solution can be simplified as follows [5]. We may choose to fix the same symbol j, $1 \leq j \leq n$, over all the node disjoint paths, but in different positions i for $2 \leq i \leq n$. So, for each path P_i, the same symbol j is fixed at the same position i in all processes on the path P_i, except for at most one. The following example illustrates the concepts (see example 3).

Example 3. Assume that we have 4-*star* system and let $s = 1234$ and $D = \{4321, 1342, 4123\}$. We construct 3 node disjoint paths P_2, P_3, and P_4 by fixing the symbol 1 ($j = 1$) at the second, third, and fourth position for each node on the path P_i, $2 \leq i \leq 4$, respectively, as follows. $P_2 = (s = 1234 \rightarrow, 2\underline{1}34 \rightarrow, 31\underline{2}4 \rightarrow, 1\underline{3}24 \rightarrow, 4321)$. $P_3 = (s = 1234 \rightarrow, 32\underline{1}4 \rightarrow, 2\underline{3}14 \rightarrow, 431\underline{2} \rightarrow, 1\underline{3}42)$. $P_4 = (s = 1234 \rightarrow, 423\underline{1} \rightarrow, 2\underline{4}31 \rightarrow, 34\underline{2}1 \rightarrow, 142\underline{3} \rightarrow, 4\underline{1}23)$.

Self-stabilizing algorithms to find node disjoint paths are proposed in [11,12,16,28]. Self-stabilizing algorithms for finding one-to-one node disjoint paths between two end-points for hypercube and mesh networks have been proposed in [11,28], respectively. A new self-stabilizing algorithm for finding two one-to-one node disjoint paths problem in arbitrary network was proposed in [12]. The basis of the algorithm was outlined in [16] as a brief announcement. It has been shown that finding the node disjoint paths is NP-hard in general graphs [13]. For n-dimensional hypercubes H_n (which has diameter $d(H_n) = n$), it was proved that n disjoint paths for the one-to-one node disjoint paths paradigm [27] and n disjoint paths for the one-to-many node disjoint paths paradigm [26] can be found in $O(n^2)$ time. For n-dimensional star graphs, (which has diameter $d(S_n) = \lfloor \frac{3(n-1)}{2} \rfloor$), it was shown that $n-1$ disjoint paths for one-to-one node disjoint paths paradigm can be found in $O(n^2)$ time [20] and $n-1$ disjoint paths for one-to-many node disjoint paths can be found in $O(n^2)$ time [8]. The time complexity of the above self-stabilizing algorithms is as follows: $O(d)$ rounds for algorithm [11] (working in mesh network), whereas the time complexity of the algorithms [12,16,28] is $O(d^2)$ rounds, where d the diameter of the network.

1.1 Contributions

In this paper, we present the first self-stabilizing distributed algorithm for finding $n-1$ node-disjoint paths between the source process s and $n-1$ other destination processes $\{d_1, d_2, ..., d_{n-1}\}$ in the n-star network. While it takes the same polynomiale $O(n^2)$ rounds to solve the same problem by the result in [5,8,29]. We propose a method based on message-passing techniques to process global information, which is more approach to reality. We adapt the approach used in [5] to ensure the disjointness of these $n-1$ paths. Unlike previous solutions, our algorithm does not utilize the cycle presentation of the permutations, making it easy to understand. Our approach is different from the previous one [5] in that the disjoint paths are constructed from the source s to the $n-1$ processes in the n-star. This makes our solution more suitable to implement. In addition, it reveals interesting functions to implement the disjointness of the paths in a self-stabilizing distributed environment.

The rest of the paper is organised as follows. In Sect. 2, we describe the distributed system model used in this paper. Then, we present the one to many node disjoint paths algorithm in Sect. 3 and its correctness proof in Sect. 4. Finally, we make some concluding remarks in Sect. 5.

2 Distributed System and Programs

Our algorithm is designed to operate on an *asynchronous distributed system* modelled as an *n-star network*. A *transposition* $\pi[1, i]$ on a permutation p, noted $\pi[1, i](p)$, is to exchange the positions of the first and the ith symbol in the permutation p. For example, if $p = a_1a_2...a_{i-1}a_ia_{i+1}... a_n$, then $\pi[1, i](p) = a_ia_2...a_{i-1}a_1a_{i+1}...a_n$. There is a link between any two processes p and q if and only if $\pi[1, i](p) = q$, for some $2 \leq i \leq n$. We will use a process identity (process name) in a star network to refer also to the permutation that labels the process. We consider the message-passing model where communication between neighboring processes is carried out by messages exchanged through bidirectional links, *i.e.*, each link can be seen as two channels in opposite directions. A *distributed protocol* for such a message passing system consists of a collection of n *local programs*, one for each processor in the system. This local program provides the ability to the processor either to perform local computations, or to send and receive messages from each of its neighbours in the n-star network. More precisely, the program consists of a collection of actions. Overall, an action is of the form: <*guard*>::<*statements*>. A <*guard*> is mainly triggered when an *input* message is received. In addition, tools like *timer* or *randomly* and *spontaneous* are used in the <*guard*>. <*statements*>, executed when a <*guard*> is activated, is a sequence of assignments/computations, invoking functions/procedures, and/or message sending. Note that an action can be executed only if its guard is activated. A message is of the following form: $(type, value)$. A message may also contain more than one value. We define the *state* of each process to be the state of its local memory and the contents of its incoming channels. The global state of the system, referred to as a *configuration*, is defined as the product of the states of processes. We denote by $\mathcal{C}$ the set of all possible configuration. An execution of a protocol $\mathcal{P}$ in a system $\mathcal{S}$ is an infinite sequence of configurations $\gamma_0, \gamma_1, ..., \gamma_i...$ such that in any transition $\gamma_i \mapsto \gamma_{i+1}$ either a process take a step. We assume that the message delivery time is finite but unbounded. We also consider a message in transit until it is processed by the receiving processor. Moreover, each link is assumed to be of bounded capacity, FIFO, and reliable (the messages are not lost and delivered UN-corrupted) during and after the stabilization phase.

3   Self-stabilizing Algorithm

In this section, we first present the basis description of the proposed solution. Given a process s and $n - 1$ other distinct processes $D = \{d_1, d_2, \ldots, d_{n-1}\}$ in the n-star system, the proposed algorithm constructs $n - 1$ node-disjoint paths $P_1, P_2, \ldots, P_{n-1}$, where P_h is the path from s to d_h, for $h = 1, 2, \ldots, n-1$. Note that the algorithm works also for $D = \{d_1, d_2, \ldots, d_m\}$ such that $m < n$. Our solution works in two phases referred to as *labeling phase* (Algorithm 2) and *One-To-Many node-disjoint paths construction phase* (Algorithm 4). The *One-To-Many* node-disjoint paths construction phase is based on the labeling process phase, *i.e.*, the progress of this phase is ensured only after the labeling process terminates successfully. During the labeling phase, each destination process d_h, $1 \leq h \leq n - 1$, in D should be labeled by a unique label j, $2 \leq j \leq n$, such that the index j is the reserved position for the symbol 1 for the processes on P_j connecting process s to process d_h. So, after this phase the set $D = \{d_1, d_2, \ldots, d_{n-1}\}$ is mapped to the set $DL = \{(d_1, j_1), (d_2, j_2), \ldots, (d_{n-1}, j_{n-1})\}$ where j_h, $2 \leq j_h \leq n$, is the label assigned to the process d_h, $1 \leq h \leq n - 1$.

During the $\mathcal{O}ne$-$\mathcal{T}o$-$\mathcal{M}any$ node-disjoint paths construction phase, we construct $n-1$ node-disjoint paths $P_2, P_3, \ldots, P_n$ from the source process s to the new labeled destination processes $(d_1, j_1), (d_2, j_2), \ldots, (d_{n-1}, j_{n-1})$ such that each path $P_j, 2 \leq j \leq n$, connects the source process s to a destination process $(d_h, j) \in DL$. For each path P_j, $2 \leq j \leq n$, we reserve a unique position j for the path, such that, for all processes on P_j (except for maximum two processes) the symbol 1 is at jth position in the permutations. In other words, we construct each path $P_j, 2 \leq j \leq n$, from the source process s to the destination process $(d_h, j) \in DL$ and keeps the symbol 1 in a fixed position j along all the processes on P_j, except for maximum two processes.

Prior to the presentation of these two phases in details, we first present Algorithm 1 which computes the shortest distance between the source s and a destination d (Function $\mathcal{D}ist(s, d)$). This metric is needed during the labeling phase. A shortest path P from a process s in the n-star system S_n to a destination process d is given by the following two rules [3]. Assuming that the shortest path P is built up to the process $p \neq d$ (initially, $p = s$), then the successor of p on P is identified as follows (See Function $NextNeigh()$ in Algorithm 1). Let x be the first symbol in the permutation of p, then (r_1) If there exists a symbol y in the kth position, $2 \leq k \leq n$, such that $d[k] = x$ (i.e., $Direct(p)$ is true), then exchange x with y ($d[k]$ denotes the symbol at the position k on a permutation d). In other words, x directly reaches its correct position in d.

(r_2) Otherwise, exchange x with the symbol y in the kth position such that y is not in a correct position in d, $y \neq d[k]$, if exists (i.e., $ByPass_p \neq \emptyset$). If multiple such symbols exist, then choose the symbol y with the smallest position in the permutation d. In other words, y, which is in incorrect position, is temporarily placed in the first position. Thereafter, it is moved to its correct position by applying rule (r_1). The Function $\mathcal{D}ist(s, d)$ computes in $dist$ (using Function $NextNeigh()$) the number of steps needed to built a shortest path from the source s to the destination d. The following example illustrates the distance computing between s and d in 5-star system (see example 4).

Algorithm 1. Distance Computing Algorithm

Input Source s and destination d.	**Output** The distance $\mathcal{D}ist(s, d)$ between s and d.
Function $NextNeigh(d : Process\text{-}ID) : Process\text{-}ID$	**Function** $\mathcal{D}ist(s, d : Process\text{-}ID) : Integer$
Predicate $Direct(p) \equiv (\exists k, 2 \leq k \leq n, :: (p[1] = d[k]))$	**Variables** $dist \leftarrow 0; p \leftarrow s;$
Macro $ByPass_p = \{k, 2 \leq k \leq n, :: p[k] \neq d[k]\}$	**begin**
begin	**while** $(p \neq d)$ **do**
(r_1) **if** $Direct(p)$ **then**	$q \leftarrow NextNeigh(d);$
$k \leftarrow j, 2 \leq j \leq n, :: (p[1] = d[j])$	$dist \leftarrow dist + 1;$
(r_2) **else**	$p \leftarrow q;$
$k \leftarrow min_k(ByPass_p)$	**end while**
return$(\pi(1, k)(p))$	**return**$(dist)$
end	**end**

Example 4. (i) The distance computing, using the path P created by the rules (r_1) and (r_2), from s to $d = 51243$ looks as follows: $P = (s = 12345 \; [dist = 0] \; (\xrightarrow{r_1}),$ $2\underline{1}345 \; [dist = 1] \; (\xrightarrow{r_1}), 31\underline{2}45 \; [dist = 2] \; (\xrightarrow{r_1}), 5124\underline{3} = d) \; [dist = 3]$. (ii) The distance computing between s and $d = 14523$ looks as follows. $P = (s = 12345 \; [dist = 0] \; (\xrightarrow{r_2}), 2\underline{1}345 \; [dist = 1] \; (\xrightarrow{r_1}), 413\underline{2}5 \; [dist = 2] \; (\xrightarrow{r_1}), 1\underline{4}325 \; [dist = 3] \; (\xrightarrow{r_2}),$ $34\underline{1}25 \; [dist = 4] \; (\xrightarrow{r_1}), 5412\underline{3} \; [dist = 5] \; (\xrightarrow{r_1}), 14\underline{5}23 = d) \; [dist = 6]$. Where the value in brackets indicate the value of $dist$ at a process, and the rule used to swap to the next process is indicated between parentheses on the arrow.

It is shown in [3] that this algorithm will always find the shortest path from s to d in S_n. It has been also shown in [3] that the diameter of S_n is equal to $\lceil 3(n-1)/2 \rceil$.

3.1 Labeling Process

The labeling phase is handled by the source process s (Algorithm 2 and Function $\mathcal{L}abeling()$). Let $D = \{d_1, d_2...., d_{n-1}\}$ be a set of $n-1$ distinct processes in the n-star network S_n. During this phase, each destination process d_h, $1 \leq h \leq n-1$, in the set D is labeled by a unique label j, $2 \leq j \leq n$. Thereafter, we denote by DL the set of the new labeled processes (d_h, j), $2 \leq j \leq n$. The index j, $2 \leq j \leq n$, associated to each destination d_h, refers to the unique fixed position of the symbol 1 along all the processes on the path P_j (except for maximum two processes) connecting s and d_h. Process p in the n-star network S_n is a (1)-$process$ if 1 is the first symbol in the permutation p. Process p in S_n is a (i_1)-$process$, where $2 \leq i \leq n$, if 1 is the ith symbol in the permutation p. The set DL is implemented using an array of structure where each element of the array in the position pos, $1 \leq pos \leq n-1$, contains the couple (id, lab) where id and lab represent the permutation (d_h) and the label (j) associated to the processs d_h, respectively. The labeling process is implemented by repeating the following three simple rules (L_1), (L_2), and (L_3). Note that the index pos is initiated to 1 and is increased each time a new element is added to DL.

(L_1) Let $D_i \subseteq D$ be the subset of all (i_1)-$processes$, $2 \leq i \leq n$, such that $D_i \neq \varnothing$; then, pick a process $d_h \in D_i$, $1 \leq h \leq n-1$ such that $\mathcal{D}ist(s, d_h)$ is the smallest among all the processes in D_i, label d_h by i and call (d_h, i) the $representative$ $process$ of the set D_i (see Function $Representative(D_i)$). If multiple processes have the same smallest distance, then choose the process with the smallest id number among them as representative process. Thus, for each $D_i \neq \varnothing$, the representative process (d_h, i) gets the position i. The process d_h is deleted from D and (d_h, i) is inserted into DL. So, $DL[pos].id$ and $DL[pos].lab$ are seted to d_h and i, respectively (See Procedure $Affect\text{-}label(Representative(D_i), i, pos)$.

(L_2) Then, for each process d_h in the set D such that d_h is a (i_1)-$process$, but not a representative process for a subset D_i, reserve a position j for d_h with $2 \leq j \leq n$, that is not already assigned to any process in D, then d_h is labeled by j. Similarly to (L_1), the process d_h is deleted from D and (d_h, j) is inserted into DL.

(L_3) Finally, for each d_h in the set D such that d_h is a (1)-$process$ reserve a position j for d_h with $2 \leq j \leq n$, that is not already assigned to any process in D, then d_h is labeled by j. Similarly to (L_1), the process d_h is deleted from D and (d_h, j) inserted into DL. Note that all (i_1)-$processes$ are labeled before (1)-$processes$. In order to illustrate the above concepts, we provide the following example (see example 5)

Example 5. Assume that we have 5-star system and the set $D = \{d_1, d_2, d_3, d_4\}$ such that $d_1 = 52143$, $d_2 = 43152$, $d_3 = 32541$, and $d_4 = 23451$. During this phase, each destination process d_h, $1 \leq h \leq 4$, in the set D will be labeled by a unique label j, $2 \leq j \leq 5$. So, by applying the Rule (L_1), we have $D_3 = \{d_1, d_2\}$ and

$D_5 = \{d_3, d_4\}$. The distances from s to d_1 and d_2 can be computed using Algorithm 1 and $\mathcal{D}ist(s, d_1) = 2$ and $\mathcal{D}ist(s, d_2) = 4$. So, the representative process of D_3 is d_1, and hence, the label 3 is assigned to the process d_1. Similarly, the distances from s to d_3 and d_4 are $\mathcal{D}ist(s, d_3) = 2$ and $\mathcal{D}ist(s, d_4) = 4$. So, the representative process of D_5 is d_3, and hence labeled by 5. Thus, after applying the rule (L_1), we have $D = \{d_2, d_4\}$ and $DL = [(d_1, 3), (d_3, 5)]$. Then, from the rule ($L_2$), the processes d_2 and d_4 are labeled by 2 and 4, respectively. Thus, after the labeling phase, the array structure $DL = [(d_1, 3), (d_3, 5), (d_2, 2), (d_4, 4)]$.

From the above, it is clear that all representative processes appear before all other processes in the array DL. In addition, the (i_1)-*processes* appear after the representative processes and before other remainder processes, *i.e.*, (1)-*processes*. In the sequel, we assume that all the processes in DL are identified based on their positions in the array DL. Thus, the process in the position one is denoted by d_1 and the process in the second position is denoted by d_2 and so on. For the sake of simplicity, each element (d_h, j) in DL is denoted by $d_h.j$, where d_h refers to the process at the position h, $1 \leq h \leq n-1$, and j, $2 \leq j \leq n$, is the label assigned to d_h. Moreover, we use the notation $d.j$, when the rank h of the process d in DL is omitted, to refer simply to a process d in DL indexed by a label j.

Algorithm 2. Labeling Process Algorithm

Input $D = \{d_1, d_2, ..., d_{n-1}\}$ be a set of $n-1$ distinct processes in the n-star network S_n.

Output DL is an array of structure of $n-1$ *labeled* processes in the n-star network S_n.

Struct D_s { id, lab }
Variables DL array [1,...,$n-1$] of D_s
Predicates (i_1)-Process$(p) \equiv (p[i] = 1) \wedge (i \neq 1)$
  (1)-Process$(p) \equiv (p[1] = 1)$
Function $Representative(D_i : Set) : Process\text{-}ID$
Begin
  return$(min_{id}\{p \in D_i :: \mathcal{D}ist(s, p) = min_{q \in D_i}(\{\mathcal{D}ist(s,q)\})\})$
end
Procedure $Affect\text{-}label(d, i, pos : integer)$
  Begin
    $DL[pos].id \leftarrow d; DL[pos].lab \leftarrow i;$
    $D \leftarrow D \backslash \{d\}; Labels \leftarrow Labels \backslash \{i\}$
    $pos \leftarrow pos + 1;$
  end

Function $\mathcal{L}abeling(D : (Set) \{d_1, d_2 ..., d_{n-1}\}) :$
  (Struct) DL array [1,...,$n-1$] of D_s)
Variables Set $Labels = \{2, ..., n\}$
Begin $pos \leftarrow 1$
(L_1) **for each** $i, i \in \{2, 3, ..., n\}$ **do**
    $D_i \leftarrow \{p \in D :: (i\_1)\text{-}Process(p)\}$
    if $(D_i \neq \emptyset)$ **then**
      $Affect\text{-}label(Representative(D_i), i, pos)$
    end if
  end do
(L_2) **if** $(D \neq \emptyset)$ **then**
    for each $d \in \{p \in D :: \neg(1)\text{-}Process(p) \}$ **do**
      pick up a label $l \in Labels$ **then**
        $Affect\text{-}label(d, l, pos)$
    end do
  end if
(L_3) **if** $(D \neq \emptyset)$ **then**
    for each $d \in \{p \in D :: (1)\text{-}Process(p) \}$ **do**
      pick up a label $l \in Labels$ **then**
        $Affect\text{-}label(d, l, j)$
    end do
  end if
  return(DL)
end

3.2 One-To-Many Node-Disjoint Paths Construction

Upon completion of the labeling phase, each process $d.j$ in DL is assigned a unique label j, $2 \leq j \leq n$, such that j is the position of the symbol 1 in all the permutations (except for at most two) of the processes on the path P_j connecting s to $d.j$. During this second phase, $n-1$ node-disjoint paths, noted by $P_2, P_3, ..., P_n$, are constructed from the source s to the destination processes in DL such that each path P_j, $2 \leq j \leq n$, connects the source process s to the destination process $d.j$. In order to carry out this task, we need to solve the following two problems: (i) We need a procedure that constructs a path from the process s to a destination process $d.j$, $2 \leq j \leq n$, and keeps the symbol 1 in a fixed position j along all the processes on the path P_j, except for at most one process. (ii) All these paths $P_2, P_3, ..., P_n$ must be node-disjoint.

The basic construction (property (i)) is referred to as *elementary construction* and is implemented basically using Function *NextNeighFix1*() (see Algorithm 3, namely the $\mathcal{O}ne\text{-}\mathcal{T}o\text{-}\mathcal{O}ne\ \mathcal{F}ix\text{-}1$ path construction algorithm) and the *message* (d, j) containing two parameters, the destination d and the position j of the symbol 1 in all the processes on the path P_j (see Actions a_{2_1} and a_3, Algorithm 4). Observe that, under certain circumstances (*i.e.*, a non-elementary construction), where the destination d is said to be *marked* (Function $Marked()$), Algorithm $\mathcal{O}ne\text{-}\mathcal{T}o\text{-}\mathcal{M}any$ disjoint paths uses another message containing three parameters (see Actions a_{2_2} and a_4, Algorithm 4). Now, we describe the elementary construction and the purpose of the second one (non-elementary construction) is discussed later. The processes in this construction exchange one type of message containing two parameters: destination d and the fixed position j, $2 \leq j \leq n$, of the symbol 1 along the processes on P_j. Once the elementary construction is started, the source process s initiates the construction of the path P_j from s to $d.j$ by sending the message (d, j) to its successor on P_j (Action a_{2_1}). Subsequently, each process p ($p \neq d$), upon receipt of this message, transmits the message to its successor process on the path P_j (Action a_3). Each process uses the function *NextNeighFix1*() to identify the successor process on the path P_j that kept the symbol 1 in the same fixed position j. The function $NextNeighFix1(d, j)$ contains also two parameters, the destination d and the position j of the symbol 1 in its successor process on the path P_j. This function is implemented by executing one of the following six rules: (r_0), (r_1),..., and (r_5) (see Algorithm 3 and Function $NextNeighFix1()$). The rules are executed in the order they are written. So, if the first rule is not applicable, then we try the next rule and so on. Assuming that the shortest path from s to d is built up to the process $p \neq d$ (initially, $p = s$), then the successor of p is identified as follows. Let x be the first symbol in the permutation of p, then (r_0) This rule is executed one time and only by the source process s, during the initialization phase. So, p is the identity process s (Predicate $Source(p)$), exchange the first symbol 1 with the jth symbol in s. In this rule, the symbol 1 is moved to the desired position j in the destination d.

Algorithm 3. Self-stabilizing $\mathcal{O}ne\text{-}\mathcal{T}o\text{-}\mathcal{O}ne\ \mathcal{F}ix\text{-}1$ path construction algorithm

Input   a source process s and a target process $d.j$ in the n-star network S_n.

Output   a Path connecting the processes s and $d.j$.

Function $NextNeighFix1(d : Process\text{-}ID, j \in \{2, ..., n\}) : Process\text{-}ID$

Predicate

$Source(p) \equiv (p = s)$
$DirectP(p) \equiv (|\ Place_p\ | = 1)$
$ByPass1(p) \equiv (|\ Swap_p\ | \geq 1)$
$ByPass2(p) \equiv ((|\ Diff\ | = 2) \wedge ((Diff = \{1,i\}) \vee (Diff = \{1,j\})))$
$ByPass3(p) \equiv ((|\ Diff\ | = 2) \wedge (Diff = \{i,j\}))$
$ByPass4(p) \equiv ((|\ Diff\ | = 3) \wedge (Diff = \{1,i,j\}))$

Macro

$Diff_p = \{k, 1 \leq k \leq n, :: (p[k] \neq d[k])\}$
$Place_p = \{k, 2 \leq k \leq n, :: ((p[1] = d[k]) \wedge (p[k] \neq 1))\}$
$Swap_p = \{k, 2 \leq k \leq n, :: ((p[k] \neq d[k]) \wedge (p[k] \notin \{1, d[1], d[j]\}))\}$

Function $Position\text{-}1(p : Process\text{-}ID) : Integer$

Begin

  $Return(k, 1 \leq k \leq n, :: p[k] = 1)$

end

Begin

$i \leftarrow Position\text{-}1(d)$

Case of ::

  $(r_0)\ Source(p) :: r \leftarrow j$
  $(r_1)\ DirectP(p) :: r \leftarrow k :: k \in Place_p$
  $(r_2)\ ByPass1(p) :: r \leftarrow min_k(Swap_p))$
  $(r_3)\ ByPass2(p) :: r \leftarrow k :: (k \in Diff_p \wedge k \neq 1)$
  $(r_4)\ ByPass3(p) :: r \leftarrow i$
  $(r_5)\ ByPass4(p) :: r \leftarrow j$

end Case of

$Return(\pi[1, r](p))$

end

(r_1) If there exists a symbol y, $y \neq 1$, in the kth position, $2 \leq k \leq n$, such that x occupies a correct position in d, $i.e., d[k] = x$ (Predicate $DirectP(p)$), then exchange x with y. In this rule, x directly reaches its correct position k in the destination d. However, in order to keep the symbol 1 in a fixed position, y should not be equal to 1, if possible.

(r_2) Otherwise, exchange x with the symbol y, $y \notin \{1, d[1], d[j]\}$, in the kth position such that y does not occupy a correct position in d, $i.e., d[k] \neq y$, if exists (Predicate $ByPass1(p)$). In this rule, we move x to a position k not occupied by a correct symbol, $i.e., p[k] (= y) \neq d[k]$. If multiple positions are not occupied by a correct symbol, then choose the symbol with the smallest position. Similarly to the case (r_1), to maintain the symbol 1 in a fixed position, y should not be equal to 1. In addition, to maintain the path P_j as shortest as possible, y should be different than $d[1]$ and $d[j]$.

(r_3) If all the symbols are in correct positions except the first symbol x and the symbol y in the j-th or i-th position (in this case the destination d is an (i_1)-$process$ and the i-th position is the position of the symbol 1 in d) such that $y = d[1]$ (Predicate $ByPass2(p)$), then exchange x with the symbol y. In this situation, we consider two cases. (a) First, $x = d[j]$, in this case d is a (1)-$process$. Then, exchange x with the symbol y, $y = 1$, in the jth position. (b) Second, $x = 1$, in this case d is an (i_1)-$process$. Then, exchange x with the symbol y, $y = d[1]$, in the ith position. In both cases, the successor process of p on P_j is the destination process d_i.

(r_4) If all the symbols are in correct positions except the ith symbol $p[i]$ $(= d[j])$ and the jth symbol $p[j] (= d[i] = 1)$ (Predicate $ByPass3(p)$), then exchange x, the first symbol in p, with the symbol y in the ith position.

(r_5) If all the symbols are in correct positions except the first symbol x $(x = d[j])$, the ith symbol $p[i]$ $(= d[1])$, and the jth symbol $p[j]$ $(= d[i] = 1)$ (Predicate $ByPass4(p)$), then exchange x with the symbol y, $y = 1$, in the jth position. In order to illustrate the elementary construction concept, we provide the following example with 8-star system and a destination $d.5$ (example 6).

Example 6. We consider the three following possible cases of the destination process $d.5$: $d.5$ $(= 53241876)$ is a representative process, $d.5$ $(= 13245876)$ is a (1)-$process$, and $d.5$ $(= 23145876)$ is a (i_1)-$process$ (in our case $i = 3$). A path from s to $d.5$ that keeps the symbol 1 at position 5 created by the elementary construction may look as follows. (a) Let $d.5 = 53241876$, $P_5 = (s = 12345678(\xrightarrow{r_0}), 52341678(\xrightarrow{r_2}),$ $2\underline{5}341678(\xrightarrow{r_1}), 3\underline{5}241678(\xrightarrow{r_1}), 5\underline{3}241678(\xrightarrow{r_2}), 632415\underline{7}8(\xrightarrow{r_1}), 8324157\underline{6}(\xrightarrow{r_1}),$ $5324187\underline{6})$. (b) Let $d.5 = 13245876$, $P_5 = (s = 12345678(\xrightarrow{r_1}), 52341678(\xrightarrow{r_2}),$ $2\underline{5}341678(\xrightarrow{r_1}), 3\underline{5}241678(\xrightarrow{r_1}), 5\underline{3}241678(\xrightarrow{r_2}),$ $\quad 632415\underline{7}8(\xrightarrow{r_1}), 8324157\underline{6}(\xrightarrow{r_1}),$ $532418\underline{7}6(\xrightarrow{r_3}), 13245876)$. ($c$) Let $d.5 = 23145876$, $P_5 = (s = 12345678 \ (\xrightarrow{r_0}),$ $5234\underline{1}678(\xrightarrow{r_2}), 3\underline{2}541678(\xrightarrow{r_1}), 2\underline{3}541678(\xrightarrow{r_2}), 6354\underline{1}278(\xrightarrow{r_1}), 8354\underline{1}276(\xrightarrow{r_1}),$ $2354\underline{1}876(\xrightarrow{r_4}), 53\underline{2}41876(\xrightarrow{r_5}), 1324\underline{5}876(\xrightarrow{r_3}), 23\underline{1}45876)$.

A (1)-$process$ $associated$ $with$ the process $d.j, 2 \leq j \leq n$, such that $d.j$ is an (i_1)-$process$, is the process obtained from $d.j$ by swapping its first symbol with the symbol 1 located at position i $(i.e., \pi[1, i](d.j))$.

Remark 1. From the above elementary construction we deduce the following remarks.
(i) If $d.j$ is a representative process of a set D_j, then all the processes of the path P_j

constructed from s to $d.j$ are (j_1)-*processes*, except s (see example 6 case (a)).
(ii) If $d.j$ is a (1)-*process*, then all the processes of the path P_j are (j_1)-*processes*, except the endpoints s and $d.j$ (see example 6 case (b)).
(iii) If $d.j$ is a (i_1)-*process* $(i \neq j)$, then all the processes of the path P_j are (j_1)-*processes*, except the (1)-*process associated with* the process $d.j$ and its endpoints s and $d.j$ (see example 6 case (c)).

Now, we are ready to present the remainder of the $\mathcal{O}ne$-$\mathcal{T}o$-$\mathcal{M}any$ node-disjoint paths algorithm ($i.e.$, the non-elementary construction). Observe that from Remark 1, if all the processes in DL are representative processes (j_1)-*processes* and/or (1)-*processes*, then the $\mathcal{O}ne$-$\mathcal{T}o$-$\mathcal{M}any$ node-disjoint paths algorithm is obviously obtained by applying the elementary construction from the source s to each destination process $d.j$, $2 \leq j \leq n$ in DL. Since for each destination process $d.j$, $2 \leq j \leq n$, there exists a distinct position j which is reserved for the symbol 1 for all the processes on the path P_j. So, each path P_j, $2 \leq j \leq n$, connecting s to $d.j$ is node disjoint from the other paths. This is illustrated in the following example (see example 7).

Example 7. Let us consider the set $DL = [(d_1 = 43152, 3), (d_2 = 23451, 5), (d_3 = 14352, 2), (d_4 = 15432, 4)]$, where $d_1.3$ and $d_2.5$ are representative processes, $d_3.2$ and $d_4.4$ are (1)-*processes*. The node disjoint paths are built using the elementary construction as follows. (i) $P_3 = (s = 12345 \; (\xrightarrow{r_0}), 32\underline{1}45 \; (\xrightarrow{r_1}), 2\underline{3}145 \; (\xrightarrow{r_1}), 5314\underline{2} \; (\xrightarrow{r_1}),$ $4315\underline{2})$. (ii) $P_5 = (s = 12345 \; (\xrightarrow{r_0}), 5234\underline{1} \; (\xrightarrow{r_1}), 423\underline{5}1 \; (\xrightarrow{r_1}), 32\underline{4}51 \; (\xrightarrow{r_1}),$ $2\underline{3}451)$. (iii) $P_2 = (s = 12345 \; (\xrightarrow{r_0}), 2\underline{1}345 \; (\xrightarrow{r_1}), 5134\underline{2} \; (\xrightarrow{r_1}), 413\underline{5}2 \; (\xrightarrow{r_1}),$ $1\underline{4}352)$. (iv) $P_4 = (s = 12345 \; (\xrightarrow{r_0}), 423\underline{1}5 \; (\xrightarrow{r_1}), 324\underline{1}5 \; (\xrightarrow{r_2}), 23\underline{4}15 \; (\xrightarrow{r_1}),$ $5341\underline{2} \; (\xrightarrow{r_1}), 3\underline{5}412 \; (\xrightarrow{r_1}), 154\underline{3}2)$.

A (1)-*process* associated with the (i_1)-*process* $d_h \in DL$, $2 < h \leq n$, (that is not a representative process) is said *marked process* (Function $Marked()$, Algorithm 4) if it is equal to the (1)-*process* associated with another (i_1)-*process* $d_{h'}$ such that $1 \leq h' < h$, $i.e.$, the path to the destination $d_{h'}$ is constructed before the path to the destination d_h. A critical step in applying only the elementary construction to construct the $n-1$ $\mathcal{O}ne$-$\mathcal{T}o$-$\mathcal{M}any$ node-disjoint paths is the *case* 5 (rule (r_5)) where for a given (i_1)-*process* $d_h \in DL$, $2 < h \leq n$, that is not a representative process of the set D_i, the (1)-*process* associated with d_h is *marked*. So, in this case, there already exists a destination process $d_{h'} \in DL$, $1 \leq h' < h$, such that its (1)-*process* is identical to the (1)-*process* associated with d_h. In this situation, the (1)-*process* associated with d_h already belongs to a previously constructed path, say $P_{j'}$, initiated by s to process $d_{h'}$ before s initiates the construction of the path, say P_j, to d_h. Therefore, the two paths P_j and $P_{j'}$ are not node-disjoint, since they intersect at the (1)-*process* associated with the two processes d_h and $d_{h'}$. We can illustrate this situation by using again the example 3 presented in Sect. 3.1 (example 8).

Algorithm 4. Self-stabilizing $\mathcal{O}ne$-$\mathcal{T}o$-$\mathcal{M}any$ node-disjoint paths algorithm

---

Input $D = \{d_1, d_2 \ldots, d_{n-1}\}$ be a set of $n-1$ distinct processes in the n-star network S_n.

Output $n-1$ node-disjoint paths connecting the identity process s and the processes in D.

Predicate (i_1)-$Process(t) \equiv ((\pi[1,i](t) = 1) \wedge (i \neq 1))$

Function (1)-$Process(p : Process$-$ID) : Process$-ID	**Function** $Marked(t, h)$: Boolean
Return $(\pi[1,k](p) :: 2 \leq k \leq n, p[k] = 1)$	**Return** $(\exists d_k \in D :: (2 \leq k < h) \wedge ((1)$-$Process(d_k) = t))$
end	**end**

Function $UMNeigh(t, h) : Process$-ID

$\quad$**Return** $(\pi[1,k](t) :: (2 \leq k \leq n) \wedge (\pi[1,k](t) \notin \{D, (1)$-$Process(t)\}) \wedge \neg Marked((1)$-$Process(\pi[1,k](t)), h)))$

end

For source process (identity process) $p = s$	For process $p \neq s$
Algorithm $\mathcal{O}ne$-To-$\mathcal{M}any(D : set)$	**Algorithm** $\mathcal{O}ne$-To-$\mathcal{M}any()$
Begin	**Begin**
$\bullet$ (a_1) **Spontaneously**	$\bullet$ (a_3) **Upon Receipt** (d, j)
$\quad$ $DL = \mathcal{L}abeling(D)$	$\quad$ **if** $(p \neq d)$ **then**
$\bullet$ (a_2) **Timeout**[]	$\quad\quad$ $Send(d, j)$ **to** $NextNeighFix1(d, j)$
$\quad$ **for each** process $d_h.j \in DL$ $(h = 1$ to $n-1)$ **do**	$\quad$ **end if**
(a_{2_1}) $\quad$ **if** $((i\_1)$-$Process(d_h) \Rightarrow \neg Marked(1$-$Process(d_h), h))$ **then**	$\bullet$ (a_4) **Upon Receipt** (d', d, j)
$\quad\quad$ $Send(d_h, j)$ **to** $NextNeighFix1(d_h, j)$	$\quad$ **if** $(p \neq d')$ **then**
(a_{2_2}) $\quad$ **else**	$\quad\quad$ $Send(d', d, j)$ **to** $NextNeighFix1(d', j)$
$\quad\quad$ $Send(UMNeigh(d_h, h), d_h, j)$ **to**	$\quad$ **else**
$\quad\quad\quad\quad$ $NextNeighFix1(UMNeigh(d_h, h), j)$	$\quad\quad$ $Send(d, j)$ **to** d
$\quad$ **end if**	$\quad$ **end if**
$\quad$ **end do**	**end**
end	

Example 8. Assume that we have 5-star system and let $DL = [(d_1 = 52143, 3), (d_3 = 32541, 5), (d_2 = 43152, 2), (d_4 = 23451, 4)]$. By Algorithm 4 and the elementary construction, the source s initiates the construction of the paths following this order, P_3, P_5, P_2, and P_4 (see example 3). (i) A path P_3 from s to $d_1 = 52143$ that keeps the symbol 1 at position 3 may look as follows. $P_3 = (s = 12345\ (\xrightarrow{r0}), 32\underline{1}45\ (\xrightarrow{r1}), 52\underline{1}43)$. (ii) A path P_5 from s to $d_3 = 32541$ that keeps the symbol 1 at position 5 may look as follows. $P_5 = (s = 12345\ (\xrightarrow{r0}), 5234\underline{1}\ (\xrightarrow{r1}), 325\underline{4}1)$. (iii) A path P_2 from s to $d_2 = 43152$ that keeps the symbol 1 at position 2 may look as follows. $P_2 = (s = 12345(\xrightarrow{r0}), 2\underline{1}345(\xrightarrow{r1}), 5134\underline{2}(\xrightarrow{r1}), 413\underline{5}2(\xrightarrow{r4}), 31\underline{4}52(\xrightarrow{r5}), 1\underline{3}452(\xrightarrow{r3}), 43\underline{1}52)$. (iv) A path P_4 from s to $d_4 = 23451$ that keeps the symbol 1 at position 4 may look as follows. $P_4 = (s = 12345(\xrightarrow{r0}), 423\underline{1}5(\xrightarrow{r1}), 324\underline{1}5(\xrightarrow{r1}), 2\underline{3}415(\xrightarrow{r3}), 5341\underline{2}(\xrightarrow{r5}), 134\underline{5}2\ (\xrightarrow{r3}), 234\underline{5}1)$.

Observe that, in the above example, the (1)-$process$ 13452 associated with d_4 is marked, since it is equal to the (1)-$process$ associated with d_2. So, the paths P_2 and P_4 are not node-disjoint paths. To alleviate such a problem, the following scheme is introduced in the $\mathcal{O}ne$-$\mathcal{T}o$-$\mathcal{M}any$ disjoint algorithm. During the construction of node-disjoint paths $P_2, \ldots, P_n$ (such that each path P_j, $2 \leq j \leq n$, connects the source s to the destination process $d_h.j$, $1 \leq h \leq n-1$, each time a marked process associated with a (i_1)-$process$ $d_h.j$ is identified (Function $Marked(d, h)$), the path P_j from s to d_h is constructed as follows (*i.e.*, the non-elementary construction). First, we need to identify a neighbour $d'.j$ of the process d_h such that the process $d'.j$ is not in DL and the (1)-$process$ associated with $d'.j$ is not marked. Note that each marked process is a (1)-$process$ contained in a previously constructed paths. Then, the node-disjoint path P_j from s to $d_h.j$ is constructed in the following two steps. First, the path P_j is constructed from s to $d'.j$. Then, the construction continues from $d'.j$ to $d_h.j$. This is implemented by the introduction of the message (d', d, j) containing three parameters d', d, and j. Hence, the (1)-*process* associated with $d_h.j$ is not included in the path P_j, whereas it includes the not marked (1)-*process* associated with $d'.j$. We can illustrate this approach by using again the example 8 (see example 9).

Example 9. From example 8, the paths P_2 and P_4 are not node-disjoint paths, since the 1-*process* associated with $d.2$ and $d.4$ are identical and equal to 13452. Let $d'.4 = 43251$ be the selected neighbour of the process $d.4$ and the (1)-*process* associated with $d'.4$ is 13254. Observe that $d'.4 = 43251$ is not in DL and the (1)-*process* = 13254 associated with $d'.4$ is not marked. A path from s to $d.4 = 23451$ that keeps the symbol 1 at position 4 created by the above approach may look as follows. First we create the path from s to $d'.4 = 43251$ as follows: $s = 12345 \xrightarrow{r_0} 42\underline{3}15 \xrightarrow{r_2} 2\underline{4}315 \xrightarrow{r_1} 34\underline{2}15 \xrightarrow{r_1} 43\underline{2}15 \xrightarrow{r_4} 53\underline{2}14 \xrightarrow{r_4} 13\underline{2}54 \xrightarrow{r_5} 4325\underline{1}$. Then, the construction continues from $d'.4$ to $d.4$ as follows: $4325\underline{1} \xrightarrow{r_3} 2345\underline{1}$

The One-*To*-*Many* node disjoint paths algorithm works as follows. After the labeling phase (Action a_1), each process in DL is assigned a unique label j, $2 \leq j \leq n$. The source process s initiates the construction of the $n - 1$ node-disjoint paths $P_2, P_3, \ldots, P_n$ such that each path P_j, $2 \leq j \leq n$, connects the source process s to the destination $d_h.j \in DL$, $1 \leq h \leq n - 1$ (Action a_2). Then, we need to consider two cases.

(a) In the simplest case, when the destination process $d_h.j$ is in one of the three following situations (*i.e.*, the (1)-*process* associated to d_h is not marked): either it is a representative process of a set D_i or, a (1)-*process*, an (i_1)-*process* and its associated (1)-*process* is not marked. In this case, the construction is elementary and is handled by the message (d_h, j) containing two parameters, d_h and j. So, once the source process s initiates this construction, it transmits the (d_h, j) message to its successor on the path P_j using function *NextNeighFix1*(). Analogously, when a process p ($p \neq d_h$) receives this message, it transmits the message to its successor on the path P_j. This is repeated until the destination d_h is reached. This is implemented using Actions (a_{2_1}) and (a_3). (b) However, when $d_h.j$ is an (i_1)-*process* and the (1)-*process* associated with the process $d_h.j$ is marked, then, as explained before (non elementary construction), we first identify a neighbour $d'.j$ of the process $d_h.j$ such that $d'.j$ is not in DL and the (1)-*process* associated with $d'.j$ is not marked. This is implemented using Function *UMNeigh*(). In this case, the construction is handled by using the message (d', d_h, j) containing three parameters: the first and the second destinations $d'.j$ and $d_h.j$ to reach, respectively, and the position j of the symbol 1 along all the processes on the path P_j. So, the source process s initiates the construction of the path P_j from s to d' by sending the message (d', d, j) to its successor on P_j (Action (a_{2_2}). Then, subsequently, upon a process p receives this message, we need to consider two cases (Action a_4). (i) If the process p is the first destination d', meaning that the first destination d' is reached, then p sends the message (d_h, j) with the second destination d_h to reach to its successor; (ii) Otherwise, the first destination d' is still not reached, then p transmits the message to its successor. Each process, upon receipt of a message, uses the function *NextNeigh-Fix1*() to identify the successor process on a path P_j that kept the symbol 1 in the same position j.

4   Proof of Correctness

We will show that Algorithm 4 constructs $n-1$ one-to-many node-disjoint paths. From Algorithm 4, each destination process $d.j$ in DL such that $d.j$ is a representative process of a set D_j, (1)-$process$, or a (i_1)-$process$ and its associated 1-$process$ is not marked (Function $\neg Marked()$), the elementary construction is sufficient to construct a path P_j from s to $d.j$ (Actions a_{2_1} and a_3). However, if $d.j$ is a (i_1)-$process$ and its associated (1)-$process$ is marked, then we need to identify a neighbour process of $d.j$ (say $d'.j$) such that $d'.j$ is not in DL and its associated (1)-$process$ is not marked (Function $UMNeigh()$). Then, the path P_j is constructed in two steps: first a path is constructed from s to $d'.j$, then from $d'.j$ to $d.j$ (Action a_{2_2} and a_4). From Algorithm 4, we can claim the following lemma.

Lemma 1. *Let $d.j \in DL$ a destination process, then Algorithm 4 constructs a path P_j from s to $d.j$ with the following properties.*
(i) If $d.j$ is a representative process, then all the processes on P_j keeps the symbol 1 at position j, except s.
(ii) If $d.j$ is a (1)-process, then all the processes on P_j keeps the symbol 1 at position j, except its endpoints s and $d.j$.
(iii) If $d.j$ is a (i_1)-process $(i \neq j)$, then all the processes on P_j keeps the symbol 1 at position j, except the (1)-process associated with $d.j$, and at most two (i_1)-processes (i.e, $d.j$ and one of its neighbour $d'.j$ in $\mathcal{N}_j$), and s.

In the sequel, we need the following definition. We say that a process sequence $(u_1, u_2, ..., u_s)$ in the n-star S_n is a *simple cycle* if all processes are distinct and (u_s, u_1), (u_i, u_{i+1}), $1 \leq i \leq s-1$, are all edges in S_n. From [4], we can claim the following result.

Lemma 2. *There is no simple cycle of the length less than six in the n-star S_n.*

Let $PrevP_j$ denote the set of all the paths built before the path P_j. We introduce the definition of the sets $\mathcal{N}_j$ and (1)-$\mathcal{N}_j$ associated with each destination process $d.j \in DL$ to facilitate the proof. Observe that each process $d.j$ has $n-1$ neighbours, one is a (1)-$process$ and the others are (i_1)-$processes$. Let the $n-1$ neighbours of $d.j$ be $d_2 = \pi[1, 2](d.j), d_3 = \pi[1, 3](d.j), d_4 = \pi[1, 4](d.j), ..., d_n = \pi[1, n](d.j)$ where $d_i = \pi[1, i](d.j)$ is the (1)-$process$ associated with $d.j$ and $\pi[1, k](d.j), 2 \leq k \leq n$ and $k \neq i$, are the (i_1)-$processes$ neighbours of $d.j$. Let $\mathcal{N}_j = \{d_k, 2 \leq k \leq n$ and $k \neq i\}$ be the set of all the (i_1)-$processes$ neighbours of $d.j$. Let (1)-$\mathcal{N}_j = \{(1)\text{-}d_k, 2 \leq k \leq n\}$ be the set of all (1)-$processes$ associated with processes in $\{d.j\} \cup \mathcal{N}_j$ such that (1)-d_k is the (1)-$process$ associated with d_k.

Lemma 3. *Let $d.j \in DL$ be a (i_1)-process, but not the representative process, of set D_i and let the sets $\mathcal{N}_j$ and (1)-$\mathcal{N}_j$ be defined as above. Then, each path P_t of the paths $PrevP_j$ contains, at most, one process in $\mathcal{N}_j$ and, at most, one process in (1)-$\mathcal{N}_j$.*

Proof. Let $P_t \in PrevP_j$ be the path that connects the source process s to the destination process $d.t$ such that t is the position reserved for the symbol 1 for all the processes on P_t (except for maximum one).

1. If $d.t$ ($t \neq j$) is a (1)-*process*, then by Lemma 1 case (ii), all internal processes of P_t are (t_1)-*processes* and $t \neq j$. Similarly, by Lemmas 1 case (iii), the path P_j contains only (j_1)-*processes*, one (1)-*process*, and at most two (i_1)-*processes* and $t \neq i$, since the position i is reserved for the representative process of the set D_i. Thus, the path P_t contains no process in the set $\mathcal{N}_j$ and contains at most one process, *i.e.*, the process $d.t$, in (1)-$\mathcal{N}_j$.

2. If $d.t$ is a (k_1)-*process* for $k \neq t$ and $k \neq i$, then by Lemmas 1 case (iii), the path P_t contains only (t_1)-*processes*, one (1)-*process*, and at most two (k_1)-*processes* and $t \neq i$. Since $k \neq j$ (because there exists a representative process for each subset D_k and D_j) and $t \neq j$ (from the labeling process), the path P_t contains no process in the set $\mathcal{N}_j$ and contains at most one process in (1)-$\mathcal{N}_j$, *i.e.*, the (1)-*process* associated with $d.t$.

3. Assume that the process $d.t$ is the representative process of the set D_i. Then, by Lemma 1 case (i), all processes except the first process s on the path P_t are (i_1)-*processes*. Thus, the path P_t contains no process in the set (1)-$\mathcal{N}_j$. To prove that the path P_t contains, at most, one process in $\mathcal{N}_j$, assume the contrary, that P_t contains two (i_1)-*processes* in the set $\mathcal{N}_j$ (*i.e.*, $d.t$ and a neighbour of $d.t$). But, the path P_t cannot contain the process $d.t$, otherwise, $\mathcal{D}ist(s, d.j) < \mathcal{D}ist(s, d.t)$, contradicts the selection of the representative process node $d.t$ in the set D_i. Thus, P_t contains, at most, one process in $\mathcal{N}_j$, the neighbour of $d.t$.

4. Finally, suppose that the process $d.t$ is a (i_1)-*process*, but not the representative process, of the set D_i. We need to consider two cases.

a. The path P_t contains only one (i_1)-process that is the process $d.t$ and one (1)-*process* that is the (1)-*process* associated with $d.t$, and the rest of the processes on P_t are all (t_1)-*processes*, $t \neq j$. So, the path P_t contains at most one process in the set $\mathcal{N}_j$ (*i.e.*, the process $d.t$) and contains, at most, one process in (1)-$\mathcal{N}_j$ (*i.e.*, the (1)-*process* associated with $d.t$).

b. The path P_t contains two adjacent (i_1)-*processes* that is the process $d.t$ and a not marked neighbour $d_k \in \mathcal{N}_t$ of $d.t$, and one (1)-*process* that is the (1)-*process* associated with d_k (*i.e.*, (1)-d_k), and the rest of the processes on P_t are all (t_1)-*processes*, $t \neq j$. In this case, not both of $d.t$ and d_k can be in the set $\mathcal{N}_j$; otherwise, the star system S_n would have a simple cycle ($d.t$, d_k, $d.j$), a contradiction with Lemma 2. So, the path P_t contains at most one process in the set $\mathcal{N}_j$ (*i.e.*, the process $d.t$ or d_k) and contains, at most, one process in (1)-$\mathcal{N}_j$ (*i.e.*, the (1)-*process* associated with d_k).

Lemma 4. *Let $d.j$ be a (i_1)-process, but not the representative process, of set D_i and let the sets $\mathcal{N}_j$ and (1)-$\mathcal{N}_j$ be defined as above. Then, for each path P_t of the paths $\mathcal{P}rev P_j$, if the path P_t contains a process d_k in the set $\mathcal{N}_j$ and a (1)-process (1)-d_l in the set (1)-$\mathcal{N}_j$, then the (1)-d_l process must be the (1)-process associated with the process d_k.*

Proof. From Lemma 3, the path P_t contains a process in $\mathcal{N}_j$ and a process in (1)-$\mathcal{N}_j$ only in the case 4.b. The process $d.t$ is a (i_1)-*process*, but not the representative process, of the set D_i. The path P_t contains two adjacent (i_1)-*processes* that is the process $d.t$ and a not marked neighbour $d_k \in \mathcal{N}_t$ of $d.t$, and one (1)-*process* that is the (1)-*process* associated with d_k (*i.e.*, (1)-d_k), and the rest of the processes on P_t are all

(t_1)-processes, $t \neq j$. The path P_t contains at most one process in the set $\mathcal{N}_j$ (i.e., the process $d.t$ or d_k) and contains, at most, one process in (1)-$\mathcal{N}_j$ (i.e., the (1)-process associated with d_k). If the (1)-process (1)-d_k is in the set (1)-$\mathcal{N}_j$, then the process $d.t$ cannot be in the set $\mathcal{N}_j$–otherwise, the process d_k is not in the set $\mathcal{N}_j$ and the process sequence $(d_t, d_k, (1)$-$d_k, d'.j, d.j)$ would form a simple cycle of length 5 in the n-star ($d'.j$ is is a neighbour $d.j$ on P_j).

Lemma 5. *Let $d.j$ be a (i_1)-process, but not the representative process, of set D_i. If the (1)-process associated with the process $d.j$ is marked, then there is a neighbour d_k of $d.j$ such that the process d_k and the (1)-process associated with d_k are not marked.*

Proof. By Lemmas 3 and 4, each previously constructed path $P_t \in \mathcal{P}rev P_j$ contains, at most, one process in $\mathcal{N}_j$ (say, d_k), and, at most, one (1)-process in (1)-$\mathcal{N}_j$, the (1)-process associated with d_k. Let $|\mathcal{P}rev P_j| = x \leq n - 2$. So, there exists x marked processes $\mathcal{N}_j$ and x (1)-processes marked processes in the set (1)-$\mathcal{N}_j$. Thus, there exists $(n - x - 1) \geq 1$ unmarked processes in the set $\mathcal{N}_j$ along with their $(n - x - 1)$ unmarked in the set (1)-$\mathcal{N}_j$, hence the result.

By Algorithms 2, 4 and Lemmas 1, 5, we can show this result by induction on the number of the node-disjoint paths previously constructed, i.e., $|\mathcal{P}rev P_j|$, such that $0 \leq |\mathcal{P}rev P_j| \leq n - 2$.

Lemma 6. *Let P_j $(2 \leq j \leq n)$ be the path constructed from s to $d.j$ by Algorithms 4, then the path P_j is node-disjoint with all paths $\mathcal{P}rev P_j$ previously constructed by the algorithm.*

Theorem 1. *Given a source s and a set $D = \{d_1, d_2, ..., d_{n-1}\}$ of $n - 1$ distinct processes in the n-star, Algorithm 4 is a self-stabilizing one-to-many node-disjoint paths algorithm and construct $n - 1$ one-to-many node-disjoint paths in at most $O(n^2)$ rounds, such that each path connects s to a process in D.*

Proof. From Algorithm 4 and Action (a_1), the source process s initiates the labeling process infinitely often. The labeling process of the set $D = \{d_1, d_2, ..., d_{n-1}\}$ uses the distance computing algorithm (Algorithm 2). In the worst situation, we have $D_2, D_3, ..., D_{\lceil n/2 \rceil} \subseteq D$ subsets such that each subset D_i ($i \in 2, 3, ..., \lceil n/2 \rceil$) contains two (i_1)-processes. So, in order to find the representative process of each subset D_i (see rule (L_1), Algorithm 2), we need to compute the distance from s to each process in D_i, i.e., $2(\lceil n/2 \rceil - 1)$ processes. Since, each distance computing needs at most $\lceil 3(n-1)/2 \rceil$ rounds, where $\lceil 3(n-1)/2 \rceil$ is the diameter of the S_n, so the labling phases requieres $2(\lceil n/2 \rceil - 1)(\lceil 3(n-1)/2 \rceil)$ rounds ($O(n^2)$ rounds). Then, from action (a_2), the source s also initiates the construction of the $n - 1$ node disjoint paths infinitely often. Then, from actions a_3 and a_4 each process participates in the construction of the paths infinitely often. From Lemma 4, the $n - 1$ node-disjoint paths are constructed in at most $\lceil 3(n - 1)/2 \rceil$ rounds. Thus, the stabilization time is $O(n^2)$ rounds.

5 Conclusion and Future Work

In this paper, we presented the first distributed self-stabilizing algorithm for finding *one-to-many* node-disjoint paths algorithm in message passing model. Two paths in a network are said to be node disjoint if they do not share any nodes except for the endpoints. Our algorithm works on n-star networks S_n. Due to being self-stabilizing, it tolerates transient faults, and does not require initial configuration. The stabilization time of our algorithm is $O(n^2)$ rounds. In this work, we merely provided an algorithm to find one-to-many disjoint paths in n-star networks. Devising distributed and self-stabilizing algorithms for hypecube is open problem that we consider as future work.

References

1. Akers, S.B., Krishnamurthy, B.: Group graphs as interconnection networks. In: 14th International Conference on Fault Tolerant Computing, Trans. pp. 422–427 (1984)
2. Akers, S.B., Krishnamurthy, B.: A group theoretic model for symmetric interconnection networks. IEEE Trans. Comput. 4(38), 555–565 (1989)
3. Akers, S.B., Harel, D., Krishnamurthy, B.: The star graph: an attractive alternative to the n-cube. In: Proceedings International Conference on Parallel Processing, St. Charles, Illinois, pp. 393–400 (1987)
4. Chen, C.C.: Combinatorial and algebraic methods in star and bruijn networks. Department of Computer Science, Texas A and M university, Ph.D. dissertion (1995)
5. Chen, C.C., Chen, J.: Nearly optimal one-to-many parallel routing in star networks. IEEE Trans. Parallel Distributed Syst. 8(12), 1196–1202 (1997)
6. Cheng, E., Gao, S., Qiu, K., Shen, Z.: On disjoint shortest paths routing on the hypercube. In: Du, D.-Z., Hu, X., Pardalos, P.M. (eds.) COCOA 2009. LNCS, vol. 5573, pp. 375–383. Springer, Heidelberg (2009). https://doi.org/10.1007/978-3-642-02026-1_35
7. Dijkstra, E.W.: Self-stabilizing in spite of distributed control. Commun. Assoc. Comput. Mach. 17(11), 643–644 (1974)
8. Dietzfelbinger, M., Madhavapeddy, S., Sudborough, I.H.: Three disjoint path paradigms in star networks. In: Proceedings of the Third IEEE Symposium on Parallel and Distributed Processing, pp. 400–406 (1991)
9. Gao, S., Hsu, D.F.: Short containers in Cayley graphs. Discrete Appl. Math. 157, 1354–1363 (2009)
10. Gu, Q.P., Peng, S.: Node-to-set and set-to-set cluster fault tolerant routing in hypercubes. Parallel Comput. 24, 1245–1261 (1998)
11. Hadid, R., Karaata, M.H.: An adaptive stabilizing algorithm for finding all disjoint paths in anonymous mesh networks. Comput. Commun. 32(5), 858–866 (2009)
12. Hadid, R., Karaata, M.H., Villain, V.: A stabilizing algorithm for finding two node-disjoint paths in arbitrary networks. Int. J. Found. Comput. Sci. 28(4), 411–435 (2017)
13. Hsu, D.F.: A graph theoretical study of transmission delay and fault tolerance. In: Proceedings 4th International Conference on Parallel and Distributed Computing and Systems, pp. 20–24 (1991)
14. Hsu, D.F.: On container width and length in graphs, groups, and networks. IEICE Trans. Fundam. Electron. Commun. Comput. Sci. E77-A(4), 668–680 (1994)
15. Hsu, C.C.: A genetic algorithm for maximum edge-disjoint paths problem and its extension to routing and wavelength assignment problem. Ph.D. thesis, NC State University (2013)
16. Karaata, M.H., Hadid, R.: Briefannouncement: a stabilizing algorithm for finding two disjoint paths in arbitrary networks. In: Stabilization, Safety, and Security of Distributed Systems, pp. 789–790 (2009)
17. Lai, C.N.: One-to-Many disjoint paths in the hypercube and folded hypercube. Ph.D. thesis, Department of Computer Science and Information Engineering, National Taiwan University, Taipei, Taiwan (2001)

18. Lai, C.N.: Two conditions for reducing the maximal length of node-disjoint paths in hypercubes. Theoret. Comput. Sci. **418**, 82–91 (2012)
19. Lai, C.N.: Optimal construction of all shortest node-disjoint paths in hypercubes with applications. IEEE Trans. Parallel Distrib. Syst. **23**(6), 1129–1134 (2012)
20. Latifi, S.: On the fault-diameter of the star graph. Inf. Process. Lett. **46**, 143–150 (1993)
21. Latifi, S., Ko, H., Srimani, P.K.: Node-to-set vertex disjoint paths in hypercube networks. Technical report CS-98-107, Colorado State University (1998)
22. Lengauer, T.: Combinatorial Algorithms for Integrated Circuit Layout. Wiley, New York (1990)
23. Ma, C., et al.: p-MDP structure against multi-failures in high-degree node based optical networks. In: Communications and Networking in China, pp. 756–760 (2013)
24. Murthy, S., Souzaand, R.J.D., Varaprasad, G.: Digital signature-based secure node disjoint multipath routing protocol for wireless sensor networks. IEEE Sensors J. **12**(10), 2941–2949 (2012)
25. Qiu, K.: An efficient disjoint shortest paths routing algorithm for the the the hypercube. In: Proceedings of the 14th IEEE International Conference on Parallel and Distributed Systems (ICPADS 2008), IEEE Computer Society Press, Vol. 4, pp. 371–384 (1999)
26. Rabin, M.A.: Efficient dispersal of information for security, load balancing, and fault tolerance. J. ACM **36**, 335–348 (1989)
27. Saad, Y., Shultz, M.H.: Topological properties of hypercubes. IEEE Trans. Comput. **37**, 867–872 (1988)
28. Sinanoglu, O., Karaata, M.H., AlBdaiwi, B.: An inherently stabilizing algorithm for node-to-node routing over all shortest node-disjoint paths in hypercube networks. IEEE Trans. Comput. **59**(7), 995–999 (2010)
29. Sur, S., Srimani, P.K.: Topological properties of star grahs. Comput. Math. Applic. **25**(12), 87–98 (1993)

Author Index

Printed in the United States
By Bookmasters